THE WAY IT WAS

By the same author:

THE WAY WE WERE: 1900–1914
THE BRITISH GENIUS (*with Peter Grosvenor*)
THE AMERICAN TAKE-OVER
THE HONOURS GAME
ANATOMY OF SCOTLAND
THE GLASS LIE
ROOT OF CORRUPTION

The Way It Was

1914–1934

James McMillan

Based on the files of Express Newspapers

WILLIAM KIMBER · LONDON

First published in 1979 by
WILLIAM KIMBER & CO. LIMITED
Godolphin House, 22a Queen Anne's Gate,
London, SW1H 9AE

© James McMillan and Express Newspapers Ltd., 1979

ISBN 0 7183 0097 1

This book is copyright. No part of it may be reproduced in any form without permission in writing from the publishers except by a reviewer who wishes to quote brief passages in connection with a review written for inclusion in a newspaper, magazine, television or radio broadcast.

Typeset by Watford Typesetters
and printed and bound in Great Britain by
The Garden City Press Limited,
Letchworth, Hertfordshire, SG6 1JS

Contents

		Page
	Introduction	11

Part I
Epilogue for an Age

I	A Time for Hate	15
II	Men at War	37
III	'Second Lieutenant unless otherwise stated'	59
IV	The Passion and the Sorrow	67
V	For Conscience' Sake	75
VI	War by every means	86
VII	The Man and the Weapons	96
VIII	Aftermath	104

Part II
Intermission

IX	Workers of the World, Unite!	115
X	General Strike	130
XI	No Licence for Saxophones	145
XII	Lure of the Silver Screen	157
XIII	Towards the Good Life	169
XIV	Morality: Old and New	191
XV	A Distressful Land	205
XVI	India and Israel: Seeds of Conflict	221

Part III
Prologue to Another War

XVII	No More Money in the Bank	237
XVIII	Believe. Obey. Fight	254
XIX	Failure of the Will	269
XX	Triumph of the Will	275
	Index	295

List of Illustrations

	Page
British volunteers in 1914	32
German volunteers in 1914	32
Desolated Western Front	33
Troops marching to the front	48
The effects of German gas	49
Women's March Past	160
Suzanne Lenglen (*Radio Times Hulton Picture Library*)	161
The wide bottomed Oxford bags (*Press Association*)	176
Noel Coward	177
Fatty Arbuckle	192
Mary Pickford	193
Gloria Swanson	208
The Thompsons and Frederick Bywaters	209
Lancashire miners on parade	240
Jarrow marches	241
Benito Mussolini	256
Hitler, Roehm and Himmler	257
Lenin and Stalin (*Radio Times Hulton Picture Library*)	257

Acknowledgements

My thanks are due to Mr Ronald Frost of the micro-film unit; and to Miss Lily Stewart for her invaluable typing.

Note

Conversion of pounds, shillings and pence into decimal coinage is as follows:—

One guinea	equals	£1.05
Six pence		$2\frac{1}{2}$p
One shilling		5p
Half a crown		$12\frac{1}{2}$p
Ten shillings		50p

Introduction

I have chosen the period between 1914 and 1934 as a sequel to my book *The Way We Were* because these twenty years represent the terrible break with the old order occasioned by the Great War, and the rise of revolutionary ardour: Communism in Russia, Fascism in Germany and Italy, nationalism in Palestine and Ireland and India – which laid the groundwork for World War II and which haunts the world of this day.

Once again I have used the microfilm of Express Newspapers to illustrate the changing modes and moods. Newspapers are the raw material of history. They are more in tune with their times than are the memoirs of statesmen which recall the clang of events in the tranquillity of the study and put the necessary gloss on the writer's participation in them. Reporters record what they saw; Cabinet minutes or General Staff appreciations what their authors want the people to think happened.

It was not infrequent for ministers to discover what was happening in politics from the columns of the press, rather than from the lips of their revered – and equally ignorant – colleagues.

At a moment when politicians and commentators were devoutly hoping that Herr Hitler would be a force for peace in the world, Herr Hitler vouchsafed in an exclusive interview with the *Sunday Express* that on no account was he going to permit Poland to keep hold of Danzig and the Corridor. Six years later he carried out his threat and launched World War II.

But while *The Way It Was* is inevitably much more political than its predecessor, the rest of life is mirrored as the papers saw it: the coming of radio and sound films; the worship of film stars; the great drink question; the bustless, thighless females and the Oxford-bags-clad males Charlestoning away. There was glitter and glamour in the twenties as well as the sullen, irremovable, irreducible army of the unemployed.

Above all there is the Great War. It would be absurd to try to encompass that milestone conflict in one part of one volume and I have not attempted to do so. What I have done is to try to light up aspects of the war: the unbelievable courage of the fighting men; how compulsory military service and conscientious objectors were treated; how our foes were viewed and finally what victory and peace meant to people.

It is a many-sided task, but newspapers are many-sided products and I have consulted a representative selection of more than a thousand. This is how it was between 1914 and 1934 as it was seen by those who were there.

PART ONE

Epilogue for an Age

CHAPTER ONE

A Time for Hate

Europe in the hot summer of 1914 was, apparently, no nearer war than it had been in any one of half-a-dozen years in the previous decade. The murder by Serbian nationalists of Archduke Franz Ferdinand, heir to the Austrian throne, and his morganatic wife at Sarajevo on 28 June was certainly deplorable, but hardly fatal to world peace. Grand Dukes had been murdered before and the rivalry of Serbia, seeking to prise the Slav provinces from foreign grasp, and the polyglot Austrian Empire which held the Slavs, had been a fact of life for so long in Europe that it scarcely roused interest. If the Great Powers had kept out of the Balkan Wars of 1912-1913 – as they had – why should they involve themselves in an Austro-Serbian imbroglio, even if it came to actual combat?

This was the view generally held by the British press, from *The Times* to the popular organs and shared by most of the policy makers in the Foreign Office.

But this time things were different. The Austrian military caste, headed by the fire-eating, mercurial Conrad von Hötzendorf, chief of the Austrian Army, was determined to put an end to Serbia's pestilential interference. The Slavs must be taught a lesson: a soldierly lesson.

So it was that an ultimatum was delivered to Belgrade making severe demands – including the right of Austrian officers to inquire into the activities of the Serbian Black Hand Society (justly suspected of being the guiding hand behind the assassination) on Serbian soil. This, and almost all the other exorbitant requirements, were, to the astonishment of Vienna, meekly accepted by the Serbian Government.

Even where there was a rejection of one or two of the most peremptory orders the defiance was tempered by Serb acceptance of international arbitration. No power could have gone further in bowing to another than did Serbia. Yet the Austrians divined that this was a ploy.

Serbia was so clearly in the wrong – spawning the gunman, Gavrilo Prinzip, who fired the fatal shot and his accomplices; condoning the most scurrilous anti-Austrian propaganda; endorsing terrorist organisations such as Black Hand – that the Belgrade Government was prepared to submit lest it bring international opprobrium down upon its head and jeopardise its relations with Mother Russia, defender of all the Slavs.

Once this particular episode was over and forgotten, however, Serbia would revert to type. Better by far, reckoned the Austrians, to push their legitimate grievance to the ultimate and force Serbia to surrender completely. A 'little war' would do the Empire no end of good by showing the lesser breeds that they could not trifle with the Germanic rulers of Vienna.

Although Serbia might even have acquiesced in the temporary occupation of the capital by Austrian troops, Vienna was adamant for hostilities. As all her demands had not been immediately and unconditionally complied with, Austria declared war on Serbia on 28 July, 1914, and set in motion the interlocking machinery of alliances.

At first it seemed that moderation would prevail. Russia, the protector of the Slavs and Serbia's natural champion, could hardly approve the murder of an Archduke. The Czar had lost a couple of his own Grand Dukes to terror. Imperial Germany, Austria's blood brother and only real ally, had no logical reason to help Vienna precipitate a European war. Everything was going Germany's way. She was the dominant industrial nation on the continent and could well, in time, fall heir to Austria and Austria's domains. Why grab the apple that was falling anyway?

However self-interest and reasonableness succumbed to elemental fury. Austria's opening bombardment triggered off Russian passion.

The huge, sprawling Empire had been humiliated to the depths of its being by the defeat inflicted on it by the Japanese – derisively referred to by Russian ministers as 'yellow monkeys' some ten years previously. Acceptance of another bitter humbling was not be countenanced.

Czar Nicholas II did not want a war. But he was as much a servant of his country's Slav sentiments as he was master of Russia's armed hosts whose honour would be tainted beyond redemption were they to turn away from Austria's challenge.

Kaiser Wilhelm II did not want a war. But the wayward, theatrical White Knight of Germany could not let down the ally he had gone to such painstaking lengths to support. He could not unsay the many colourful phrases about 'shining armour', 'drawn swords', 'Germany's place in the sun', now that the moment of truth, and destiny, had arrived. His people, heady with industrial triumphs, were not averse to a final solution of Europe's balance of power and some military leaders (not all, for Helmut von Moltke, Chief of the General Staff, was not panting for battle) yearned to put into action the Schlieffen Plan that would turn France's left flank by a massive invasion of the Low Countries and crush the French before the ponderous Russians even completed mobilisation.

The French President Poincaré probably *did* want war. He would not be President for ever and he was desperately eager to see the provinces of Alsace and Lorraine, lost to Germany in the war of 1870, regained for France. Many Frenchmen shared his view. Some did not. But they were Socialists and when – as it happened – they were deserted by their socialist 'brothers' in Germany they flung in their lot with the nationalists to save the Motherland.

The British were the most pacific of all. The Government, headed by H. H. Asquith, was almost solidly for peace. 'Almost' because Winston Churchill, First Lord of the Admiralty, had long recognised that war with ever-expanding, ever-demanding Germany was inevitable. Most of his colleagues, however, were in favour of closing their eyes in prayerful anticipation of something turning up. The Liberal administration had come to an 'understanding' with France to counter German aggression but were not willing to understand the full implications of the arrangement. Nearly all the Ministers were ready to join Mr Asquith in his policy of 'wait and see'.

The key that turned the whole terrible clanking machinery of war was the railway timetable: the fear of each great power of being caught out by the speed and stealth of his opponent's preparations. Thus as soon as Count Berchtold, the dandified Austrian Foreign Minister, had despatched his declaration of war to Serbia (in French, the language of diplomacy) Russia found it incumbent on herself to mobilise as a counter to Austrian mobilisation. The Germans then mobilised so as not to be caught off-balance by the Russians. The French mobilised so as not to be caught wrong-footed by the Germans. And the British? They hesitated, while the Kaiser, who had long convinced himself that his grandmother's country (Queen Victoria was his grandma) would never fight Germany, furiously scribbled on a despatch from his ambassador, Prince Lichnowsky, in London: 'England reveals herself in her true colours. . . . England alone bears responsibility for peace or war.'

The cause of the Kaiser's fury was the British declaration that if France were drawn into a war against Germany 'a new situation would be created and it would not be practical for the UK to stand aside for an indefinite period'. In other words, British neutrality could not – as the Germans believed – be taken for granted.

What finally swung the still-dithering Liberal Cabinet in favour of war was the German invasion of Belgium, a country whose neutrality had been guaranteed by the powers, including Germany and Britain.

For eighty years this little bilingual nation had enjoyed precarious independence. Owned by Holland, occupied by France, coveted by Germany (as an avenue for the invasion of France) and regarded as vital to British security, Belgium was the touchstone of European intentions.

German intentions were becoming increasingly clear in the early years of the twentieth century, as tiny wayside railway stations were extended into virtual junctions capable of handling tens of thousands of soldiers a day. But until either France or Germany actually *moved* against Belgium, Britain was uncertain what to do.

When Germany delivered her ultimatum to Brussels, demanding the right to move troops across the country into France, the Cabinet in London swung decisively in favour of war. David Lloyd George, the brilliant, emotional Chancellor of the Exchequer, had been strongly inclined towards non-involvement until Belgium was threatened. Then the sympathy of one from a small country – Wales – for those of another small country welled up and overflowed. Those tending towards war – Asquith, Grey the Foreign Secretary, Haldane at the War Office – were confirmed in their beliefs and fears. Churchill had already mobilised the Fleet. A united Cabinet (the pacifists, including the Lib-Lab member, John Burns, resigned) delivered a note to Berlin on 4 August requiring the Germans to quite Belgium on pain of war with the British Empire. When no reply was received hostilities automatically commenced.

Would Britain have gone to war if Germany had not invaded Belgium? Probably yes: probably too late, and certainly as a divided Empire. Ultimately Britain could never have lived with German occupation of the Channel ports and with a conquered France's naval power added to Germany's own vast fleet. The fear of that alone would have driven Britain to war. But by the time a distracted, quarrelsome cabinet had made up its mind the Germans would have been deep into France and the British Expeditionary Force (small, but superbly well-trained) could well have been too late to help save Paris.

Belgium was the catalyst. The rape of 'brave little Belgium' and German Chancellor Bethmann-Hollweg's remark 'you are going to war over a scrap of paper' aroused the passionate concern of almost all Liberals who now found themselves at one with the Conservatives who had long regarded war with Germany as inevitable. Hatred of militarism fused with patriotism and the Imperialist ideal. The Empire – which was at war with Germany the moment the King-Emperor signed the declaration – was galvanised into action in prideful recognition of the Mother Country's stand for 'decency, integrity and the protection of the weak'. The greatest Empire in history moved to support the mist-shrouded islands off North-West Europe. The roll call of territories is a measure of what that meant in terms of power.

India (embracing India, Pakistan, Bangladesh, Sri-Lanka, Burma)
Malaya
Singapore
Borneo and a host of Pacific islands
Australia
New Zealand
Canada
South Africa
much of West Africa
much of East Africa
The West Indies
Gibraltar
Malta
Cyprus

Expatriates in their thousands rushed home to join the crusade and millions in India and the colonies prepared to fill the Imperial ranks.

It was however in Europe, the killing ground itself, that enthusiasm broke all bounds. Paris, Berlin, St Petersburg and Vienna were gripped by war fever. The press reported a similar surge of joyous patriotism in Britain on 4 August:

> The spirit that moves the nation was seen in a rush of offers of military or civil service in defence of the country. A stream of men poured into the various recruiting offices and headquarters.
>
> The spirit showed itself, too, with a subtle and ennobling exaltation when an immense crowd in Birdcage-walk bared their heads as the colours of a regiment of Guards were brought on parade in the barrack-square. Only a flag – and the phlegmatic Briton is not used to make displays of emotion before material things. But to-day – a symbol! a sacred thing, a whisper of England's soul, and the London crowd 'bared their heads'.

Many books have been written about the terrible innocence of these days; of a generation reared in peace aching for the excitement of war, eager to get away from the humdrum routine, to do and dare; to be with mates in a great adventure and stand taller with the girls.

Yet the first recruiting advertisement, appearing on 5 August, offered none of this boyish romanticism:

Your King

and Country

need You.

Will you answer your Country's call? Each day is fraught with the gravest possibilities, and at this very moment the Empire is on the brink of the greatest war in the history of the world.

In this crisis your Country calls on all her young unmarried men to rally round the Flag and enlist in the ranks of her Army.

If every patriotic young man answers her call, England, and her Empire will emerge stronger and more united than ever.

If you are unmarried and between 18 and 30 years old will you answer your Country's call? and go to the nearest Recruiter – whose address you can get at the Post Office, and

Join the Army

To-day!

The newspapers' approach to this was necessarily ambiguous. They mirrored prevailing public opinion: that the Russian steamroller would roll the Germans flat, that the British blockade would starve the enemy into early surrender (a headline was: 'Hamburg Starving'), and that if you didn't join up straight away you wouldn't see any action as the war would be over by Christmas.

The press was not alone in viewing the war as a short-term affair.

The British director of Military Intelligence, General Sir Henry Wilson, thought the Entente (Britain, France and Russia) would settle the hash of Central Powers (Germany and Austro-Hungary) in four weeks. The French deputy Chief of Staff, General Berthelot, was aghast at such pessimism: he could not see his country's foes lasting beyond three weeks.*

---

* Lord Kitchener, the new War Minister, was the sole military figure to dissent from the 'over by Christmas' optimism. He solemnly avowed that the war would last at least three years.

First reports from the front tended to bolster this confidence. The Russians were pictured as advancing irresistibly into East Prussia (as they were – lured to their doom in the marshlands of the Masurian Lakes) while the French, according to Alphonse Courlander, special correspondent:

> After forty-four years the French are in Alsace. They have advanced more than twenty miles from the frontier in the direction of Belfort, and have driven the Germans out of Altkirch and Mulhausen.
>
> The battle was superb. For years the French soldiers have had memories of Alsace bursting within them, and this was the tempest that swept the Germans away.
>
> The French troops dashed forward like madmen, frenzied with victory. They made magnificent bayonet charges right up to the mouths of the guns. It is impossible to hold them back.
>
> 'You could not keep them back with chains,' wrote General Joffre a few days ago to the Minister of War, concerning his men. 'They speak not of decimating the enemy with gun and rifle fire, but of fierce bayonet charges. They dream of bayonet charges.'
>
> It was always French bayonet charges that routed the Germans.
>
> Artillery galloped into battle at terrific speed. Infantry advanced under cover of the field guns, opening fire as they neared the German trenches. Then all the French fighting blood was stirred, and there was one great cry: *'En avant à la baionnette!'*
>
> Officers were literally unable to hold back the impetuous troops, who advanced in one wild charge, shovelling the Germans out of their trenches at the point of the bayonet.

In their death-or-glory attack on Alsace, the French – still wearing blue tunics and red pantaloons – suffered 300,000 casualties in a week. They did not re-occupy the province, or Lorraine, until the war was over.

The British newspapers waited impatiently for the British Expeditionary Force to go into action.

Lord Kitchener's message to the troops was prominently displayed:

> 'The operation in which you are engaged will for the most part take place in a friendly country, and you can do your own country no better service than in showing yourself in France and Belgium in the true character of a British soldier.
>
> 'Be invariably courteous, considerate and kind.

'Never do anything likely to injure or destroy property, and always look upon looting as a disgraceful act.

'You are sure to meet with a welcome and to be trusted. Your conduct must justify that welcome and that trust.

'Your duty cannot be done unless your health is sound, so keep constantly on your guard against any excesses. In this new experience you may find temptation both in wine and women. You must entirely resist both temptations and, while treating all women with perfect courtesy, you should avoid any intimacy.

     Do your duty bravely
     Fear God
     Honour the King
          KITCHENER, Field Marshal'

When British troops did go into action, courageously and with considerable effect in the latter part of August, reporters brought the war to every household:

1 September, 1914:
A young infantryman spoke of the joy in the British ranks at Mons on the first day of the battle when they completely checked the German advance.

'The "sausages", as we call them, didn't know quite so much about us then,' he said, 'and thought that their odds of two to one were sufficient, but they had a lesson. I suppose they imagined our shooting was as erratic and wide as theirs – the worst I've ever seen – for they came straight ahead without bothering much about taking cover.

'We had the time of our lives shooting the silly beggars down, and on the first day there weren't quite enough of them to force us away by sheer weight of numbers, although they continually repeated their desperate attacks.

'We stopped them every time, but on Monday they came rolling up in huge masses which must have put us in a minority of one to three, four, and eventually five, I should imagine.

'To give the devils their due – and they are devils when they get a chance to vent their rage on our wounded – they don't seem the least bit to mind being shot. The awful gaps caused in their ranks by our carefully directed fire are immediately filled up, and they rush straight ahead in the face of a regular hail of lead, but the sight of cold steel seems to unnerve them absolutely.

'We were marching hour after hour, and what we had to carry

was enough to kill an ordinary man. Fancy doing thirty or forty miles with 91 pounds on your back.'

A few days later Henry Roberts cabled his experiences of four days inside the Allied lines as the British and French fell back on Paris before the German onslaught:

At Soissons I came on a private who had been in the Sunday fighting and had lost his way.

'The first man down on Sunday,' he said, 'gave us a bit of a shock. It was strange to see Bill, who had lent you a fag only two minutes before, rolling against you like a drunken man and saying nothing. It gave you a sort of feeling that I can't describe, and then you just say to yourself, "It's them bloody Germans what's doing it," and you ain't going to let 'em do more than you can 'elp.

'When two or three of the boys are down in your company, you get used to it. With one ear you think 'ow you are goin' to get your own back, and with the other you listen to your officer.'

And even though he was in the middle of a battle, Mr Roberts kept his English hauteur:

I was held up by a French corporal's guard. The corporal was officious, and I was not inclined to bandy many words with him, save to remind him that he was impertinent; whereupon I was taken from my car and brought before a young officer, who ordered me, without further ado, to go back whence I came. My papers, he said, were all right, but back I must go. So I went back half a mile and made a detour, coming to Soissons by another road.

It was from this despatch that the first stories of German atrocities, true or false, were reported by civilian refugees fleeing the fighting:

Through this straggling procession ran the terrible tale of German brutality that serves to announce the coming of the Teutonic host. The women with pale set faces told of the tales of terror that had come to them from 'over there'; how young girls had been torn from their mother's embrace to disappear among a brawling crowd of German soldiers – to disappear for ever or to be returned wrecked and pitifully broken for life; of the shooting of husbands and fathers who, in their frenzied agony, dared to thrust a protecting hand to save their children from the bestial ravishers of youth and innocence; of the mutilating of young boys; of the fiendish behaviour in a hundred ways of these hell hounds let loose on a peaceable countryside. And the stories, losing nothing of their terrible nature, had driven these people on, with renewed speed, to their hoped-for haven of safety.

The travails of French, Belgians, Serbs and Russians made the British feel guilty and it was almost with a note of relief that the *Express* announced on 4 September, 1914:

BRITISH CASUALTIES NOW OVER 10,000.

The casualty lists* which were to become such a tragic part of the daily newspapers had not yet dulled the senses; they were still part of the 'necessary sacrifice'. And there was a chauvinistic note added by the local correspondent in Antwerp:

> I have received information from two independent sources with respect to the prisoners held by the Germans at Maubeuge.
> The thirty thousand French prisoners are guarded by two hundred Germans.
> There are seven Englishmen prisoners there and these are carefully watched by thirty Germans. My informants left me in no doubt as to the accuracy of these figures.

At the end of the first week in September, the French Army, somewhat tardily aided by the British GOC, General French, drove the Germans back at the Battle of the Marne and ended the Kaiser's hopes of winning a decisive victory in the West. The stunning reversal of German fortunes naturally launched a wave of optimism:

GERMANS STAMPEDING OUT OF FRANCE

proclaimed the *Express* of 15 September, 1914. A jocular note was adopted:

Joffre to the Kaiser: *Must* you Go?

---

* The first officer to fall was Archer-Shee, the real life central figure of Terence Rattigan's *The Winslow Boy*. Falsely accused by the Admiralty of forging a postal order while at Dartmouth, he joined the Army.

After the victory of the Marne, the Allies and Germans raced to the sea, each seeking to outflank the other. By the beginning of November, the trench lines were established which were to last, with but slight variation, for four years.

With the Western Front in stalemate, the *Express* contracted a neutral journalist, an American, to observe and report on Germany. 'His instructions,' said the *Express*, 'are to write exactly what he sees and not to gild pills if they are bitter.' The first of these remarkable wartime despatches appeared in the issue of 23 November, 1914:

> The comfortable night boats of the Netherlands Zeeland Company are now used for the day service from Folkestone to Flushing. During the passage almost every man, woman and child sits searching the sea for mines. Every now and then a passenger points out some object seen in the water as one of these dreaded mines, which an ever calm and undisturbed Dutch steward or sailor explains is simply an empty case thrown overboard by a passing steamer.
>
> At Flushing the travellers bound for Germany find a train running through to Goch, the German frontier station.
>
> German passengers returning home from England are, of course, chiefly female. When leaving London they all have a hunted look. It is only when over the German frontier that they feel absolutely safe and free, and it is curious suddenly to hear the louder and more open conversation all over the train, to see faces brightening up, to hear sighs of relief everywhere, and tales told of hardship and suffering and broken-up homes – tales, I am sure, often exaggerated through nervous tensions.
>
> A great number of these women, whose male relatives are interned in England, have been assisted by philanthropic societies who provide them, on payment of a small sum (I believe 12s 6d) with a second-class ticket to the German frontier.
>
> What struck me more than anything else on the way to Hamburg was the most admirable arrangements made by the German Red Cross Society for the soldiers. At every station of any importance depots have been provided on the platforms, with hot and cold drinks and food for the travelling soldiers, and these are handed to them in their compartments by men and women attendants.
>
> Hamburg is a revelation to me. With its shipping industry at a complete standstill, the great export and import trade of Hamburg is suspended (thanks to the British blockade) and one no longer sees the hundreds of wagons and lorries going to and fro that in the days

of peace filled the streets of Hamburg with the clatter of commerce.

My first thought, in view of these conditions, was that I should find the people longing for peace, and my surprise was great when, meeting members of different classes, I could see that one and all had but one idea, to fight the enemy to the last, and, above all, to battle implacably against the hated Englishman.

The feeling against England is one of bitter hatred. Hamburg, which used to be nicknamed in Germany 'a suburb of England', and where Englishmen always had preferential treatment, now curses England, the country which, to its mind, is responsible for the war.

The correspondent went on to Berlin, where he reported:

It is a delusion to imagine Berlin as a city of mourning. It is nothing of the kind.

Yet in all the public places in Berlin a serious tone reigns. No bands play now in the fashionable restaurants, and this is not on account of orders from the police authorities, but merely as an expression of the general feeling that in these days, when the whole country is engaged in such a serious war and the flower of its manhood is fighting at the front and so many people have lost relatives or friends, music and general gaiety are out of place.

For the ladies it is not fashionable to be too elegant, more simple tailor-made suits being the dominant note. Though life generally is much more simple than it used to be, there is a general tendency towards advising the moneyed classes not to diminish their staffs of servants more than is necessary, nor to live so economically as to bring trade in articles more of a luxury than of absolute need to a standstill.

Many of the larger private establishments, keeping as a rule a huge staff of menservants, are employing female servants to take the place of the men who have joined the army.

Every one has read in the newspapers recently about the hatred of Germany for England.*

England, they believe, has been preparing this war, jealous of German trade and of Hamburg's prosperity. Men and women all alike say: 'We do not mind now whether we may be ruined, whether

---

* A popular German book of the time was Hindenburg's *Entry into London*. The German hymn of hate had the lines: 'We have one enemy and one only—England.'

our sons, husbands, and brothers are killed: we shall give all and everything we have to carry on the fight, we shall either be victorious or we shall die; we are fighting for our existence.'

Only those who have been in Germany and have heard the expression of that hatred from German lips can realise its almost incredible intensity. Their eyes blaze like the eyes of a wounded tiger, and they can scarcely express themselves, so fierce and overwhelming is their rage.

There will be nothing left of London worth looking at, they tell you, when the German Army has done with it. It will be a blackened ruin, and there will not be a public building left with one stone standing on top of another. It will be consumed with fire cast upon it by the German fleet of aeroplanes, and all that the Londoners will have left will be eyes to weep with.

The correspondent went on to praise Germany's methods for transferring labour from war-hit industries to war-intensive ones, to commend the country's efficient and humane treatment of the wounded – including Allied wounded – and to set Germany up as an example of devoted patriotism.

It is impossible to imagine a like mission being financed by a British newspaper in the Second World War. By then the official propaganda machinery had taken over the news management of total war.

However, while the *Express* was ready to publish this extremely fair comment from the other side of the hill it was still implacably resolved to prosecute the war to the hilt, and to chastise those whom it regarded as failing in their duty.

Lord Haldane, the former War Minister, was one. He had expressed pro-German views and, according to the *Express*, had cut down on the Army when he should have been building it up. 'The man who knew Germany best did the least to protect Britain.'

Bowing to press hostility, Haldane finally quit the Government. Whether he could have done more to sharpen the Army's readiness in the face of a pacific Cabinet intent on retrenchment and reform is debatable. But he held the office and he had to bear the burden of responsibility. Those like A. C. Benson, the author and son of the Archbishop of Canterbury, who recanted their sympathies for Germany were welcomed back to the fold. By the late autumn of 1914 the spirit of 'he who is not with me is against me' was abroad in the land and the Home Front was alive with rumours:

Members of the Regular and Territorial forces should be cautioned in the strongest terms against accepting cigarettes from ostensibly kind-hearted strangers.

It is stated that several cases have already occurred in which members of his Majesty's forces have been engaged in conversation by persons professing friendliness towards them, and have received from these persons cigarettes which have afterwards been found to be drugged.

The *Express* did, however, specifically deny that any Russians had landed in Britain – with or without snow on their boots.

The German bombardment of Louvain had aroused world-wide revulsion and now columns of the papers were filled with samples of alleged German atrocities:

At Lier de Sante Marie the Germans broke into a chapel in which four priests were conducting mass. On the plea that they required the chapel as quarters for their troops the enemy seized the priests whom they accused of not concluding the service quickly enough, and made them prisoners.

On the following day, the soldiers forced the priests to march ahead of them, and eventually the four men were killed.

At Renaix the Germans broke into a private house and found the entire family hiding in a cellar. They first violated and then cut the throats of two girls.

They then cut the ears off a boy, subsequently inflicting on him unnameable mutilations.

The hatred that the Germans were reported to feel for England was now being reciprocated, summed up in a widely circularised war poem, addressed to the Kaiser, by Mr Henry Chappell, a Bath railway porter:

> But after the Day there's a price to pay
> For the sleepers under the sod,
> And Him you mocked for many a day –
> Listen, and hear what He has to say:
> 'Vengeance is mine, I will repay.'
> What can you say to God?

The resolve of the soldiers was displayed by letters, extracts from which were published in the newspapers. Private Bartlett of the Royal Canadian Dragoons wrote:

Dearest Father and Mother, – Just a few lines to let you know that I am ordered to the front. We will leave as soon as the first contingent is ready.

I earnestly beg of you not to worry about me, for, whatever happens, I am going to show them that there is not a yellow streak in me. I hope and trust to pull through safely, but if I go under it will be one consolation to you to know that I did a little good before I went.

I know, dad, in your heart you would be proud of me, and to know that I am acting as a man, and I want you not to let mother worry about me. Cheer her up for God's sake, and don't let her worry, but try to make her see things as I do.

From Private A. McGillcray:

I saw a handful of Irishmen throw themselves in front of a regiment of cavalry trying to cut off a battery of Horse Artillery. Not one of the poor lads got away alive, but they made the German pay in kind, and anyhow the artillery got away.

Every man of us made a vow to avenge the fallen Irishmen. Later they were finally avenged by their own comrades, who lay in wait for the German cavalry. The Irish lads went at them with the bayonet when they least expected it. Some of them howled for mercy, but I don't think they got it. In war mercy is only for the merciful.

Major Charles Yate of the King's Own Yorkshire Light Infantry was awarded the Victoria Cross posthumously:

When all other officers were killed or wounded he led his nineteen survivors against the enemy in a charge in which he was severely wounded. He was picked up by the enemy, and has subsequently died as a prisoner of war.

Yate had earlier written in an article, 'Moral Qualities of War':

'The spirit in which soldiers must go forth to war – not dreaming of the homecoming, the medal. These are distant and problematical. Nearer and more probable are the enemy and the tomb.'

Rage at the enemy was stirred up by stories such as this one, which appeared in the spring of 1915:

The *Daily Express* has received the following letter from a British officer, who is now a prisoner in Germany. We can vouch for its authenticity, but for obvious reasons it is impossible to give the officer's name:

It is almost impossible to give a detailed account of my captivity in a letter, for the treatment and the conditions have been so varied. Speaking generally, we have been treated usually as German private soldiers are treated, sometimes as naughty schoolboys, sometimes as criminals, and only on rare occasions as officers.

There were no proper arrangements to provide us with food. Red Cross men, and women too, many times poured hot coffee on the ground sooner than give it to Englishmen, even though they were wounded.

At several stations we were exhibited like wild beasts to the mob, who were permitted to jeer and spit at us. Twice I was struck. At the station two wounded British officers were so weak from hunger and pain that we obtained permission from our guard to take them into the restaurant. One of them we practically carried there, fainting.

Unfortunately, the station kommandant was in the restaurant. The moment he saw us, cursing us and abusing both us and our guard, he sent us straight back to the train. I saw much worse treatment meted out to an unfortunate French priest, an old man over sixty years of age, who travelled part of the way with us. I have since heard that he died the night we left him. If ever any man was murdered he was.

My experiences were in no way unusual. On my arrival at ——— I learned those of many other British officers. Many had a much worse time than I did.

And again:

A French doctor, who was for five months a prisoner in one of the invaded towns of the north, has managed to cross the lines. He brings a remarkable story of the reign of terror under the Huns.

The governor of the town was a man of extraordinary brutality, who went out of his way to cause suffering to the people. He was particularly terrible after lunch, a meal which usually consisted of a box of sardines and a bottle of champagne.

The fines inflicted on the inhabitants afford instances of his petty tyranny. A man found carrying a copy of a French newspaper had to pay £40; an old man who had no room to give a German officer, but who offered to pay for his room at an hotel, was fined £4.

When the trunk of a tree was found placed across a railway line the unhappy inhabitants had to pay a fine of £1,200, and the neighbouring villages were fined £100, and the money had to be forthcoming within forty-eight hours, otherwise the mayors would have been shot.

The effect of a barrage of news items like this – true and false, partly true, partly false – was to change the British from a tolerant, easy-going people into a fierce and vengeful one. The folk at home vented their feelings on the only Germans they could get their hands on – the enemy aliens who had not taken the escape boat to Holland and who had not yet been interned:

> There were a large number of outbreaks of disorder in Manchester and Salford yesterday, led by men and women whose indignation had mastered them and who sought to wreak vengeance on the property and persons of Germans.
>
> In some cases premises occupied by Germans were stormed and considerable damage was done, but in others the demonstration took a less violent form. Workmen refused to continue to work alongside Germans, and a factory employing a considerable number of Germans was forced to close on the peremptory orders of an angry body of dockers.
>
> A number of arrests were made . . .
>
> Liverpool presented a scene of turmoil late on Monday night, when crowds of men and women, many of them fashionably dressed, systematically wrecked shops and houses in the occupation of Germans, destroying any furniture or valuables they could find.
>
> Premises were looted by hordes of men, women, and children. In one instance a piano was dragged into the street and was used to accompany topical songs which the crowd sang lustily.
>
> The state of public feeling in London was illustrated at the West London Police Court yesterday, when George Gray, a private in the Middlesex Regiment, was accused of being drunk and disorderly and of breaking a plate-glass window, the property of Peter Nell, a baker, of Goldbourne-road, North Kensington.
>
> A policeman said that he saw Gray surrounded by a large crowd. He was waving his arms about and shouting: 'Set about them!' meaning the baker's shop.
>
> 'I suppose the baker was a German?' said Mr de Grey, the magistrate.
>
> 'I suppose so,' replied the policeman. 'Gray took his left boot off and threw it through the window. When I arrested him we were followed by a hostile crowd of people, who threw stones and filth.'

Inspector Travers said that he had great difficulty in inducing Mr Nell to charge Gray. Mr Nell was not present in court.

'He is afraid of these people?' said the magistrate.

'Yes,' answered the inspector. 'The demonstration was against three German shops in the vicinity.'

'It is very regrettable,' said the magistrate, 'but it is my duty to keep the peace. It is due to the horrible and abominable conduct of the Germans against harmless and innocent people.'

'Feeling is becoming very strong,' said Inspector Travers.

'I hope the Government will do something for the safety of Germans,' said the magistrate.

The charge of breaking the window was withdrawn, and Gray was fined 5s, for being intoxicated.

*

The Germans proved by deeds – notably the sinking of the *Lusitania* – to be their own worst enemies in the battle for the hearts and minds of neutral America and what was called the world's 'conscience'.

When a German U-boat sank the British liner *Lusitania* in May 1915, Berlin was honestly astonished at the violent reaction from the USA. Admittedly scores of Americans – among them Charles Frohman who produced *Peter Pan* (the boy on whom Barrie's character was based, George Llewelyn-Davies, had been killed on the Western Front the previous month) – had been drowned but that, to the official German mind, was their own fault for travelling to England on a British ship which, the Germans alleged, was carrying munitions. And hadn't Germany warned the Americans in newspaper advertisements against sailing in the ship? Did the Americans not realise that unrestricted submarine warfare was the Reich's only appropriate reply to the British naval blockade which was strangling the economic life out of the Central Powers?

That the Americans were enraged at the Germans was beyond question: 'Savages drunk with blood' was the *New York Times*' comment. 'Wholesale butchers,' opined the *Herald*. 'The law of God and the law of nations have alike been trampled upon,' quoth the *Evening Post*. The event, however, was not sufficient to swing America away from neutrality. Two years were to pass before the USA entered the war on the side of the Allies.

Meanwhile the sinking of the *Lusitania*, in which many more British

Volunteers (British)
Britain alone among the contestants in 1914 relied entirely on volunteers. More than 2,000,000 were forthcoming.

Volunteers (German)
German civilians in training and looking uncommonly like their foes. Note the modern-looking block of flats.

Desolated Western Front
"In a few days we move up to a place where we do not know what awaits us, but where we know many of our comrades have found their graves......" from a soldier's letter home.

than Americans were killed, provoked the bitterest anti-German riots yet in England:

> Anti-German rioting spread like wildfire yesterday. Shops were wrecked and looted in almost every district of London and in many provincial towns, and scores of Germans were attacked and hunted in the streets.
> An enormous amount of damage was done in the East End. Premises were absolutely wrecked and stripped of every article, even pianos being taken away. Two shops were afterwards set on fire.
> Special constables and mounted men were called out to assist the police, but it was quite impossible to control the crowds of thousands of persons in so many districts, and looting took place under the eyes of the police.
> A specially summoned meeting of the Cabinet was held yesterday to consider the question of interning all alien enemies.

For their own safety, the Cabinet decided that all enemy aliens should be interned. But this action, though it assuaged the mob's fury, did nothing to lessen the hatred for anyone or anything German:

> A spirited protest against Councillor Wertheim, a naturalised German, resuming his seat on the Hampton District Council was raised at the meeting of the council last night.
> At the beginning of the meeting, Councillor William M. Bailey, the vice-chairman, asked the chairman how long he and his colleagues would have to submit to the indignity of sitting at the same table with a German.
> 'I have tried to keep my temper in the past,' said Councillor Bailey, 'but in consequence of what has happened in the last few days I find it impossible to do so any longer. I do not know how Mr Wertheim can have the impudence and cheek to come and sit by the side of respectable Englishmen.'
> Mr Wertheim claimed that his sons had enlisted in the King's Army, and that his daughter was attending the wounded in France, while he had been in England for forty-nine years.

No one was spared, from humble town councillors to the highest in the land.

Sir Edward Speyer, Privy Councillor, Chairman of the London

Underground, trustee of King Edward's Hospital Fund and a British subject for nearly thirty years, wrote to Mr Asquith:

> For the last nine months I have kept silence and treated with disdain the charges of disloyalty and suggestions of treachery made against me in the press and elsewhere. But I can keep silence no long, for these charges and suggestions have now been repeated by public men, who have not scrupled to use their position to inflame the over-strained feelings of the people.
>
> I am not a man who can be driven or drummed by threats or abuse into an attitude of justification. But I consider it due to my honour as a loyal British subject and my personal dignity as a man to retire from all my public positions.
>
> I therefore write to ask you to accept my resignation as a Privy Councillor and to revoke my baronetcy.

Prince Louis of Battenberg, First Sea Lord and the man technically responsible for keeping the Fleet mobilised after its review in July 1914, had to go because of his German connections. Even long dead and renowned figures like Richard Wagner were pursued, as this letter to the *Express* demonstrates:

> You reported an incident which occurred during the holding of a crowded concert at Queen's Hall on Good Friday. It consisted of a passionate protest from a woman in that audience against the use – in this instance the exclusive use – of German music in England, at a time when Germans were merrily occupied in torturing and slaughtering our fellow countrymen.
>
> I am proud, sir, to emerge from the anonymity of your report disclosing myself as the author of that protest. I had gone to the Queen's Hall in the knowledge that I would hear some good music, and in ignorance of the fact that it was possible to hold a successful concert in the heart of the British Empire on a day dedicated to the Prince of Peace, at which thousands of Englishmen and Englishwomen would gather and vociferously applaud a Gargantuan feast of Hunnish melody.
>
> My unpremeditated outburst, with its final cry of 'Shame!' on that occasion finds an echo in my heart as I write this, for reflection leaves me entirely unrepentant. I would this same echo, this same natural abhorrence of the Hun and all his works, which even the worship of the arts cannot excuse, would find a hearing in many other hearts.
>
> In that happy case, such insults to our patriotism as that concert to the glory of Wagner then would never again be perpetrated.
>
> Baroness Helene Gingold.

On 11 October, 1915, the Germans committed a crime which was also a colossal blunder. They executed Nurse Edith Cavell by firing squad. She was not the first woman to be judicially killed. The French, for example, had shot one Margueritte Schmitt for spying for Germany. But Nurse Cavell's execution for helping Allied prisoners to escape from Brussels where Miss Cavell ran a hospital evoked special horror because she saved lives (Schmitt was a paid hireling). The Spanish and American ministers in Brussels did their utmost to save Edith Cavell. Their efforts prompted Herr Zimmermann, Under-Secretary for Foreign Affairs, to justify the German action with a telegram to the American Associated Press which merely confirmed Germany's reputation for callous brutality:

> I see by the British and American press that the shooting of an Englishwoman and the conviction of several other women in Brussels for treason have created a great impression, and that we are being severely criticised.
>
> No law book in the world, least of all those dealing with war regulations, makes such a differentiation, and the female sex has but one preference, according to legal usage – namely that women in a delicate condition may not be executed.
>
> Countless British, Belgian and French soldiers are now again fighting in the Allies' ranks who owe their escape from Belgium to the activity of the band now sentenced at the head of which stood Miss Cavell. With such a situation under the very eyes of the authorities, only the utmost severity can bring relief, and a Government violates the most elementary duty towards the army that does not adopt the strictest measures. These duties in war are greater than any other.
>
> The sentence has been carried out to frighten those who presume on their sex to take part in enterprises punishable with death. Should one recognise these presumptions, it would open the door for the evil activities of women, who are often handier and cleverer in these things than the craftiest spy.

Even Hermann Ridder, editor of the *Staats Zeitung*, the German language paper in the USA, could not bring himself to condone his Government's idiotic infamy. 'There are times,' he wrote, 'when German commanders may do things in the heat of war in which even their own people will not support them.'

The Bishop of London preaching in Trafalgar Square called for three million recruits 'who will know the reason why this poor Englishwoman was murdered. God's curse is on the nation that tramples underfoot and defies the laws of chivalry.'

The Germans with their use of poison gas, indiscriminate U-boat sinkings and the execution of Edith Cavell put all the weaponry of propaganda into the hands of their foes. They really did seem a nation – to quote a contemporary description – possessing 'the cruelty and ferocity of their Mongol origin, springing, as they do, from the Genghis Khan who settled in Prussia.'

On the battlefield, however, the Germans were far from losing the war. They were showing themselves to be superb soldiers who could match the Allies in courage, out-machine them in armaments and hold them – even at odds of 4-1 – on the Western Front while they inflicted defeat after defeat on the half-armed Russians in the East.

It was the sheer professionalism of the German Army which gave the Allies such a hellish time in trying to break through. Even the newspapers, eager as they were to trumpet victories, could not disguise the horror of trench warfare.

CHAPTER TWO

Men at War

By December 1914 the Allied Armies in the west – overwhelmingly French – faced the Germans in a line of uninterrupted trenches from Switzerland to the North Sea.

'Line' is however a simplistic description. The French system was a form of grid with front lines linked to reserve lines by means of communication trenches; with transverses, 'kinks', to prevent the whole trench being enfiladed by enemy fire, with dug-outs deep in the earth where officers and men could rest safe from all but a direct hit by heavy mortar or large calibre shell. And the whole was protected by masses of barbed wire, reinforced by machine-gun emplacements and redoubts formed by ruined farms or villages.

Such a village was Neuve Chapelle twenty miles inside France from the Belgian frontier. This battered spot was chosen for the first major British push of the war, designed to take the village and the ridge beyond which commanded the plain containing Lille, Roubaix and Tourcoing, three of the richest towns in occupied France.

The dream of the staff was to break through the enemy's fixed defences so that the cavalry could roam free, dealing death and destruction on the fleeing Hun (it was never quite clear what the German cavalry was going to do in these circumstances).

So in early March the regular British Army, reinforced by scores of Territorial Army battalions, all with strong local affiliations, prepared to attack Neuve Chapelle. Six weeks later the newspapers were permitted to publish a despatch for general release by the London News Agency:

> The dawn which broke reluctantly through a veil of clouds on the morning of Wednesday, 10 March, seemed as any other to the

Germans behind the white and blue sandbags in their long line of trenches about the battered village of Neuve Chapelle.

For five months they had remained undisputed masters of the position.

For weeks past the German airmen had grown strangely shy. On this Wednesday morning none was aloft to spy out the strange doings which, as dawn broke, might have been described on the desolate roads behind the British lines.

From ten o'clock of the preceding evening endless files of men marched silently down the roads leading towards the German position, through Laventie and Richeborg St Vaast, poor shattered villages of the dead, where months of incessant bombardment have driven away the last inhabitants and left roofless houses and rent roadways.

Watch the troops go by. Here some Indians, dark faces beneath slouch hats, kukris slung behind their waist belts.

Not Gurkhas these – they are further down the road – but Garhwalis, a tribe akin, of similar cast of face with a strong Mongolian strain, but men of sturdier build. Here are the Leicesters, the 'Tigers' as they call them from their badge, here Territorials of the Royal Fusiliers, here the Lincolns and the Berks, the silver cross of the Rifle Brigade, the star and bugle of the Scottish Rifles, the Black Watch in their bonnets, the Northants, the Worcesters, heroes of Ypres.

Halted by the roadside are the Middlesex, the West Yorks, the Devons; every burr from Land's End to John o' Groats is heard on these deserted highways.

Two days before, a quiet room, where Nelson's prayer stands on the mantelshelf, saw the ripening of the plans that sent these sturdy sons of Britain marching all through the night. Sir John French met the army corps commanders and unfolded to them his plans for the offensive of the British Army against the German line at Neuve Chapelle.

The whole experience of this war has gone to show that infantry cannot advance against machine-guns defended by barbed-wire entanglements. A machine-gun, firing 600 shots a minute, can reap down advancing infantry like ripe corn. A great general has truly said that two men with a machine-gun can hold up a brigade. Concentrated artillery fire is, therefore, the indispensable preliminary to an offensive in the present trench warfare. . . .

God! How the time drags! The aeroplanes glitter soft. Here and there a bird sings. Subalterns are glancing at their watches. . . . Then hell breaks loose. With a mighty hideous screeching burst of noise, hundreds of guns spoke.

In some places the troops were smothered in earth and dust, or even spattered in blood from the hideous fragments of human bodies that went hurtling through the air. At one point the upper half of a German officer, his cap crammed on his head, was blown into one of our trenches.

Words will never convey any adequate idea of the horror of those five-and-thirty minutes. When the hands of the officers' watches pointed to five minutes past eight, whistles resounded along the British lines. At the same moment the shells began to burst further ahead, for, by previous arrangement, the gunners lengthening their fuses, were 'lifting' on to the village of Neuve Chapelle so as to leave the road open for our infantry to rush in and finish what the guns had begun.

On getting out of their trenches the Middlesex were a little crowded. As they pressed forward to the attack they were suddenly swept by a diabolical fire from two machine-guns posted at either end of the German trench so as to cover their converging fire a patch of about 200 yards front. In this zone no man could live. But the Middlesex were men of grit. They did not stop. They got as far as the wire. They hacked at it, tore at it with their hands until they were raw and bleeding and their uniforms rent to tatters.

From their starting point right up to the wire they left a deep lane of their dead and dying 120 yards long, a sight so poignant that men, coming suddenly on that bloody trail, broke down and wept at the sheer pity, the undying glory of it.

Ultimately a number of positions, including Neuve Chapelle, were taken. Then, as always happened, came the enemy's riposte. The Germans too could, alas, die with valour.

The German counter-attack was a ghastly business.

The slaughter was sickening. In front of one of the brigades the Bavarians, coming along at the ambling trot adopted by the German infantry at the assault and bawling 'Hourra' in the approved fashion, blundered into the fire of no fewer than twenty-one machine-guns. The files of men did not recede or stagger. They were just swept away. One moment one had the shouting, ambling crowd before one's eyes; the next moment where it had been lay a writhing, convulsed pile of bodies heaped up on the brown earth.

When day broke amid the rattle of machine-gun and rifle fire, the German corpses were used to make ramparts behind which the wounded took cover.

With hopes high and courage undaunted our troops went forward again against the German line protecting the ridge.

Here it was that the 6th Gordons lost their colonel, Lieut-Colonel Martin. A subaltern, hearing he had been killed, hastened to his side and found him still alive, lying in the open behind the trench, with a bullet in his back and sinking fast. He was suffering grievously. The young officer fetched the colonel some morphia, which eased his pain.

'Thank you,' said the dying man, 'and now my boy, your place is not here. Go about your duty.' So he dismissed him, and died a little while later, a very gallant gentleman.

The courage of these men, many of them new to battle, and their extraordinary achievements is summed up in the citation for just one of the VCs awarded for valour in the four-day battle:

> No 15624 Lance-Corporal Wilfred Dolby Fuller, 1st Battalion Grenadier Guards.
>
> For most conspicuous bravery at Neuve Chapelle on 12 March, 1915. Seeing a party of the enemy endeavouring to escape along a communication trench, he ran towards them and killed the leading man with a bomb; the remainder (nearly fifty), finding no means of evading his bombs, surrendered to him.
>
> Lance-Corporal Fuller was quite alone at the time.

Now this despatch, while glowing in its praise of British gallantry, disclosed the tragic weakness of the Army's preparations. The German wire in many places was not cut: lack of co-ordination between the second stage of the artillery barrage and the infantry prevented the probable capture of the Aubers Ridge.

Neuve Chapelle was fought by men who had at least trained for war – and some of them had experienced it – yet, despite tremendous bravery, they made little impression on the German defences. Why? Because behind the front-line troops Britain was still mentally at peace, governed by peace-time politicians with industry still geared to 'business as usual' and the workers to striking as usual.

Mr Asquith, the Prime Minister, was so ignorant – or so wilfully misinformed by the Munitions Committee of the Cabinet headed by Lord Kitchener – that he told a meeting in Newcastle on 20 April, 1915, 'I do not believe that any army or navy have ever entered on a campaign or been maintained during a campaign with better or more adequate equipment.'

The shells that failed to flatten the German wire at Neuve Chapelle were not adequate. Many of them did not go off, thanks to faulty fuses and detonators.

British industry was so woefully lacking in accurate machine tools for modern armaments that whole factories had to be re-equipped from America.

As for the workers, in the very week of Neuve Chapelle 10,000 Clyde engineers were on strike to gain an extra two pence an hour.

Their fellow-workers on the battlefield were paid one half-penny an hour for risking their lives twenty-four hours a day. In the week after Neuve Chapelle 10,000 Merseyside dockers went on strike because they had to wait until the following Saturday for payment for weekend work. They regarded this delay as intolerable and consequently refused to do any weekend work until it was rectified. On the day of Mr Asquith's speech at Newcastle, South Wales miners' delegates voted in favour of a national strike to secure a twenty per cent war bonus. One of the miners' arguments was that the patriotic considerations had not prevented the coal owners from taking advantage of higher coal prices.

Yet within a year many of the very men who had struck were in the forces, the miners, especially, providing huge contingents of Kitchener's New Army and 'backward' industry had thrust itself forward to such a degree that it was able to provide three million shells for that Army to fire in one day's battle alone (Napoleon had 20,000 at Waterloo).

The creation of the Kitchener Army forged from young men who came from a long line of civilians was a miracle of improvisation. Alone among the contestants Britain maintained the voluntary system. For a year and more it was enough. Men flocked to the colours in such numbers that the recruiting offices were engulfed. The Army and the supply services could not cope.

Between 28 August and 3 September, 1914, four infantry battalions – 4,000 men in all – were recruited by Lord Derby in Liverpool. They were all 'Pals' battalions, made up of men who worked together: as clerks in Cunard shipping, or in shops or warehouses or tramway depots.

As soon as 100,000 men had been processed (cleared as fit for service and given an arm band) they were designated K1 or K2 – Kitchener 100,000; Kitchener 200,000. Then their training began, largely composed of interminable route marches.

But, gradually an army of 1,500,000 was created to relieve the regulars and Territorials, most of whom had gone more than a year in France without any home leave.

Not all groups were as forthcoming as the Cunard clerks. By April 1915 only 122 out of 1,800 professional footballers had joined up. Perhaps they could hardly be blamed, considering the disproportionate effect on their lives of even a minor war injury. However the authorities soon brought regular league matches to an end and the recruiting figures picked up.

The trench life these men from factories, fields and offices were about to experience was vividly described in news items like these:

> Of the smaller trench annoyances few are more worrying than the plague of rats. Shelter and trenches, no matter where they are made, whether in woods, or open fields, or on the mountainside, become immediately infested with the objectionable creatures. In one case within my personal knowledge they drove a French officer out of a comfortable and commodious dug-out in to a damp and melancholy one which was to some extent protected from them by sheets of corrugated iron. The plague had attained considerable dimensions before a really organised attempt was made to deal with it, and there were many cases of rats actually biting men who were chasing them down the trenches.
>
> Terriers have proved of considerable assistance. Trains full of dogs have been despatched to the front, and poison has been fairly effective. Lately a reward has been offered for every dead rat brought in by men in the trenches, and regular battues have been organised. In a single fortnight one army corps alone has disposed of no fewer than 8,000 rats. At a halfpenny a rate this has involved an expense of over £16, and it was certainly money well spent.
>
> The sport of rat catching on such very advantageous terms has proved very popular among the men, who now suggest that the standing reward offered for the more dangerous and more exciting form of sport involved in the capture of a German machine-gun should be raised to a higher figure.

As can be seen from that, and other items, the public was informed: sometimes in melodramatic prose, some times in matter-of-fact, almost jaunty, narrative of what was going on at the front. Yet the gap remained unbridgeable between those who had been there and those who hadn't.

The *Express* even sent a young woman correspondent, Jane Anderson, to visit the French sector (the French were more responsive to reporters and, of course, to women). She was to give the woman's eye view. She described the horizon blue of the French officers' tunics, the darker blue of the *poilus'* helmets and then, having made her gesture towards the 'woman's world' she arrived at the nub of the matter as it would strike anyone, male or female, coming to this strange, implacable, fearful place:

We came to the front. And it was well in accordance with my ignorant conception of such matters that I did not know we had arrived. The car stopped. I saw the narrow road reaching out straight in front of us, and, close by, a narrow break in the barrier. The chauffeur climbed down and opened the door. Some officers appeared at the opening where the canvas strips were fastened back. They apologised for the car having been late, asked me if the drive had been bad.

We started to walk along a muddy path through the fields. The path broadened, the mud deeper at every step, a grey clayey mud which dried in white patches on the officers' boots and the blue cloth of their topcoats.

'It will be worse soon,' the lieutenant assured me, smiling. His English was perfect.

He was right. The border of the field was a bank of earth, like a levée. As we neared this, the mud, over which a thin surface of rain floated, was like a paste, not like solid ground. It swirled underfoot and spattered over the wet grass.

Two sentries waited at the levée, which was barricaded. They stood at attention as we passed through the narrow tunnel which was their post. I asked the captain who was walking beside me how far we were from the trenches, and as I asked him we stepped out from under the low roof of the tunnel and on to a strip of mud from which a trench opened directly. I don't know why this should have appeared to me such an astonishing fact. But I had never realised that the front was identical with a muddy field full of rank weeds. I had conceived in my mind some fatal line of demarcation, some point of divergence between a peaceful earth and the black territory of war. It was a conception, without reason, founded on no information, no logic; but it seemed neither just nor fitting that human beings should walk through a meadow and step into war.

She had arrived at the start of the grid system and as she walked forward towards the actual front line:

I stepped down into this trench. It was deep, with shallow spade marks showing in the clay. It was more solid underfoot than the half-frozen ground of the field. But it was wet, although miraculously clean.

I walked along slowly because the trench swerved suddenly: it was not a straight line but a long succession of slow curves. When I looked back, the place where I had walked but a moment before was hidden.

'This is,' said the captain, 'a boyan' (a communicator trench). 'But it is fortunate that there is mist this afternoon because you may go to the front line. It is a quiet day.'

As he said this, calling it out to me because I was walking a little in advance, a slow and rolling sound, like the sound of thunder which rolls very low on the horizon, was carried down to us across the flat earth.

'From this point we hear the guns speak plainly,' said the captain. 'The minenwerfers.'

I waited, thinking that this sound of distant firing would cease; that it was but for a moment that those thunderous waves rolled down through the trenches towards us. But they did not cease. Steadily, neither increasing nor diminishing, that distant thundering lay always to our right.

For a long time I could distinguish no one of the individual sounds of which it was composed. It was confused, vast, non-resonant, like detonations in an immense vacuum. But little by little I separated the crunching of the shells as they struck and the overlying vibrations which preceded or followed the explosions. . . .

The network of wire overhead stopped abruptly. There were firing steps cut into the wall.

These steps were no more than ledges spaded out, ledges upon which several men might stand in a row. The parapets were higher, thrown up more evenly and solidly.

Beside some of the ledges there were little doors which opened into the clay walls. These led into the dug-outs, and the commandant opened one of them, calling to one of the men within. A *poilu* appeared suddenly in the black opening, silhouetted sharply against the solid wall of darkness.

The commandant sent him back for some candles and we followed him down into that enormous black hole. The ground shelved abruptly under our feet.

The *poilu*, standing by a table, lighted a candle, and the thin flame illumined irregular walls of earth lined with bunks, one above the other. These were heaped with grey blankets. Telephone wires were strung in rows of three, with open plugs; a funnel-shaped stove, in which a slow fire burned, glowed in one dim corner. The air was thick, wet and heavy. I saw in the flickering candlelight some men moving out of the black shadows which seemed to descend upon us from an invisible ceiling. The place was cavernous; I saw the shadowy bodies of men disappear, but when we followed them I saw that they had only turned and gone up some rude steps into another communication trench than the one by which I had entered. However, that black dug-out filled me with terror, with nameless forebodings. The daylight and the yellow ditches which I had seen did not look like war, but this great cavern hollowed out of the earth for the housing of thirty men was peopled with horrors. That human beings should be reduced to living in such hideous burrowings in the face of the earth!

'Guns . . . trenches . . . dug-outs . . . the sea of rusty red barbed wire that comes up to a man's helmet.' Jane Anderson described the scene vividly and truthfully But it was the news despatches that conveyed the real horror. Like this one from an interview with Private David Jones of the Canadian Light Infantry recuperating in a Cardiff hospital:

'We were playing football,' he said, 'about three miles behind the French trenches, not far from Ypres, when our eyes began to smart and to water, but we did not know what it was.

'Presently we saw a crowd of refugees from Ypres coming along the road. The Germans are coming through Ypres,' they said. The Canadians immediately fell in and fought all through Thursday night.

'I had been working in the Welsh collieries before I went to Canada, and I know something about the effect of gas. This German gas at first seemed to have the same effect as ammonia on the eyes, but it became stronger and blinded us. Then the breathing of the fumes was deadly.

'I knew that vinegar was a good thing, so I got a bottle of pickles and poured it on my handkerchief, which I placed in my mouth, and that gave me great relief.

'Some of our men, however, were going crazy, and I saw a trench full of Algerians who had been killed by the fumes. The Germans in this instance had used hand grenades made up like sausages. They flung them into the trenches, and so soon as they burst the smell caused the men to collapse and die.

'The gas in its effect is just like black damp, and when you are at close quarters you are laid out immediately. This is not fighting; it is absolute murder.'

Another Canadian describing the poisonous bombs said to me:

'The smoke they exude is a yellowish green colour, much the same as the smoke from lyddite, but it does not mix with the air. It seems to stop dead unless it is carried like a feather on the wind.

'The French were unable to live in their trenches, and many of our men went down. Aeroplanes, too, dropped bombs full of stupefying gas.'

The response to the Germans' use of poison gas was typically – uproariously – British:

The new request of the War Office was the topic of conversation in every place where women met yesterday. The great stores – notably Selfridge's, Harrods, Whiteley's and Gamages – were thronged throughout the day with women anxious to buy materials and learn how to make respirators.

Thousands of women asked if they could buy them ready made, so that no time might be lost in sending them to Belgium and France. In the early morning, while the first inquiries were being made, experiments took place in dozens of West End workrooms to arrive at the most efficient and expeditious method of shaping materials into respirators.

By noon the respirators appeared in hundreds of windows. Several shops in the City showed them as wax models.

Harrods were particularly busy during the day selling materials for the respirators and also in booking down orders for ready-made pads.

Every woman who makes a respirator must be careful to observe the directions. For the convenience of those who would like to see the process in detail, Messrs Selfridge have arranged to give a practical demonstration at their Oxford-street premises throughout to-day.

A woman demonstrator will be in attendance in the surgical instrument department on the ground floor from 10 am onwards, showing how the absorbent cottonwool should be cut, placed in absorbent cotton gauze, and stitched.

In the same department the firm will from today onwards have a collecting basket into which respirators may be placed. Any number may be placed in the basket, so long as the number is clearly stated on the outside of the package. They will be sorted and despatched to the chief ordinance officer in multiples of 100.

Unhappily amateur improvisation was not enough – and it typified the whole approach to what was to become the greatest battle ever fought by a British Army: the Somme.

Security was lax; frequently non-existent. On 1 June, 1916, one month before the Big Push was due Mr Arthur Henderson, President of the Board of Trade, told munition workers in Leeds:

'I have been asked why the Whitsuntide holidays have been postponed until the end of July. How very curious we all are! It ought to be sufficient that we are only asking for postponement until the end of July. That fact ought to speak volumes.

'I say this on the authority of the Minister of Munitions, who has done so much to bring it about, that in stocks of ammunition, machine-guns, heavy guns of the highest standard, and shells of the biggest calibre, we stand better to-day than we have ever done, and I venture to say, better than he in his most sanguine moment ever expected we should do.

'If need calls, and our men in the trenches are in a position to respond, their powers of endurance, their heroism, their military capacity, with the supply of all kinds of munitions, will, I hope, enable them to strike the hardest blow yet struck on behalf of the Allied cause.'

There could hardly have been a more obvious give-away that the British Army was preparing for a massive offensive than Mr Henderson's 'wink-is-as-good-as-a-nod' speech.

Some months previously Lord St Davids, a former Welsh Liberal MP, had alleged that the General Staff had failed the troops in the battle of Loos – another of those interminable and bloody battles to capture a 'feature': a hill, or a ridge on the Western Front. There were, he said, no reserves to exploit the breakthrough; no effort to reinforce success and cut one's losses with failures.

These were criticisms of tactics, of military methodology. Much graver were his assertions that the General Staff were lazy, snobbish good-for-nothings:

'Our staff has been crowded with men of rank, men of position, and men of money.

'The men I allude to had been out of the Army for years, had retired to take up politics or business or to amuse themselves in social life, but for years have had no experience of soldiering, and these have been crammed into the Headquarters Staff.

'Men have been appointed because they could give a good "tip" as to a winner in the racing world.

'Our Army is not anything like so large as the French Army, and yet our Headquarters Staff is five or six times as large as the staff of General Joffre.

'Then ladies, it is said, have visited the British headquarters. Does the Government defend the presence of any ladies at the General Headquarters of the British Army in France – the thinking machine of the British Army?

'Owing to the playing of bridge many officers are later for their duties in the morning. Here we are sending our sons to risk their lives and to be directed by men who cannot be early at their offices because they are late the previous night at bridge.

'These things are spoken about in the Army; it is time they should be said in public.'

Much of what Lord St Davids alleged was refuted by Government spokesmen, but their defence of the staff did not alter the hatred felt by the front-line officers for those in the rear who made the decisions to attack but bore none of the consequences.

The tragic toll of these young front-line officers was revealed in a newspaper paragraph the very day before the Somme offensive was launched:

'The number of Old Harrovians known to have served or to be serving at present is 2,815,' said Lord George Hamilton, speaking at the Governors'-day commemoration at Harrow School yesterday. 'The casualty list represents 25 per cent of this total. No less than

Troops on the March

On the march from rest areas to the front. In the early days of the war men marched as many as 40 miles a day carrying 91 pounds on their backs.

Gas

"I had been working in the Welsh collieries before I went to Canada and I knew something about the effect of gas. This German gas at first seemed to have the same effect as ammonia on the eyes, but it was stronger and blinded us...." Pte. David Jones, Canadian Light Infantry.

21 per cent have gained honours or promotion. Four have received the Victoria Cross.'

Losses such as these – and they were largely of the trained regulars or Territorials – diminished the small stock of British leaders available at zero hour for the Somme.

The men who would go over the top that day were overwhelmingly Kitchener's New Army: deployed (at General Joffre's request) on a fifteen-mile front. Fourteen British divisions faced five German. But the three to one advantage was more than cancelled out by the thoroughness of German preparation; the depth and robustness of their defence system and the killing power of the machine-gun: so truthfully perceived by the special correspondent who had observed the battle of Neuve Chapelle fifteen months before.

In Britain's New Army, training was so rudimentary that sophisticated fire plans – even assuming the Royal Artillery was expert enough to have laid down creeping barrages thirty yards ahead of the advancing infantry – would have been useless. The much maligned staff had to cope with realities and those dictated simple brute strength of bombardment: a week of firing, reaching a crescendo in the hour before the assault. Add to the Army's basic unreadiness for such a trial as the Somme the natural confusion of battle: total lack of communications (land-lines destroyed, wireless not fully developed) and the smoke which blotted out the landscape and it is easy to understand why things went wrong.

That they went catastrophically wrong was hidden from the people at home at the time. The big breakthrough never took place. The first day's fighting, the bloodiest ever recorded in British history – 21,000 dead and 39,000 wounded – was reported cautiously by John Irvine, the special correspondent with the British troops, operating north of the Somme River which ran at right-angles to the battlefield, and triumphantly by reporter H. J. Greenwell with the French forces to the south of the river. The only real triumph of the Somme, however, was the unbelievable valour of the men who fought it.

This is how Irvine saw things:

With the British Army in the field (1 July, noon)
The great day of battle broke in sunshine and mist. Not a cloud obscured the sky as the sun appeared above the horizon – in the direction where the German trenches lay. But, anon, a purple haze

crept up, which grew in intensity as the morning advanced, and the view of distant objects was veiled in obscurity.

The night passed quietly in our trenches. The enemy submitted in silence to the ordeal of our terrific gunfire. No doubt he knew that it was a prelude to a great event, and that whatever might be his powers of retaliation later, for the time being he must be content to wait and endure.

From a ridge a little to the west of Albert, overlooking the town and commanding a wide view of the beautiful undulating country, I witnessed the last phase of the bombardment which preceded the advance. It was six o'clock (summer time) when we arrived there. The guns had been roaring furiously all through the night. Now they had, so to speak, gathered themselves together for one grand final effort before our British lions should be let loose on their prey.

The sound was that of raging pandemonium, and one felt almost inclined to sympathise with the soldier who remarked to a comrade: 'Pity the poor German devils in the trenches who are copping this lot.' 'Serve them right,' was the reply. 'I hope they'll be sorry now they started the war.' The mist at first was too thick to note through the telescope the falling of the shells. For half-an-hour we heard nothing but the ceaseless crashing and booming of our guns, great and small, and saw nothing but the flashes of fire from their muzzles.

A perceptible slackening of our fire soon after seven was the first indication given us that our gallant soldiers were about to leap from their trenches and advance against the enemy. Non-combatants, of course, were not permitted to witness this spectacle, but I am informed that the vigour and eagerness were worthy of the best traditions of the British Army. I have myself heard within the past few days men declare that they were getting fed up with life in the trenches, and would welcome a fight at close quarters. Thus it may be taken as certain that our men entered into the grand assault in the true spirit of a sane and cheerful manliness. Death might come or suffering, but the soldier recks not concerning these things; he hears only the call of duty and he does it.

We had not to wait long for news, and it was wholly satisfactory and encouraging. The message received at ten o'clock ran something like this: 'On a front of over twenty miles, north and south of the Somme, we and our French allies have advanced and taken the German first line of trenches.

8 pm

I have just returned from the front line of some of the most desperate points of the battle. Let me say at once that the day's operations are entirely satisfactory to ourselves and our allies. There have been a few disappointments, but, on the whole, they have been counterbalanced by unexpected gains. We have ploughed deep into the German lines.

The Germans evidently realize what they are up against, and are fighting grimly inch by inch. While there is every reason to believe that the secret of our plan of campaign has been rigidly excluded from their ken, all the evidence points to the fact of their complete preparedness, and though our success may be assured, a speedy ending to the battle is not at the moment to be looked for.

The taking of the first trenches referred to in my previous message was in some places comparatively easy – almost a walkover. It was only when our men bit deeper into the enemy's defences that they were brought face to face with difficulties: but their indomitable pluck and perseverance have triumphed over what have been in some cases almost superhuman obstacles.

A description of the French part of the enterprise came from H. J. Greenwell who, having been with attacking Allied troops, visited wounded *poilus* in Paris:

I spoke this afternoon with dozens of men tucked into white hospital cots, who at 7.30 yesterday morning felt their hearts thumping against their ribs and wondering what the next few seconds had in store for them.

In the French attacking force all the men were given two days' iron rations and a second supply of water. The ammunition supply was doubled, gas masks and mouth pads were made ready for emergency, dressings were inspected, and all men ordered to wear clean underwear in order to prevent the infection of wounds. Thursday and Friday were spent in writing letters.

During Friday night they had nothing to do but watch the shells of Allied gunners bursting with absolute precision along the whole front. The Germans were firing, too, and the earth rocked like a railway platform when an express rushes through.

Amid the terrible din the men lay down, with their knapsacks on, and had a meal of sardines, bread and cheese. Afterwards came the order 'Stand to arms,' and they began filing through the trenches.

Suddenly a whistle was blown and a whispered command was passed along the ranks to fix bayonets. The whistle was blown again twice. Men adjusted their straps and shook hands. Everybody wore a fixed grin.

Twice again the whistle sounded, and all rushed for the trench wall, eager to be out first and get it over. Like runners panting to reach the tape the men struggled into the roaring hell. Above the tick-tacking of machine guns, the rattle of rifle fire, and the grinding smashes of bursting shells, came the roar of men's voices, 'En avant. Vive la France!'

Nearing their first goal the men were faced by a wall of bursting seventy-five shells from the supporting artillery – a wall formed of black clouds in their lower edges tinged with flames of green and red. The smoke curtain shut out the sunlight. Lumps of metal and earth descended in showers.

As they came nearer the wall they had to brace themselves on the rocking ground, like sailors in stormy weather. Then the fire curtain suddenly jumped like a jerky cinema film, rose, and fell on another trench further on. Nothing was left in front of our men but desolation. Everything had been flattened out of existence. The men leaped across the ruined trenches and rushed towards the wall of smoke and fire.

This drama was repeated again and again always with the same success. The men approached the curtain, saw it lift, and fall further on. Our gunners' range was perfect.

In this cyclone of fire it was not possible to give a spoken command, and everything was done by gesture. When the officers lay down the men followed suit. The officers waved to the right or the left to show the direction which the advance was to take.

The losses of both British and French troops in the great battle south of the Somme have been extraordinarily light.* I am able to make this statement on the authority of a high military personage, and have supplemented the information by the evidence of my own eyes.

I have already visited three hospitals which were entirely evacuated in preparation for the offensive, and was delighted to find that hundreds of beds were vacant. I have also seen efficient hospital trains all ready to bring back men from the Somme battle-

---

* This was true. The French were experienced troops and they had easier ground to traverse. British soldiers co-operating with their allies also suffered fewer casualties than their comrades to the north.

field. Thanks to what our gunners have done, not half the trains prepared have been in use. In fact, it is no exaggeration to say that never has any offensive been so cheaply carried out.

The bitterly disappointing results of the battle of the Somme – a penetration of five miles at the maximum for the loss of 170,000 fighting men over four months – brought Britain's political leadership to crisis point. Effectively, 1916 marked the end of 'civilian' Britain and the emergence of an armed nation dedicated to total war.

General Sir John French, Commander of the Expeditionary Force in France, had been displaced by the beginning of the year. With his straggly white moustache, bulging blue eyes and bow legs – he was a cavalryman – French has been pictured as the very model of an insensitive old military duffer. He was rather the product of a colonial school of wars (he distinguished himself in South Africa) and the victim of circumstances. The battles he fought in 1915, notably Loos, which raised the fury of his critics, were forced on him by the appeals of the Allies and the promptings of his own Cabinet.

Baulked of a quick victory in the West by defeat at the Marne and the stalemate of trench warfare, Germany turned east to maul the Russians. Poorly armed, pitifully short of supplies of all kinds, the Czar's armies wilted under the blows. The loss of Russian territory to the German-Austrian attackers was trifling, perhaps one-fiftieth of the land yielded twenty-five years later to the Nazis, but when gains and losses in the West were measured in yards the surrender of miles was unendurable.

Moreover, Russia was politically unstable. There was a peace party (to which the Czar's wife, of German birth, was believed to be not unsympathetic) and a strong and growing undercurrent of social revolution.

Russia, the 'steamroller' of 1914 had become, by 1915, the sick man of the alliance. Everything had to be done to keep her in the war for, without her, the re-inforced German armies in the West would leap forward and destroy France. Hence the repeated British and French assaults on the Western Front designed, as much as anything, to relieve the Russians of remorseless German pressure by forcing the German High Command to keep up its strength in the West.

Hence, too, the Dardanelles campaign aimed at opening a route to Russia to supply the Czar's heroic troops, who by January 1915 had one week's supply of shells left (firing at the rate of 45,000 a day and producing at the rate of 35,000 a month).

Turkey had entered the war on the side of the Central Powers and opened a fresh front against Russia. But Turkey had also presented an opportunity to Britain: to force the Straits, take Constantinople, reach the Black Sea and provide a warm water route to Russia, incidentally knocking Turkey out of the war on the way.

This plan commended itself to Winston Churchill, First Lord of the Admiralty, who wanted to use 'his' Navy and avoid the ghastly slogging match in the mud of Flanders. The plan was carried out but was so badly bungled through lack of Navy–Army co-ordination (a month elapsed between the naval bombardment and the landing of troops) that it effectively ruined any opportunity for an alternative to attrition in the West: every alternative being dismissed as 'another Dardanelles, another expensive sideshow'.

Churchill, as originator of the scheme, bore the brunt of the blame for failure. He was sacked from the Government, quitting the Duchy of Lancaster when informed he was not to serve on the War Council, thus joining Sir John French in the wilderness.

French went quietly – from command in France to a sinecure at home; his place being taken by the granite Scot, Sir Douglas Haig, a solid advocate of grinding the Germans down. Churchill went eloquently, as testified by his resignation speech to the Commons:

'I began to direct the attention of the First Sea Lord and other naval advisers to the possibilities of action in Turkish waters. The Dardanelles stood out as incomparably the most decisive operation that was open. Of course, from the beginning we all recognised that a joint naval and military operation by surprise was the best way of attacking the Dardanelles. As early as 3 November – over a year ago – we obtained from the War Office their appreciation of the number of troops necessary to seize the Gallipoli Peninsula by a joint amphibious coup de main.

'On 30 November I sent a minute to my noble friend, Lord Kitchener, offering to congregate transports for 40,000 men – that is to say, for the first echelon of an army for the purpose in Egypt on the chance of their being wanted, as I could see that the situation was developing in the direction of an attack in the Eastern Mediterranean on the Turkish Empire.

'We were informed that no army was available, and further, in the early discussions which took place among us, and also at the War Council, it was clearly the prevailing opinion they should not be used for attacking the Gallipoli Peninsula.

'Yet in the early days of March it became clear that military operations might be required and that military support would be forthcoming.

'I asked Lord Kitchener directly whether it was understood that he assumed responsibility for the military operations, by which I meant, the measuring of the force required to achieve success, and to that he replied in the affirmative.

'All through the year I have offered the same counsel to the Government – undertake no operation in the west, which is more costly to you in life than to the enemy; in the east Constantinople, take it by ships if you can or by soldiers if you must: take it by whatever plan, military or naval, commends itself to your experts; but take it, and take it soon. [Cheers.]

'The situation is now entirely changed and I am not called upon to offer any advice upon its aspects but it seems to me that if there were any operations in the history of the world which, having been begun, it was worth while to carry through with the utmost vigour and fury, with a consistent flow of reinforcements and larger disregard of life it was the operations so daringly and brilliantly begun by Sir Ian Hamilton in the immortal landing of 25 April. This is all I have to say about the Dardanelles.'

Both Churchill and French paid the penalty of being in the most exposed position as a divided and distracted civilian administration failed to deliver.

The dominant personality in the first eighteen months of the Great War was Lord Kitchener. Asquith was the Prime Minister, but Kitchener was the Warrior King. Unfortunately Asquith had imposed no discipline on his Cabinet – as Churchill did in the Second World War – and never really allowed the so-called War Council to get a grip on all the factors: moral fervour, industrial, commercial, financial, political that make for totality of struggle.

Kitchener on the other hand dabbled in things he knew little about. As War Minister he looked upon himself as War Dictator (which he assuredly was not); he was reluctant to delegate responsibility and he drew the fire of Lord Northcliffe's *Daily Mail* – it was publicly burnt on the Stock Exchanges for accusing Lord Kitchener of ordering the wrong kind of shells. Lord Kitchener even tried to impose his views on such recondite issues as temperance.

The Drink Question was guaranteed to rouse all kinds of passions: boozing males v. female abstainers; brewery supported Tories v. Liberal non-conformists. So it had been before the war. Now the Devil Drink was blamed for inducing a lack of martial spirit. Lord Kitchener of Khartoum, he was affectionately known as K. of K., opened the campaign on 15 March, 1915. In a speech to the House of Lords he declared:

> 'We have unfortunately found that the output is not only not equal to our necessities, but does not fulfil our expectations, for a very large number of our orders have not been completed on the dates for which they were promised.
>
> 'While the workmen generally have worked loyally and well, there have, I regret to say, been instances where absence, irregular time-keeping, and slack work have led to a diminution in the output of our factories. In some cases the temptations of drink account for this failure to work up to the high standard expected.'

The King followed with this message a fortnight later:

> 'We have before us the statements, not merely of the employers, but of the Admiralty and the War Office officials responsible for the supply of munitions of war, for the transport of troops, their food and ammunition.
>
> 'From this evidence it is without doubt largely due to drink that we are unable to secure the output of war material indispensable to meet the requirements of our army in the field, and that there has been such serious delay in the conveyance of the necessary reinforcements and supplies to aid our gallant troops at the front.
>
> 'The continuance of such a state of things must inevitably result in the prolongation of the horrors and burdens of this terrible war.
>
> 'I am to add that, if it be deemed advisable, the King will be prepared to set the example by giving up all alcoholic liquor himself and issuing orders against its consumption in the Royal Household, so that no difference shall be made, so far as his Majesty is concerned, between the treatment of rich and poor in this question.'

It was, however, David Lloyd George, the Chancellor of the Exchequer and voice of perfervid Welsh non-conformism, who hammered and hammered away at the issue: in speeches to the shipbuilding employers, to the Trades Union Congress and finally to the Commons on 30 April, after the battle of Neuve Chapelle had exposed the shortcomings of British shells and the shortage of munitions. He spoke to the House after a strong campaign by the brewers who placed this advertisement in the newspapers:

> 'Beer "fills the bill" because it is a healthful beverage – pure and very refreshing. The sedentary may drink a little; those who take reasonable exercise may drink it freely and without harm.
>
> 'Dr Davy, when President of the British Medical Association, declared that "a meal of cheese, bread, and light beer is infinitely more scientific than a meal of bread, tea and jam."
>
> 'And it is a temperance drink. Mr Lloyd George has said it. Beer-drinkers know it. All over the country Chief Constables have reported a notable decline in drunkenness last year, but the consumption of beer increased by about half-a-million barrels. You would not get these two facts together unless beer was a temperance drink.
>
> 'Ale should not be rejected by throwing at it the word "alcoholic". Alcohol is so frequent in nature that, without much exaggeration, we might say that it is almost omnipresent. It is found in ginger-beer to a quite appreciable extent, and even in new bread. It is the extent of the dilution which is the important matter. And the dilution in modern light beer is very great, with the result that there is just enough to give a pleasant stimulating property to the beverage, but not enough to injure or intoxicate, unless most extravagant quantities are drunk. That is the ground of its claim to be a temperance drink.'

Lloyd George also knew that to rake up the drink question *as a party issue* would revive fears that the Liberal Government was about to hold an election (one was due in 1915). He further knew that a coalition was on the cards. But Lloyd George was resolved to stir the sluggards: something which would do him no harm with his prospective Conservative partners.

So he began: 'Politically I am prepared to take a pledge never to touch drink. Every Government that has ever touched alcohol has burned its fingers in its lurid flame ... but drink is doing more damage than all the German submarines put together.' He instanced loss of production in the shipyards where some men were producing less than in peace-time because greatly increased wages allowed them to drink more than ever and to absent themselves from work on Mondays.

Excessive drinking was to blame. He instanced the publican in Scotland who filled 100 bottles of whisky every Saturday night for his shipyard customers to take home and consume on Sunday when the pubs were closed. His solution was to impose a doubled surtax on spirits and *heavy* beer, a quadrupled duty on wine and for the State to take over pubs and brewing in certain areas of special importance to the war effort.*

A key phrase in Lloyd George's speech, and one that foreshadowed his rise to supreme power in the direction of the conflict was: 'Wars are now waged not by armies but by nations, and nations must therefore be under discipline like armies. . . . There are 2,000,000 men who have voluntarily surrendered their liberty to serve their country. . . . I propose measures as an act of discipline for the whole country.'

Here was the foretaste of things to come: the transformation of liberal, easy-going England into a resolute, disciplined force, reminiscent of Cromwell's commonwealth and thus able to fell militarist Germany.

---

* One of these places was Carlisle, a vital railway junction. The pubs remained State-controlled until the 1960s.

CHAPTER THREE

"Second Lieutenant unless otherwise stated"

Never a day passed (until 1918 when the papers were reduced to four pages) but the Press printed columns of killed and wounded headed simply: '2nd Lieutenants unless otherwise stated', or 'all privates except otherwise stated'. The appearance of the lists caused widespread grief and anxiety. The flower of the country, the best of the best, were being mown down by the tens of thousands and to these anonymous daily intimations of tragedy were added reports of the great and the humble which gave personal poignancy to the growing feeling of irredeemable loss.

Items such as:

It is reported by the War Office that more than 50 heirs to peerages have been killed in the fifteen months since the outbreak of War:

*

VICTORIA CROSS
Boy, First Class, John Travers Cornwell,
(died 2 June, 1916 from wounds in action at Jutland)
Mortally wounded early in the action, Boy, First Class, John Travers Cornwell remained standing alone at a most exposed post, quietly awaiting orders, until the end of the action, with the gun's crew dead and wounded all round him. His age was under *sixteen and a half years*.

*

A grief-stricken mother who has already lost three out of her four soldier sons sent a letter to the Queen begging that her youngest boy might be kept on home service.

The Queen was touched by the pathetic appeal and the bereaved mother received the following letter:

Buckingham Palace.

Madam, – I am commanded by the Queen to say that her Majesty is glad to be able to inform you that Private Walter Payne, of the Bedfordshire Regiment, will shortly be transferred to a home service unit.

The Queen deeply sympathises with you in the loss of your other three sons.

*

Mr Smallwood, the newly-elected MP for Islington, told in the course of his speech in the House of Commons last night a story of treatment he received in France which will cause the whole country to rise in shocked indignation. He said:

'I was summoned to France to see my last son (Mr Smallwood lost all his sons in the war) after he had been wounded for the third time. I saw him in hospital in the authorised hours – from two to five.

'The boy was very nearly gone, and I begged that I should be allowed to stop the night. But after sitting concealed behind a curtain for three hours, I was turned out by the matron, who refused to allow any appeal.

'The boy died the same night.'

Famous figures were not spared. One after another, from Prime Minister Asquith's household to those of most of his supporters and opponents in the Commons and Lords, there was scarcely a home untouched by death at the front. A leading article headed, simply, 'The Sacrifice' illumined the loss of one such noble family, that of Lord Rosebery's:

Mr Neil Primrose is the latest of the brilliant young men who have lost their lives for their country. There are no words capable of expressing the tragedy of the passing of youth with all its potentialities unfulfilled. A gay spring, a few days of summer – and then the end. Mr Primrose was born for distinction. To the advantages which he inherited he added outstanding charm of character. The whole nation grieves with his stricken father, now counted with the pathetic army of fathers doomed to go on living with a band of ice round their hearts. Yet the nobility of the sacrifice cannot be forgotten. It is something to be counted with the young men who have, since August 1914, given their all for England – with the poets, the dreamers, the clean-souled youth from the castle and the cottage who have died with their faces turned towards the dawn. Grief is for those left behind, not for them.

Another, and even more widely known name was that of Lauder:

> Mr Harry Lauder, the great comedian who has made millions laugh, yesterday received news that his only son, Captain John C. Lauder, of the Argyll and Sutherland Highlanders, was killed in France on 29 December.
>
> It was only the day before that an article written by Mr. Lauder was printed in the *Sunday Herald* beginning 'When my son comes home from war –'
>
> No father could have been fonder or prouder of his only son. He, who once worked in a mine, then became a music-hall singer, and achieved fame and riches, cherished the hope that his son would be a Scottish laird – when he came home from the war.
>
> 'I hope,' he wrote, 'to see him established up in the north as a decent Scots laird, growing the nation's meat, and, as the years go by, growing the nation's men. That's life, that's reality. But most of your doings in town are just a cinema show.'
>
> Perhaps at the very time that Mr Lauder was looking through those words in proof his son was dying for his country.

Rudyard Kipling, master of the short story, poet of the Empire, the man who had written at the outbreak of war:

> There is but one task for all –
> One life for each to give
> What stands if Freedom falls?
> Who dies if England lives?

lost his son in the Ypres salient. John Buchan, the novelist joined the ranks of mourners:

> Mr John Buchan, the novelist and historian, who was recently appointed Director of Information under the Prime Minister, has lost both his brother and his business partner in this week's fighting. His brother was Lieutenant Alastair Buchan of the Royal Scots

Fusiliers, and his partner in the publishing firm of Nelson was Captain Nelson of the Lothian Border Horse.

Lieutenant Buchan, who was only twenty-two years of age, and went straight from college to the ranks, fell this week while leading his company.

Captain Nelson was the most brilliant Rugby footballer of his time. He was captain of the Oxford Rugby fifteen and of the Scottish Rugby fifteen.

The princes of the Church yielded up their quota :

The Bishop of Exeter (Lord William Cecil) received news yesterday that his eldest son, Randle William, had been killed in action.

The Bishop's fourth son, Lieutenant Edward Rupert Cecil, Bedfordshire Regiment, was killed in 1915, and his second son, Captain Victor Alexander Cecil, has twice been wounded. The third son is in the RFC.

Far from weakening the resolve to continue the war, the lengthening casualty list re-inforced determination to see it through. Sacrifice took on something of a holy order. It has been fashionable, since the 1920s, to dismiss this as rather naive propaganda dished out by blood-thirsty elders or warfevered females sitting safe at home and in no way reflecting the views of the men in the trenches. And yet how to explain this letter, typical of many, written in 1916 after two years of Flanders agony, told and re-told by returning soldiers and war correspondents?

> In a few days we move up to a place where we do not know what awaits us, but where we know many of our comrades have found their graves . . . I go forward looking to God and trusting by His help to do my duty. If the call comes I am prepared and shall go without a pang of sorrow, unless that of leaving you and the great many friends who have been so good to me. It is a great cause for which so many have already gone : one for which it is a privilege to pay the last great sacrifice. But God grant the result may be lasting peace.
> (sgd) John Cunningham

He was killed within the week. He had come to serve the 'great cause' from Hamilton, Ontario.

The old sweats, the veterans of a hundred trench raids, were not downhearted; they had evolved their own gallows humour as this despatch makes plain :

The unvarying cheeriness of men wearied to the point of numbness is one of the most lovable characteristics of that lovable personality – the British soldier. The *poilu* is quick to see a joke, and quick to enjoy it, but Tommy alone rises above all circumstances of hardship and horror in this hard and horrible war to a pinnacle of light-heartedness.

No enemy can hope ever to defeat a people whose sons are of such stuff as the wounded lad who urged the stretcher-bearers to hurry because he could not die there – 'there' being the icy morass of No Man's Land – because he'd catch his death of cold!

To fight or work or march all day and then find 'someone had blundered' in the matter of providing a hot meal produces a silence in the ranks.

I have heard that silence shattered by a gust of laughter, however, when a slow, affected 'Oxford' drawl informed the hungry men that 'We can't give you wine, and we can't give you beah, but we can give you three – hearty – British cheahs!'

Sometimes the comedy is one without words, as in the case of the lonely bomber who sat on the parapet of a sap calmly hurling death at a German trench. Below him were a group of his own wounded and some German prisoners being searched, their hands above their heads. With a bomb in his right hand the lonely bomber reached down his left, grasped a burly German arm, turned it towards him and coolly noted the time on the wristlet watch!

There are, one knows, gentle people who regard death and its circumstances as too reverent a subject for humour's arrows, but they are not in the Army. If sometimes the humour is grim, it never fails to provide for harassed nerves that priceless sedative – laughter. I remembered once in a death-strewn gap where body was piled on body, and the working party sent to clear it stumbled and fell over things that once were men, a great shout of laughter went up as we noticed a dead arm and hand, palm uppermost, stretching out from the sap wall, bearing a card with the words: 'Give it baksheesh!' The well known cry of the Egyptian beggar coupled with that supplicatory palm was irresistible, and not all the horrors of the deadly sap could restrain our mirth.

If our soldiers laugh, with little reverence, in the face of death, it is not callousness, but the working of a generous and ardent spirit which sees clearly, and, seeing, is unafraid.

That is probably as true a description of the front-line Tommy – the one immortalised by Bruce Bairnsfather – as can be found anywhere. It was, however, the voice of innocent, clear-eyed heroism that moved public opinion to the belief that volunteers alone should no longer be called upon to bear the terrible burden. This letter, published in October 1915, gave expression to what many were thinking:

The mother of the late Lance-Corporal Leonard Keyworth, VC, of the 24th London Regiment, has received the following message from Lieut-Colonel J. Eustace Jameson, her son's commanding officer:

Your son was one of the highest examples of unselfishness and devotion to his comrades and to duty. Among the many acts of bravery which have been performed by our gallant soldiers his will stand out prominently, and his name will be enrolled among the bravest of the brave.

He returned to duty at his own request after he had received his VC, and notwithstanding all the well-earned praise and commendation that were showered upon him, his one desire was to return to the front to help his comrades. Surely such a splendid and heroic death will help us in our hour of need to get recruits for the battalion in which he served and of which he was an honoured member?

He has taught us all a lesson – a lesson that should go home to the hearts of those who up to the present have not come forward to serve their country.

Such letters buttressed and personalised the psychological campaign already launched by the authorities to stimulate recruiting:

THE MAN
TO BE PITIED

Now that the eyes of the Nation are upon the men who honour themselves by *serving* their king and country, how sad is the lot of the man who cannot go!

He knows that his Country thinks of the men who have answered the call. He envies them the great opportunity which he has missed. They were of a soldier's age: they were physically fit: *and they went*.

After the War is over *they* will be able to hold up their heads. Their womenfolk and their children will be proud of them.

But *he*! He who had no part in this great honour. No crowds will cheer him through the streets. He will hear the praise of other men's courage and patriotism; but he will have no share in it. His lot is hard. He is to be pitied.

Are *you* going to be pitied or praised? If you are physically fit – don't be pitied.

ENLIST TODAY
GOD SAVE THE KING.

*

A CALL
FROM
THE TRENCHES
(Extract from a letter from the trenches):

I saw a recruiting advertisement in a paper the other day. I wonder if the men are responding properly – they would if they could see what the Germans have done to Belgium. And, after all, it's not so bad out here – cold sometimes, and the waiting gets on our nerves a bit, but we are happy and as fit as fiddles. I wonder if ——— has joined, he certainly ought to.

Does '———' refer to you?
If so
ENLIST TO-DAY
GOD SAVE THE KING

Caustic comments were written by observers of the passing scene:

I stood on Wimbledon Hill on Sunday afternoon and watched the crowds passing on their way to the common.

As I gazed it became borne in on me that quite a large percentage of the men were young and obviously unmarried. Sometimes they were in batches of three and four, laughing and joking together, cigarette in mouth and cane in hand; sometimes they were accompanied by a bright-faced girl hanging on an arm and chattering the soft nothings that make love's young dream ...

It was stated a few weeks ago that separation allowances had been issued to 900,000 cases. Think of it! Nine hundred thousand volunteers who have women and children dependent on them! And yet there are young men free as the air, without a soul in the world to worry about, who are still out of uniform.

The young men who have not voluntarily answered the call must be compelled to step forward. Every man between nineteen and thirty years of age who is unmarried and without ties should be called to the colours willy-nilly.

The male view however was a faint echo of the fury of the women at those who 'dodged the column'. It was the women who 'gave' sons and brothers, husbands and sweethearts. They it was who received the dread telegram, who wept and bore up and wept again – in private. And it was the women, stepping in to fill the gaps in the labour force caused by men volunteering, who dramatised the war.

CHAPTER FOUR

The Passion and the Sorrow

White feathers were women's first weapon to shame men into joining up. The white feather was a cock-fighting term denoting a degenerate strain in the cock that sported one. Such a cock was regarded as a poor fighter and in the nineteenth century 'to show the white feather' was applied to soldiers who acted in a cowardly manner. By handing feathers to young, apparently fit, men in the street, the women very often inflicted thoughtless pain. Some of the men offered white feathers were soldiers home on leave and taking the opportunity of wearing civvies (many stopped this and wore their uniforms instead); others had volunteered but had not yet been called to the colours due to shortage of equipment; still others were unfit. The White Feather campaign was disgraceful and indiscriminate but it *was* effective and it did express, albeit in a waspish fashion, women's dedication to the war.

It was not for nothing that women were used in recruiting posters to propel men into the forces. The best known World War I poster was the pointing finger of Kitchener, so drawn that it seemed to follow the passer-by; but the most dramatic was one depicting women waving to their khaki-clad men under the caption 'Women of Britain say "GO".'

Female stars of the music hall sang songs specially composed to win recruits:

'I joined the Army yesterday.' 'Goodbyee, don't Cryie.'
'If you'll only take the Shilling.'
    A new ditty is being sung at the Oxford Music Hall by Miss Marie Lloyd, who is never happier than when she is presenting characters of the 'Arriet' type.

There is real humanity as well as homely humour in Miss Lloyd's cockney lass, who vows that she loves her 'bloke John' all the better 'now yer've got your khaki on.'

The sentiment is driven home with such effect that the song is encored repeatedly.

Occasionally women carried their zeal against the dodgers a little too far, as was recounted in this bizarre incident:

How an aggrieved little wife thrashed her Socialist-pacifist husband with a strap down a street for 150 yards was described at Eastbourne yesterday, when Mrs Nellie Bishop was summoned by her husband, Thomas Bishop, for assault.

Although the bench sympathised with Mrs Bishop, they had to fine her, but they fixed the fine at the minimum of 2s 6d and readily granted her plea for separation order.

The wife explained that she thrashed him in the street because the shop was not large enough for her to do so properly.

'I have lived a terrible life since he became a Socialist,' she continued. 'He is a Socialist starver, and that is why I thrashed him.

'I cannot remember the last occasion on which he gave me money, although he is saving himself. I even bought my own wedding ring. His motto is to get everything for nothing.'

But women were not content to exhort and excoriate; they flocked to fill the ranks left vacant by workers who went off to war. The formidably impressive suffragette movement was switched overnight from an agency of rebellion against male domination into a weapon of war against the Kaiser. Emmeline Pankhurst, and more particularly her daughter Christabel, became avenging angels (although Sylvia, the second daughter, went the other way and embraced pacificism.) Delicately-reared women rushed to train as nurses. Their servants departed for the munition factories, presaging the social change that was to overtake the middle classes, as one member dolefully reported:

MAIDSERVANTS AND MUNITIONS
The Servantless Life of the Future
by Mary Mortime Maxwell

'You cannot have any servants unless they are mentally or physically deficient!'

A woman superintendent was showing me over a great munitions factory, and she was telling me something about the former occupations of the girls I saw at work among the cartridges and other things to be sent to the front. She told me of the large number of girls employed under her who had left domestic service. I had sighed and said:

'That's why I and hundreds of other women have to do our own housework.' She had replied laughingly that that was certainly the 'why' of it.

Employers were emphatically enthusiastic about the new labour force:

'Any fears that may have been entertained of women's capacity for warwork have been dispelled long ago. We are now employing thousands of women, of all sorts and conditions, in munition-making, and, frankly, we have nothing but praise for their work.

'They are steady, intelligent, industrious workers, very interested in their work, and excellent timekeepers. I have no hesitation in saying that in the particular grade of work in which they are employed, these women have already shown themselves quite as able as men. We are glad to have them in our employ.'

A director of Messrs Vickers, paid the above striking tribute to the battalions of women, each a thousand strong, who are now engaged in 'doing their bit' for their country in making shells and other munitions for their husbands, brothers, sweethearts, uncles, cousins, and friends at the front.

Some idea of the confidence reposed in the women munition-makers may be gathered from the fact that they are now entrusted with both shrapnel and high-explosive shell making.

The pay and hours are those which obtain in the district works where the women are employed, and no discrimination or preferential treatment of any sort is shown to them.

Shell-making, particularly shell-filling, may seen to the uninstructed lay-mind a hazardous sort of occupation, but the women who do it declare that it is no whit more dangerous than, say, serving behind the counter in a milk-shop.

The running of shops, delivery services, farms, tramways, all were competently taken over by women. They showed themselves especially adept with cars:

'So completely is the profession of motor driving passing into the hands of the feminine sex that even schoolgirls are becoming chauffeurs.'

This statement which was made by the secretary of the British School of Motoring affords some idea of the manner in which women are taking up the work of men 'for the duration of the war' and, maybe, after.

The 'goddess in the car' who, in leather habiliment, is now seen driving a heavy motor lorry or an ambulance wagon, was pursuing a far different life a few months ago.

'Among the hundreds of women who have passed through our classes and are still receiving instruction,' said the seceretary of the school 'are those who used to be :

Typists   Actresses
Governesses   Shop Assistants
Dressmakers   Social Workers.

'Titled women are taking up the duties of a chauffeur with avidity, while even schoolgirls are anxious to learn to drive. The latter obtain their certificates when they are seventeen. There are quite a number of feminine drivers doing duty in France and Flanders.'

Films played a part in making war-work attractive :

'The physical strength of many beautiful girls as shown by their feats reproduced on the films is a great surprise to those who cling to the old idea that the athletic girl loses all her womanly charm and elegance,' said Miss Irene Miller, the scenario writer at a meeting of the Stoll Picture Theatre Club.

Miss Miller believes that if it had not been for the 'cowboy girl' on the films women would not have been so ready to take up the new kinds of war work which require physical strength and the wearing of trousers. Breeches as worn by film actresses are inoffensive and not without charm, as the munition makers and the land girls were quick to observe.

Some women continued with the traditional support to men at war : food and sex. Tuck boxes went out to the trenches, each one for ten men containing :

Two glasses of potted meat – chicken and ham,
    turkey and tongue, etc.
1 tin Milkmaid 'café-au-lait'

1 packet Nestle's nut-milk chocolate
1 tin smoked sardines
1 tin smoked sardines in tomato
1 tin Oxford sausages
1 pot campaigning Bovril
½ lb ginger chips
½ lb mixed drops – acid, peppermint, etc.
1 tin opener

and, of course, there were socks, balaclavas, and comforters of all kinds by the millions. In 1915 there were mittens to spare – but fewer than 300,000 steel helmets. The women had not taken over the War Office!

Sex naturally loomed large as millions of men, uprooted from their homes and facing death at the front came back to Blighty for a spell of leave greedy for 'companionship', and for experiences to relate to their mates on return to France. The newspapers warned about 'teenage harpies' preying on tired warriors but condoned natural passions, a sentiment not shared by Church leaders:

'The present time is a moment when the sacredness of the marriage law is most seriously threatened,' the Bishop of Oxford declared. 'I cannot but feel that the controversy which has arisen under the title of "War Babies" indicates a very widespread laxity of sentiment and feeling with regard to sexual matters.'

'We have newspapers with immense circulations advocating what is practically free love, using the stress and strain of the present difficulty to advocate it most strongly,' said the Bishop of Chelmsford; and the Bishop of London, who declared that there was no place where morality was greater than among the people of Bethnal Green, added:

'The women of that part feel it very much that mistresses are to be treated, under the regulations, for allowances to soldiers' dependants like wives. It has been bitterly resented by the whole of the East End of London.

'The newspapers which are taking up the question are not representative of all of the working classes, who are absolutely disinclined for one moment to endorse the line which these newspapers have taken.'

Lady Gwendolen Cecil gave voice to the puritan ethic:

'There is no peculiar sanctity attached to illegitimate births even when the father is a soldier.

'I am afraid that in many cases the appeal (in the interest of the children) is merely a veil for a less creditable sympathy with the mothers. A girl's loss of purity is assuredly a subject for infinite sorrow – but not for sentimental condonation. Among a large proportion of these mothers an even sterner attitude is probably called for.

'Do not let us be frightened by the accusation of Puritanism. A touch of it is a valuable element in the national character. And even in its extreme forms it is better than sentimental sympathy with vice.'

Top brass in the Army too was concerned about the moral tone (and the increasing incidence of venereal disease.) General Sir Horace Smith-Dorrien deplored falling standards in certain theatrical establishments:

'I refer chiefly to the music-halls and some of the revues. The kind of thing I mean – the exhibition of girls in too scanty clothing, and indecent suggestion – is to be found in some houses of this character.

'I have been told that in one of the leading military centres the music-hall presents entertainments which scarcely veil the indecent.'

A jauntier view of the sex urge was taken by the maids of Bo'ness on the Firth of Forth:

Two girls tossed on Saturday night to decide which of them should be the bride of a soldier.

The soldier is a man who fought at Mons, and is now discharged through disablement. He was to have been married at Bo'ness on Saturday night. The feast was prepared, and more than a hundred guests assembled, but the bride did not appear.

Two girl friends offered to fill the breach, and the soldier agreed to accept either of them. A coin was tossed up to decide which should be the bride, and the choice, curiously enough, fell on one of the girls who was an old sweetheart of the soldier.

The wedding with the substitute bride will take place this week.

However the infinitely tragic side of the relationship of men and women to the war was the one that found most frequent expression in the newspapers. Items very similar to these appeared again and again:

Worry over a young man who was at the front was said to be responsible for the death of Ellen Mary Taylor, a seventeen-year-old girl on whose body, which was found in the Thames, an inquest was held at Windsor yesterday.

Mrs Annie Taylor, with whom Taylor lived for twelve months, said that the girl, who had once threatened to drown herself, had a young man who was serving at the front. He had told the girl that he would write every eight weeks, and that if she did not hear from him in that time, it would be because he had been killed.

A photograph of a young man was found on the girl's body, hidden underneath her blouse.

*

'Oh, mummie, I have done for myself. I am going to Cecil.'

These were the dying words of Mrs Sybil Catherine Griffin, the eighteen-year-old widow of an officer, who shot herself with a sporting gun at Chester-terrace W.

It was stated at the inquest at Marylebone yesterday that she had been married only seven months when her husband, an officer in the Gordon Highlanders, was killed.

A verdict of 'Suicide while of unsound mind' was returned.

*

'I consider that I only did my duty, as I did in France,' said Henry Stephen Graham, a private in the Machine Gun Corps, Expeditionary Force, France, when he was charged with the wilful murder of his wife, Gladys Ann Graham, by shooting her at Great College-street, Camden Town.

When Graham, who is only twenty-one, was remanded at Clerkenwell Police Court yesterday, it was stated that at the police station he said:

'I shot her with my service revolver. I went to France about sixteen months ago, and soon after I heard that she had sold up my home with the exception of a few things. She had left the baby to be looked after by anybody, and was leading an immoral life. I have letters to prove it.'

The overpowering feeling as the war entered its second winter was: 'Why should my man (son, boyfriend) go off to the war while her man (son, boyfriend) goes scot free to earn big money' (in Belfast shipyards, for example, the semi-skilled were taking home £15 a week, equivalent to £180 in the late 1970s). 'Why should the British Empire maintain the voluntary system while France, Russia, Germany and Austria call all their men to the colours?'

Women were not the only force pushing the country towards conscription but they were the most vocal, and wives whose husbands had been killed or mothers who had lost sons (Annie S. Swan, a popular novelist of the time, wrote a poem grieving that she had no son to give) presented an unanswerable argument to the politicians.

CHAPTER FIVE

For Conscience' Sake

By August 1915 more than 2,000,000 men had volunteered to serve in the British forces: the greatest voluntary levy en masse in history. The motives that impelled this surge to battle were complex and various. We have already discovered the influence of wives, mothers and sweethearts. Indeed women were themselves urging the conscription of women for work on the land ('educated women of the leisured and professional classes should be compelled to undertake work in the fields' – Women's Institute Conference on the land, May 1916). But there were many other factors prompting men to volunteer. Primarily there was simple patriotism. The motherland was in danger and men rallied to the flag from the four corners of the world. There was the excitement and challenge of a whole new experience, to which Rupert Brooke gave tongue:

> Now God be thanked who has matched us with his Hour
> And caught our youth, and wakened us from sleeping.

Liberation from dull routine or hopelessness was a universal reaction to the war. In Munich a dilettante artist and poor itinerant fell upon his knees to 'thank God for deliverance'. His name was Adolf Hitler. He promptly volunteered for a Bavarian regiment.

In the first heady days it was a matter of holding back the flood of recruits in Britain as elsewhere. As the months passed, the continentals drew in their already trained classes of conscripts while Britain, still relying wholly on the voluntary system, had to assure potential soldiers that their services were still required.

Early recruiting for Kitchener's Army was based on posters, handbills, newspaper advertisements, rousing speeches from local notables and was everywhere undertaken by the military: it was, quite literally, taking the King's shilling from the recruiting sergeant.

Lord Derby – he who had recruited so many battalions in Lancashire – early saw that a more systematic method was needed. Patriotic ardour was not enough; reliance on able-bodied young men seeking thrills and novelty was not enough; women's pleas, even their fury at 'shirkers', were not enough.

In October 1915 the Derby scheme was launched and the press explained its outlines:

> Civilians, instead of soldiers, will be responsible.
>
> Pink form canvassing will be carried out by the local committees on lines similar to the canvassing at a general election. Political agents of all parties and municipal and civic authorities will help.
>
> The number of men needed from each district will be supplied to the committees.
>
> Every 'unstarred' man will receive a letter from Lord Derby, so that he may not be able to say that he was not called on to join.
>
> The canvass and returns will be completed by 30 November – six weeks hence.

Dovetailing local recruiting committees with local Parliamentary constituencies made use of existing door-to-door contacts. It was a thorough combing-out exercise: 'starred' men being those who because of age, health, essential war work, married status, dependents, etc., were not expected to volunteer. Unstarred men were expected to enlist – and the clear implication was that if they did not they would shortly find themselves conscripted. Many of the men were quite ready, even anxious, to serve but as letters to the press showed separation allowances were wholly inadequate where the joiner was the bread-winner.

Derby's scheme yielded a million men to raise the voluntary total to 3,000,000 in January 1916. It was not sufficient. More than half-a-million eligible men had not come forward and Lord Derby commented: 'It will not be possible to hold married men to their attestation unless and until the services of single men *have been obtained by other means.*'

Public pressure for compulsory universal military service was now intense. Some idea of how strong it was may be gauged from this exchange in court:

A youth complained to Mr Fordham at the West London Police

Court on Saturday that people had insulted him for two or three months.

'They tell me I ought to be in the Army,' he said.

'I quite agree, if you are strong,' said the magistrate.

'Yes, but I am not old enough,' said the youth. 'I am only seventeen.'

'Some chaps of sixteen have gone into the Army,' said the magistrate.

'I have an invalid father,' protested the youth.

'I cannot prevent people telling you that you ought to be in the Army,' said the magistrate. 'Nearly every man who can go thinks he ought to go.'

The magistrate eventually granted a summons for assault against a neighbour.

Single men who had no intention of volunteering were buying khaki armbands (evidence that they had attested their willingness to serve) at sixpence a time merely to buy a few weeks of comparative peace from the sniping of girls friends and soldier mates.

Finally, in May 1916, Parliament passed the General Compulsion Bill making military service obligatory on all males between 18 and 41. It came into operation in June, almost two years after the war had started.

That the United Kingdom had fought so long on the purely voluntary system was a tribute to love of country, but it was also a cause of deep divisions between the relatives of those who had gone and the men who had not. And when conscription did arrive it too proved divisive for, while continental populations had long grown used to compulsory service, it was wholly alien to the British tradition and violently resented by a considerable section of the community.

Pacifism, of a religious or political nature, was strongly in evidence throughout the whole of the Great War. Although it was very much a minority sentiment, it represented part of the strong non-conformist vein in the British character.

Before the war had begun men and women of pacifist leanings took a full page advertisement in the *Manchester Guardian* warning Englishmen 'to keep out of France's war'. This isolationist view diminished with the invasion of Belgium and not a few of the signatories to that appeal were shortly afterwards in khaki themselves.

Next came the Committee of the International Conference of Women, derisively nicknamed 'The Peacettes'. They maintained that if the women of the world could only get together they could get their menfolk to stop fighting. Neutral Holland was the chosen meeting place for British housewives and German Hausfraus but such contacts as did take place were abortive.

A few Churchmen took their stand against the shedding of blood. Such a one, fairly typical, was the Reverend R. J. Campbell of the City Temple who issued these extracts from his sermons to the nation via advertisements in the newspapers:

' "Where was God when my only son was bayoneted in the face, and left to bleed in agony," cries one heartbroken mother.

' "If prayer were any use would the child I bore with so much anguish be torn to pieces by German shells and shriek for death to end his torment?" wails another.

'And then to talk of God and Heaven! – *Are we fools?*'

Surely and steadily however the movement against the war took on a political tone. The Labour movement itself was split. One of its leaders, James Ramsay MacDonald, was against the war (he was asked to resign from his Scottish golf club, and refused). Others like Arthur Henderson were staunch in support of the struggle against Prussian militarists. The intellectuals of the Fabian Society, the Left's brain trust, were also split: H. G. Wells, for example, was a strong pro-war champion; Bernard Shaw less so.

Out-and-out foes of the war were to be found in the ranks of the Independent Labour Party, heirs to the old extreme Social Democratic movement with its international links to comrades abroad. The *Express*, in common with other papers, saw the hand of Germany in anti-war propaganda circulating in Britain. That was not altogether unreasonable as the Germans had every reason to promote defeatism among the Allies and were indeed to use the greatest revolutionary of them all – Lenin – to help bring about the collapse of Russia. Blamed as tools of the Germans were: the Union of Democratic Control; the Stop-the-War Committee; the Fellowship of Reconciliation; the No-Conscription Fellowship. This sample of the pacifist appeals in 1915 is taken from a leaflet 'The Military Ideal':

Young man. The lowest aim in your life is to be a good soldier. The 'good soldier' never tries to distinguish right from wrong. He never thinks, never reasons; he only obeys.

A good soldier is a blind, heartless, soulless murderous machine.

He is not a man, he is not even a brute, for brutes only kill in self-defence.

All that is human in him, all that is divine in him, all that constitutes a man, has been sworn away when he took the enlistment oath. His mind, his conscience, and his very soul, are in the keeping of his officer.

No man can fall lower than a soldier – it is a depth beneath which we cannot go. Young Man, don't be a soldier or a Territorial – be a MAN.

Those who took the promptings of 'The Military Ideal' to the troops were liable to be severely punished under the Defence of the Realm Act. Alphonso Samms, a Council workhouse official from Sheffield, got two months in jail for telling a wounded Canadian trooper 'not to butcher people' and urging another to revolt against 'the masters who are benefiting from the war'.

The No-Conscription Fellowship issued advice to its members on how to fill in the National Register which preceded the launch of the Derby recruiting scheme: 'While registering as a citizen in conformity with the Government demand I could not, for conscientious reasons, take part in military service or in any activity necessitating the taking of the military role as in the production of munitions.'

As the country moved towards conscription the whole issue of 'conscience' took on a new dimension. Who was genuinely a conscientious objector on religious, moral or political grounds, and who simply a dodger?

The Reverend G. T. Sadler of the Union of Democratic Control gave his interpretation of the Christian attitude:

'On the question: What should we do if the Germans attacked our wives? There are many things a Christian might do, viz. speak calmly and firmly to the bully, calling him "friend' and not "you vile beast." Clasp him and call for others to help. But the first thing to say to those who argue for wars of self-defence is to say that the cases are not parallel. If there be no armed resistance there is no killing. In Brussels there was no killing, and few, if any atrocities, for Brussels was undefended. Just recently some have been shot after trial; but because of disturbances. Belgium pluckily resisted Germany, but would not have been attacked had she still more pluckily refused to fight, and had France and Russia refused the result would have been spiritually marvellous. The Germans would have killed no one . . . If we stopped the war now and made a give-and-take peace no Germans would come to our homes at all.'

A week later, on 12 January, 1916, a poetically-minded correspondent replied in the press:

> Really I cannot kill the so-called Hun;
> My conscience bids me conflict rude to shun
> What though he bayonets children, poisons wells
>   and tramples peaceful cities into hell? –
>   He is my brother
>
> The *Lusitania*, Belgium's silenced chimes,
> And all the Newgate Calendar of crimes
> That he so loves, are very sad, of course.
> Still, I could never think of using force
>   Against my brother.

Punishments grew more and more severe as the war dragged on:

> John Maclean,* an ex-school teacher of Govan, was found guilty at Edinburgh yesterday on four out of six counts of making seditious speeches calculated to prejudice recruiting and impede the production of munitions at public meetings in Glasgow and Govan, and was sentenced to three years penal servitude.
>
> He admitted that he had called Lloyd George a liar, and that he used the words 'bloody English capitalists', but he pleaded that the latter was merely a classical expression.
>
> The jury, after an hour's consideration, returned a unanimous verdict of 'Guilty', on four counts.
>
> In passing sentence, the Lord Justice General pointed out that Maclean had been convicted before of an offence against the Defence of the Realm Regulations, and the light sentence then passed had evidently failed as a warning.

Militant protestors responded by circulating leaflets calling on workers to down tools in opposition to the Conscription Act. Workers did no such thing, but when the Act came into operation there were considerable numbers of men who applied for exemption though very few did so for purely political reasons – they knew only too well how the local

---

* After the war Lenin appointed him honorary Soviet Consul in Glasgow.

military service tribunals, composed of municipal, legal and army representatives, would have treated them.

Here is the first report of the workings of the tribunals in 1916:

> Interesting arguments were put forward yesterday when the first conscientious objectors appeared before the tribunals under the Military Service Act.
>
> At Westminster R. T. Shirley, a twenty-year-old book-keeper, asked for total exemption from service on the ground that his conscience objected to war.
>
> 'What religious body do you belong to?' asked the mayor.
>
> 'I am a Wesleyan,' replied the applicant.
>
> 'I have not heard before,' remarked a member of the tribunal, 'that it is part of the creed of Wesleyans that fighting is a wicked thing.'
>
> 'Would you rather that your mother and sister should suffer than that you should kill a German?' asked Mr Davis, the military representative.
>
> 'I would protest, but would not kill,' returned the applicant.
>
> 'I want to conduct cases of conscientious objection in the spirit in which they should be conducted,' said Mr Davis, 'but I do not think that in the present case there is sufficient evidence to satisfy the tribunal that the applicant has a bona-fide conscientious objection.'
>
> Then the applicant changed his ground. He said that he suffered from nerves and had a weak chest.
>
> 'That is a matter for the military doctors,' said the mayor, and passed to the next case.
>
> A conscientious objector at Northampton expressed his willingness to serve in the Royal Army Medical Corps or Army Service Corps.* He was exempted from combatant service.
>
> Other interesting applications heard during the day included the following:
>
> One of two partners in a City firm. Put back for a week for the partners to decide between themselves which of them shall go.
>
> Scoutmaster and head of a boys' institute. 'We absolutely refuse. This is the worst case we have had before us.'
>
> Pawnbroker's manager 'most useful in catching thieves.' Refused. 'He may be useful in capturing Germans.'

---

* Conscientious objectors who served with front line medical services often performed acts of outstanding bravery.

Young man who wished to get married at Easter and to earn enough money in the meantime. Must serve at once.

Young man supporting his mother. Two of his brothers have been killed in the war, and another is in the Army. Exempted.

Civil servant, who thought he ought not to leave his mother 'in these days of Zeppelin alarms'. Refused.

Typical of the exchanges which took place between bona fide pacifists and the members of the tribunal was one involving Westminster and a leading activist with the No-Conscription Fellowship, Mr H. L. Bacon:

Mr Bacon stated that he believed in the sacredness of man. 'I consider it as big a crime to murder a foreigner in warfare,' he said, 'as it is to murder one of my fellow-countrymen.'

'We all believe in the sacredness of human life,' said the chairman, 'but this is rather a different position. We are face to face with war, and the defence of the country necessitates that men should be trained in the defence of their homes. If an enemy threatened to kill your mother, and you were standing by and a rifle was lying beside you, what would you do?'

'That is a difficult question to answer; it depends on the state of one's mind at the time,' replied Mr Bacon.

The chairman: Although the soldiers are fighting in France, it practically means that they are at the door of your home. What would you do if they were actually?

'I should protest,' said Mr Bacon, 'but not kill if I could possibly help it.'

The clerk: Suppose a Zeppelin was overhead dropping bombs, and you were at an anti-aircraft gun, what would you do? – 'I do not suppose I should stop it.'

But you would have an opportunity of saving your mother's and sister's lives. You would stand by, with a gun at your hand, and allow your home to be destroyed and your mother and sister killed? – Yes, I think I would.

He was excused from combatant service.

An impudent fellow from Woking, proprietor of a pig breeding business was granted exemption on the grounds that looking after the nation's food stock was work of national importance. On being asked if he could not find women to look after the animals he replied that the women would need more looking after than the pigs. The all-male board agreed with him!

Some well-known people took the pacifist line. James Maxton, later MP for Bridgeton, went to jail for his pains – and sent a letter to his comrades apologising for his absence from a meeting 'as I am confined to my room.' The Dunn family of hatters roused the ire of the *Express*:

> Mr G. A. Dunn – who has made a fortune out of the 3s 9d hat – and his four sons constitute the most remarkable family of conscientious objectors in the kingdom. The sons conscientiously object to hats, and are growing apples instead, while Mr Dunn senior has a conscientious objection at least to part of his own business.
>
> The sons, who have obtained exemption from military service, are:
>> Randolph Ellis Dunn
>> Clifford Arthur Dunn
>> Howard Oswald Dunn
>> Lloyd Stafford Dunn
>
> All live at the Aubreys, Redbourn, the home of their father. They were granted exemption by the Hertfordshire Appeal Tribunal. We take the following account of the proceedings from the *Herts Advertiser and St Albans Times*:
>
> Mr Frampton (barrister) appeared for the appellants, and claimed for them absolute exemption. They were the sons of a gentleman who was very prosperous in business, and their ages ranged from twenty-five to tweny-nine years. They held the belief that to destroy life in any form would be destroying part of the Creator. They had held these views conscientiously for years.
>
> The tribunal had not to consider whether the view they held was sound, but whether they really held that view. They had all had an opportunity of entering a flourishing business where they could have made a fortune for themselves, but they had preferred to live according to their principles.
>
> The appellants were questioned in turn.
>
> The oldest stated, in reply to Mr Reynolds (one of the tribunal) that he did not go into his father's business because he objected to commerce. He admitted, however, that he sold vegetables that he grew.
>
> Asked by Mr Gape (another member of the tribunal) if there were not officers' caps displayed in the windows of their father's business, one of them claimed that the allowance they received came

from that portion of the business that was not concerned in any way with the war.

Replying to the chairman (Mr E. B. Barnard) they stated that they obtained their views through abstaining from a meat diet, which made them see things in a different light.

They further declared that they would refuse to kill rats or mice even if they attacked their crops. If they saw a cat killing a rat they would try to prevent it.

Exemption was granted on condition the appellants undertook work on a farm.

A young man in Nottingham was given 'duty which will not bring him into contact with bloodshed' when he pleaded that he would never dare kill a fly and always ran away if he saw a woman faint or fall ill in the street.

So, in many cases, it is clear that the tribunals allowed conscientious objection on grounds other than those sanctioned by religious belief. Even so, some of the 16,000 conscientious objectors in the Great War were forcibly shipped to France and when they still refused to obey military orders were sentenced to death – the death sentences being commuted to penal servitude by the Commander-in-Chief, France.

In accordance with the Army Acts the objectors were then obliged to spend their jail terms in civilian prisons in England. Later 'conchies' who utterly refused to do any war work went straight to prison where they were frequently harried unmercifully by the conventional convicts, though given special treatment in the form of one day's leave per month, a concession which roused the wrath of the good folk of Plymouth who objected strongly to objectors from nearby Dartmoor having any free time whatsoever.

During the Great War – with one outstanding exception – opposition to total war came from what may be loosely called 'the Left': hard Marxists who wanted a war between the classes to replace the 'Imperialistic struggle', soft Liberals who stood aghast at the slaughter and honestly believed that 'goodwill' could somehow triumph over the test of blood and iron.

The exception was Henry Charles Keith, fifth Marquess of Lansdowne. He was the very epitome of stern, aloof, unyielding Tory diehard. A former Governor-General of Canada, Viceroy of India, Foreign Secretary in Lord Salisbury's Cabinet, leader of the last-ditch opponents to reform of the Lords, Lansdowne had organised the meeting at which Tory leaders had agreed to offer the Liberal Government of 1914 unconditional support to go to war on the side of France. Lansdowne himself had served on the War Council after the Conservatives joined in a coalition with the Liberals in 1915. However Lansdowne dissented from the doctrine of war-to-the-death propounded by Lloyd George. He circulated a memorandum in autumn 1916 outlining the criteria for a negotiated peace. Asquith, still Prime Minister, concurred with it. Then Asquith fell and was replaced by Lloyd George. Lansdowne, no longer a member of the War Council, fell silent, only to return to the matter, publicly, in November 1917 when he published a letter in the *Daily Telegraph* advocating openly what he had urged in private.

The letter (which Lansdowne had discussed with his Conservative colleague and Foreign Secretary, Mr A. J. Balfour) said the Allies should assure Germany of its right to remain a great power and promise to settle international problems by agreement in a new association of nations. Two years earlier such a call from such a source, endorsed by men like Asquith and Balfour *might* have prompted a reply from Germany. By November 1917 there was not the faintest chance of that happening. Russia, convulsed by revolution, was reeling out of the war. France had bled to such a degree that sixty of her regiments had mutinied. Italy had been shatteringly defeated at Caporetto. America had declared war but had not yet partaken of it. The Germans were winning. They were in no mood to talk of negotiations. The conqueror does not discuss. He commands. Moreover the Lansdowne letter suggested Britain, the only effective combatant, was weakening in resolve to continue the hostilities.

In these circumstances, Lansdowne's noble effort to save a remnant of the old civilisation was universally condemned. The *Express* put the sentiments of millions into one single sentence: 'A war half won, a peace by negotiation, could only mean gigantic world preparation for a conflict more horrible and hideous than that through which we are now passing.'

The horrible, hideous war was a global struggle in the sense that America, Russia and the colonial possession in Asia and Africa were involved. But overwhelmingly it was Europe that was fighting and dying. And France, perhaps more than any other nation the representative of European culture, was suffering most of all.

CHAPTER SIX

War by every means

'Audacity, audacity, always audacity' was the watchword of the mighty armies which flung themselves at each other in the autumn of 1914. Later, weapons would be forged and methods used that would make people vomit at the memory of the Great War, but in its opening phases gallantry and selflessness shone through. Nowhere was sublime heroism shown in greater measure than by France.

In listing the reasons why the Allies won pride of place must go to France – for making sure the Allies did not lose the war in the first few weeks.

Desire for revenge for the defeat of 1871 and the recovery of Alsace and Lorraine motivated the French in their mad, glorious attacks to regain the lost provinces in the first week of the war. They were giving expression to the patriotism voiced by schoolboys of Paris who had addressed this appeal to the French Prime Minister in March 1913:

'We are the soldiers of tomorrow and the day after tomorrow, and we wish to assure you, sir, that we are ready to sacrifice joyfully for France's life and France's glory three years of our youth.

'We hope that when the question of the three years' service is discussed by Parliament no one will dare to use as an argument against it the burden which a modification in the present state of affairs would place on the shoulders of the youth of France.'

Few, in England at any rate, believed that the huzza-ing 'frogs' would prove themselves as unyielding in defence as they were magnificent in offence. For France's image in 1914 was that of *opera-bouffe;* a slightly absurd theatricality given flesh by the actual proceedings in a French criminal court as France mobilized for war.

The man at the centre of these proceedings was the Finance Minister (and former Prime Minister) Joseph Caillaux. His wife had shot the editor of the *Figaro* newspaper, Gaston Calmette, to prevent him publishing old love letters from her to Joseph when they were both married to other people. She fired five shots into Calmette and then, at the trial, delivered herself of the immortal excuse: 'I did not think I had hit him, a revolver like that goes off by itself': a defence that was somewhat punctured by the evidence of the gunsmith who sold her the weapon: 'She shot at a silhouette in our gallery and hit it three times at a distance of eight feet.'

When Caillaux's first wife, the woman scorned, entered the witness box to testify against the accused, the *Daily Express* special correspondent gave full vent to Gallic exuberance:

I cannot imagine scenes more pulsing, more vibrant with human passion.

No novelist or dramatist would have dared to conceive such a situation as that into which the principal players in the great human tragedy were thrust today.

It was life; real, naked life stripped of all its illusions and shams. All the hidden truths were laid bare.

There was a man, once Prime Minister, once Finance Minister, and even now the most powerful politician in France – he might have been President of the Republic, so triumphant was his career – and here out of the past rose all the intimate life, the private secret things of the man himself. His love affairs and tenderness were pitilessly exposed before the world in which all these things had happened.

They were exposed by the wife from whom he had been divorced –Mme Gueydan – and he, M. Joseph Caillaux stood in the court, but a few paces away from her while the woman in black who is now his wife, was in the dock accused of murder.

A free woman in the court, the first wife, dark haired with the pallor of a southerner, her eyes burning with long-harboured hatred for the other woman who is loved by the man who once loved her. There is no doubt of her hatred. It was living and hissing and relentless in every word of her evidence.

'I didn't know that my husband ever had a mistress,' she said once and that word 'mistress' darted out like the forked tongue of a snake in two envenomed syllables, while she looked at that other, the fair-haired white-faced woman in the dock who shot a man for her husband's sake.

Madame Caillaux's defence lawyer, Monsieur Labori, summed up his client's case by claiming she suffered from a split personality. She was, he said, a female Jekyll and Hyde who had committed the murder in a sub-conscious state. His oratory – or Madame Caillaux's piteous appearance – won the day. The jury acquitted her ... presumably the gun had gone off by itself.

Her husband returned immediately to active politics and, as the Germans reached the Marne, urged the French Government to make peace and leave Germany free to fight England. Frustrated in this policy he went off to South America, ostensibly on a purchasing mission, actually to treat with the enemy for which offence he was arrested.

Joseph Caillaux exemplified sly corruption and his wife hysteria. Fortunately for the Allies they were not typical of France.

Without French endurance: on the Aisne in Champagne, above all at Verdun – the most appalling battle in the whole war – there would have been no Western Front and no possibility of victory. It was the French who possessed the finest medium artillery – the 75 mm; who provided Marshal Foch, the organiser of victory, who took supreme command of the British, American, Belgian and French armies in 1918; who were led by the most implacable of Germany's foes in the stooping figure of Georges Clemenceau, 'the tiger' who became France's Premier in 1917.

Excepting the short-lived breakdown of French morale and discipline in 1917, brought on by an ill-conceived offensive, the French Army was the mainstay of the Allied front for the first three years of the war. Long after the tunes of glory had faded France could take pride in the chilling, fatalistic resolve of her fighting men. One day, in January 1917, her foremost air ace, Lieutenant Georges Guynemer – with more than 30 kills to his credit – was asked: 'You have the Legion of Honour, the Military Medal, the Silver Cross – what other decorations can you possibly win?' 'The Wooden Cross,' he replied.

France lost one-fifth of her entire mobilized fighting force. Proportionately her death toll of 1,350,000 was by far the heaviest of the combatants. The sacrifice of 1914–18 was her undoing in 1940.

In 1914 France was fighting for her life. Her territory had been violated; the Germans were bent on taking Paris. Russia was under no such compulsion when she sent two armies into East Prussia to relieve the pressure on the French. She did so out of loyalty to her ally.

Her armies, led by Generals Rennenampf and Samsonov, were destroyed. But they achieved their objective. Two corps of the German forces designated to make the German right-wing 'punch' were transferred to the east to save Prussia. The Germans faltered in the West – and were lost. They might have been defeated on the Marne regardless of events in the East: what is certain is that without an eastern front the Germans would have triumphed in the West in 1915. Russia bled so that the West might live. By the time the Bolsheviks took Russia out of the war – in the winter of 1917/18 – America was in on the Allied side. Petrograd had kept faith.

What of Britain? Once the war was deadlocked by the trenches in the West the weapon of decisive importance came into play: the blockade.

In the annals of war few instruments are more indiscriminate than starvation – and few are more efficient. The civilian population is the principal victim, for any sensible government will make sure the armed forces are reasonably well fed. But, in time, letters from home will begin to affect the morale of the fighting men. Production of munitions will be affected by physical deterioration and the will to win will be gradually sapped. Men and women will endure the most appalling suffering if they believe the alternative to be death or slavery, as the Russians did in Leningrad from 1941–43 and the Germans – bombed day and night – did in 1943–45. But if the alternative to slow starvation, or at least grievous malnutrition, is tolerable then the cry 'Why go on?' will finally drown the beat of the drum.

Starving the Germans into submission was a perfectly understandable strategy for the Royal Navy. If you must fight a war then fight to win. The British Fleet was far larger than any other. So long as it remained *in being* the Germans could not invade the United Kingdom nor could they trade with the rest of the world outside Central Europe. They would be denied raw materials, fuel and food. Gradually their stocks would run out and they would be forced to sue for peace.

If, as Mr Churchill, then First Lord of the Admiralty, suggested in *The World Crisis,* the German Admiralty really believed that the Royal Navy would seek out the less numerous but still extremely strong German fleet in its Baltic lair, then the German admirals were very stupid men. The Royal Navy could only lose from such foolhardiness, gaining little if it destroyed quiescent German ships, risking all if it in turn were destroyed. It was said of Admiral Jellicoe, Commander of the Grand Fleet, that he was the only man who could lose the war in an afternoon. He needed only to stay away from a German killer stroke to ensure that Germany was gradually strangled.

Within weeks of the war opening the German mercantile marine was swept from the oceans. The German surface warships on the high seas were either sunk, rendered impotent or obliged to make fleeting pinprick attacks. Even the U-boats made little impression and did nothing to check the successful transfer of the British Expeditionary Force to France. Later, of course, the U-boats were to have a profound effect on Britain's chances of survival. But initially all the naval cards were in the hands of the British Admiralty.

We have already seen (see page 25) the impact of the blockade on Hamburg by the winter of 1914. Steadily over the following months stories were published of increasing shortages in Germany. Much of the material was propagandistic, to counter the continuing tale of German military victories. This report, however, published in May 1916 is a significant admission of the first small cracks in the German Home Front:

> The following is the report of what recently happened in Berlin, published in the Berlin newspaper, the *Berliner Zeitung am Mittag*. In view of the German official denials that the British blockade is causing a state of famine and the claim that there is plenty of food in the country, this German report is particularly valuable. It states:
>
> 'Demonstrations which occurred last night at Charlottenburg had very unpleasant consequences. After the streets round the Wilmersdorferstrasses and Pestalozzistrasse had been closed by the police, the excited crowd slowly withdrew. In the night, however, the mob assembled again, and began to wreck the butter and fish shops in the neighbouring streets, which were not guarded by the police.
>
> 'Thus, about 1 a.m. they smashed the windows of the butter shop, "Märkische Perle" at the corner of Schlüterstrasse and Pestalozzistrasse, stormed the shop, and plundered and destroyed almost all it contained.
>
> 'Then the crowd passed into Schlüterstrasse, to the next corner, to the butter shop of Martha Wolter, where it contented itself with banging all the signboards together. Meanwhile part of the crowd had stormed Hucke's butter shop in Grollmannstrasse. A soldier tried to resist the stormers, but was hurled by the raging mob through the window.

By January 1917 the situation had deteriorated and the *Express* reported:

The misery of the little towns of north-western Germany is terrible, despite the continual smuggling of food stuffs from Holland – a work in which the German sentries take an active hand, either by helping the smugglers to cross the frontier line with a fee varying from 5s to £5, or by smuggling goods themselves with the co-operation of the Dutch professionals. The sentries often use the services of children whom they send into Holland to fetch bread, milk, and meat 'for their parents'. The children receive a few coppers, while the soldiers sell the goods at many times their real value.

My correspondent, a neutral American, visited Buchholtz and tasted the 'bread' the local bakers sell there. He affirms that it is unfit even for horses' food but the population have seen no other bread for eighteen months. Two ounces daily of this stuff, which tastes like india-rubber and is made of sweepings of rice and sawdust, is the chief nourishment of the poor population of Western Germany. Meat and milk are hardly ever seen except on the tables of the well-to-do.

Cologne prides itself, like every other German city, on being the best organised town in the empire. In reality special precautions are taken, because many neutrals and many soldiers pass through the place, and the Government does not wish to give either too dismal an impression. In reality the women of Cologne are driven to despair by famine, for famine there is. This is the 'bill of fare' for Cologne people as arranged by the authorities under the card system:

Bad bread (daily)	8 ozs
Sugar (weekly)	22 ozs
Meat, including bones (daily)	$1\frac{1}{4}$ ozs
Fats and substitutes (weekly)	13–14 ozs
Butter (weekly)	2 ozs
Potatoes (daily)	18 ozs

The potato ration only appears five times a week; on the two other days the same weight of cabbage, generally decayed, is substituted. One egg every fortnight is allowed.

People in Cologne have not had milk for four weeks, except children under six, who receive less than a pint daily. There has been no genuine coffee for months, only an undrinkable substitute made with barley, and sold at a high price. Beans, rice, and dried vegetables are unheard of.

Every market day rioting takes place between the buyers, and often between the buyers and the police. On 12 December, two women were killed in the open market place of Cologne by revolver shots from the police because they were quarrelling about the dearth of food.

The *Dusseldorf Generalanzeigst* publishes a remarkable warning from Herr Georg Gothein, a member of the Reichstag, on 'world starvation'. He admits that food is very scarce in Germany.

There were exaggerations in this despatch but serious undernourishment *was* a growing factor in Germany's ability to wage war. Hence the launching of unrestricted submarine warfare as the only means of hitting back at the British (who had mined the sea approaches to Germany) even at the risk of bringing America into the war.

German frightfulness at sea had been tried before – notably the sinking of the *Lusitania* in 1915 – but had been abandoned partly out of deference to America, partly because of the 'counter-frightfulness' of the British who had used armed cruisers camouflaged as innocent American merchantmen and sank U-boats which came to the surface to attack legitimate British mercantile targets. Evidence for these alleged British atrocities was contained in an affidavit submitted by US citizens serving aboard British merchant ships.

So severe had the blockade become during the winter of 1916 – Britain was refusing to let even medical supplies from the USA through – that Germany reluctantly decided to re-introduce and extend indiscriminate submarine attacks. Kaiser Wilhelm's Government probably reckoned that Washington would grudgingly accept the German action because President Woodrow Wilson had himself enunciated 'freedom of the seas' policy comparable to Germany's and had denounced Britain's practice of forcibly examining neutral ships as 'unwarranted, inquisitorial, illegal and indefensible'. (Mr Wilson's inaugural address January 1917.)

Consequently Berlin's conditions, published 1 February, 1917, for control of trans-Atlantic traffic to the UK were severe. The US was limited, for example, to one sailing weekly between Falmouth and New York; every steamer to be painted and bedecked according to German instructions, to be illuminated at night and to shun the transport of contraband ('only rich American females seeking English lordlings will be permitted,' observed one German newspaper). Failure to comply with Berlin's orders would result in immediate sinking.

As will be seen, the impact of this 'insult' on American opinion and White House policy was far greater than Berlin had foreseen. But had Germany any choice? She *had* to break the blockade or go down.

Malnutrition was such that rickets – weakness of the bones – among children was designated 'the English disease'. *Vorwarts*, the Socialist journal, was suppressed for reporting: 'Many people are dying of sheer hunger. Sixty million people are suffering. They will not always remain silent. Germany is on the verge of catastrophe.' Even the conquest of wheat-rich Rumania was not enough to compensate for the denial of essential foodstuffs, fertiliser and raw materials from sources outside Europe. In her struggle to survive Germany *had* to play the U-boat card. In so doing she made America's entry into the war against her more likely. What clinched US involvement, however, was the same brutal stupidity that had characterised Berlin's handling of the *Lusitania* sinking.

Parallel with unrestricted U-boat warfare, the German Foreign Office offered an alliance to Mexico and Japan to 'take on' the USA if America abandoned neutrality and sided with the Allies. Thanks to the British decoding system directed by Admiral Hall of Naval Intelligence, the infamous telegram from Herr Zimmermann, Germany's Foreign Minister to Herr von Eckhardt, the German representative in Mexico City, was fed to the American newspapers. The telegram said:

Berlin, 19 January, 1917

On 1 February we intend to begin submarine warfare without restriction. In spite of this it is our intention to endeavour to keep the United States neutral. If this attempt is not successful, we propose an alliance on the following basis with Mexico:—

We shall make war together, and together make peace.

We shall give general financial support and it is understood that Mexico is to reconquer her lost territory of New Mexico, Texas, and Arizona.

The details are left to you for settlement.

You are instructed to inform the President of Mexico of the above in the greatest confidence as soon as it is certain that there will be an outbreak of war with the United States, and suggest that the President of Mexico shall on his own initiative communicate with Japan, suggest the latter's adherence at once to this plan, and at the same time offer to mediate between Germany and Japan.

Please call to the attention of the President of Mexico that the employment of ruthless submarine warfare now promises to compel England to make peace in a few months – (signed) Zimmermann.*

Within five weeks of the disclosure of this plot America was at war with Germany and a major Allied objective had been achieved.

Until the climacteric events of February/March 1917 the USA was in no wise belligerently minded. President Wilson had actually won the election of 1916 on the slogan 'The Man who kept America out of the war'. His Republican opponent was still more resolute in holding fast to American non-involvement in Europe's squalid squabble. Nor was there any overpowering reason of self-interest to drive the US to hostilities. Just the reverse. Economically the European war was a boon and a blessing to Wall Street. After a year industrial securities stood at an all-time high. For example:

	August 1914	*1915*
Crucible Steel	17	79
New York Air Brake	55	116
Westinghouse Electric	62	112
American Locomotive	19	56½
Bethlehem Steel	32	300

Orders placed by the Allies were fuelling an export-led prosperity. In 1916 America's foreign trade broke all records with overseas sales leaping $1.5 billion. On a number of occasions the US was angrier at Britain than at Germany. Mr Wilson frequently adopted a pose so lofty that he seemed to sprout a halo:

> 'America must have the consciousness that on all sides it touches elbows and touches hearts with all the nations of mankind. The example of America must be a special example – it must be an example not merely of peace because she will not fight, but because peace is a healing and elevating influence in the world, and strife is not.
>
> 'There is such a thing as a man being too proud to fight: there is

---

* Mexico had a long standing feud with the USA which had taken huge areas of Mexican territory. Mexico probably gave harbourage to German submarines in the South Atlantic. The Japanese connection was a piece of wishful thinking. Japan was actually at war with Germany and it seems likely that German agents in South America had been consorting with some anti-American Japanese not – at that time – representative of their country.

such a thing as a nation being so right that it does not need to convince others by force that it is right.'

Thus moral righteousness combined with economic advantage to keep American isolationist (who can doubt that the UK would have adopted precisely the same policy had she been in America's place?). What brought America in was the British Naval blockade of Germany.

So, on two counts, the blockade must be reckoned the decisive weapon: it weakened Germany to exhaustion at its most vulnerable point, the Home front and by provoking Berlin into 'frightfulness' at sea and anti-US adventuring in Latin America brought the US into the war.

A considerable period however passed before American troops took the field in France. This despatch is dated 27 October, 1917, – more than six months after Congress declared war:

Mr J. W. Pegler, the United Press correspondent with the American troop says:

> The Sammies are fighting side by side in the trenches with the *poilus*. A red-headed artillery captain and his gunners will share the fame of firing the first shell. The captain gave the command, the gunner jerked his lanyard, and the shell screamed towards a German battery precisely at six o'clock on a misty morning.
>
> The infantry restlessly awaited in billets behind the lines until the evening, when they swung through the rain-swept muddy street of a tiny village, shadowy forms disappearing down the road towards the trenches.
>
> Some attempted to sing 'Tramp, tramp, tramp! the boys are marching' and others shouted 'Shut up! the Boches will hear you.' Silence fell except for the rumbling of a rolling kitchen.

By May 1918, more than a year after America's entry, US forces at the front line numbered a mere 85,000 and the British and French had to supply most of the heavy arms and aircraft. Thereafter American soldiers flooded into the forward areas and the sight of those splendid, fit, fresh young men, battalion after battalion, brigade after brigade, division after division inflicted devastating damage on German morale and was unquestionably a major war-winning factor.

Yet there may well not have been a Western front to reinforce had Britain not sloughed off the peace-time attitudes of Mr Asquith.

CHAPTER SEVEN

The Man and the Weapons

Herbert Henry Asquith was the last of the patrician Liberal leaders: a man cast in the mould of Gladstone without the latter's holier-than-thou aspect, but also, alas, without his habit of temperance either.

David Lloyd George was the antithesis of Asquith. He was a little Welsh solicitor on the make with the charm of a nightingale's song, enough ambition to match the rest of the Commons and a genius for intrigue, inspiration and administration. In addition he had the killer instinct in war and politics. This final quality proved his strongest asset – and Asquith's undoing.

The nub of their quarrel was the central direction of war policy. Lloyd George argued that a small, four or five, member War Council *with total power over every aspect of the war effort* was essential. Asquith didn't want to sacrifice old colleagues and downgrade others. There was a despairing attempt at a compromise: a War Council chaired by Lloyd George but subject to Asquith's over-riding veto as Prime Minister. This was clearly unworkable as it would have meant two hands on the tiller. So the crisis came to its pre-ordained climax at the beginning of December 1916.

Mr Asquith, no mean manoeuverer himself with eight years of experience of the premiership behind him, told a hushed Commons that 'His Majesty the King, acting on the advice I have given him this morning (4 December) has approved a reconstruction of the Government.' Asquith's intention was to let Lloyd George go ahead to try to form an administration: fail, and leave Asquith much strengthened to resume the reins of power. Mr Asquith however had reckoned without Andrew Bonar Law, the taciturn Scots Ulster Canadian who led the

The Man and the Weapons

Conservative Party. Bonar Law favoured Lloyd George and he was a politician of a very rare species indeed. He was without personal ambition.

When King George sent for him – as it was the monarch's constitutional duty when Premier Asquith handed in his resignation (part, of course, of the Asquithian ploy) – the *Daily Express* concluded that Bonar Law was the new Prime Minister. The *Daily Express* moreover had a special contact, Max Aitken, soon to be Lord Beaverbrook and already part-owner of the *Express,* who was Bonar Law's closest friend. And this is what the *Express* had to say on the morning of 6 December:

> Mr Andrew Bonar Law, the new Prime Minister, who is fifty-eight years old, is of Canadian birth, the son of a New Brunswick clergyman, and a business man. He was an iron merchant in Glasgow for many years before he entered politics, and his success in that sphere gave him a grip of trade and commerce which has been of great service to the House of Commons.

Bonar Law refused the post and insisted on serving Lloyd George who, to everyone's surprise, succeeded in winning over enough of his own Liberal Party to form a coalition administration with the Conservatives. And within hours the country was experiencing a tighter grip and a new realisation of sacrifices.

> The announcement by the Board of Trade that it is proposed shortly to make an order prohibiting the consumption of meat, poultry and game on certain days lends added interest to the fact that the King has set an example to the country in this respect.
>
> The King and the royal household have for sometime past had two meatless days a week.
>
> 'His Majesty always does the right thing at the right time,' said Colonel Lockwood, MP, chairman of the Kitchen Committee of the House of Commons.
>
> 'We all ought to eat less, and it is certain that if we do not do it of our own accord we shall be compelled to do it. Before long we shall have a weekly national meatless day – if not two – and we shall all be the better for it.'

Two months later Lord Davenport, the food controller, recommended everyone to eat less and laid down a scale for each member of a household:

Bread .... 2 loaves a week
Meat .... $2\frac{1}{2}$ lbs a week
Sugar .... $\frac{3}{4}$ lb a week

'The nation,' he said, 'is placed on its honour to observe these conditions. If all else fails the machinery for rationing is ready.'

It seems astonishing that in the third year of the war, with the U-boats on the rampage rationing was still resisted by the authorities. Lord Davenport's successor, Sir Arthur Yapp, gave his reasons in a speech at Harrods in November 1917:

'It is not at all certain that rationing is fair to the poor, and I do not believe the poorer classes would benefit by it so much as others.

'I realise that I have undertaken as difficult a task as I possibly could have done. One section of the community is saying "It's all bluff!" and the other, "Why don't you ration us forthwith."

'There are a lot of great difficulties in connection with compulsory rationing. One of the difficulties would be forged tickets. In the first year of rationing in Germany 6,000,000 forged tickets were in circulation.'

Sir Arthur Yapp appealed to the people to observe the following rules:

Use no cream except for infants and invalids, and as little milk as possible.

Take no sugar in tea and do not take tea more than once a day.

Use not more than one egg a day in any form.

Do without bread at the midday and evening meals.

Use potatoes in place of bread.

Bacon and ham, which are essentially the foods of the working classes, should be used sparingly.

Be as careful as possible with dried fruits, for they came from the danger zone.

During the Christmas festivities be as careful as you possibly can.

'We must win through with this campaign by Christmas, or else in all probability we shall have compulsory rationing, and we do not want that if we can help it.'

Unwillingness to introduce rationing was really indefensible: merchant shipping losses to U-boats reached a peak of 849,000 tons – 423 ships – in April 1917 and even though the convoy system cut the sinkings, Britain's food supplies were insufficient to go around fairly at reasonable cost. Inevitably envy grew of those able to take advantage of 'rationing by price' and hoarding was made a criminal offence:

> Miss Marie Corelli, the novelist, was fined £50 and £21 costs for sugar hoarding at Stratford-on-Avon yesterday. The defence was that the sugar was used for jam making.
> It was stated that Miss Corelli, whose household consisted of seven persons, was able to obtain sugar locally, and from Lipton Limited in London.
> On this basis Miss Corelli's household was entitled during the period named, to thirty-two pounds of sugar, but she had obtained 183 pounds independently of preserving sugar to which she was entitled.
> After evidence of sugar purchases had been given a police constable described his reception at Mason Croft, Miss Corelli's house, when he went to see her about large deliveries of tea and sugar.
> 'I hear you have been accusing me of hoarding,' said Miss Corelli to the police constable. 'It has come to a fine thing if women cannot live in their homes without being interfered with by the police.
> 'I think you police are overstepping your duty in visiting my house. You are upsetting the country altogether with your food orders and what not. Lloyd George will be resigning to-morrow, and there will be a revolution in England in less than a week.'
> Lady Mabel Gore-Langton, of the Glade, Englefield Green, was fined £80 for obtaining food in excessive quantities on various dates since last April.
> When the house was searched the police found:
>
> | | |
> |---|---|
> | 125 lbs of tea | 23 lbs of currants |
> | 35 lbs of coffee | 44 lbs of sultanas |
> | 11 tins of syrup | 7 lbs of raisins |
> | 12 tins of condensed milk | 20 lbs of sugar |
>
> The tea, with the exception of a few pounds, has been confiscated. The household consisted of twelve persons, including servants.
> Superintendent Meers asked Lady Mabel: 'Do you know that most poor people have obtained only 2 ozs of tea weekly, and sometimes under that, for the last three months?'
> 'I am sorry to say that I do not,' was the reply.

Finally on 25 February, 1918, compulsory rationing of most basic foods was introduced accompanied by price controls. The lesson of the failure to secure minimum amounts of food for everyone at acceptable prices was learned. Rationing was applied within four months of the outbreak of World War II.

A measure of how Britain was scraping the barrel by mid-1918 may be gauged from this item of news:

> Four or five pounds of wool, in the form of combings, may be obtained in a year from long-haired dogs, such as old English sheepdogs, samoyeds and chows. A toy pom will yield in the year about two pounds of wool, equal to the finest vicuna, worth 8s or 9s a pound.
>
> So-called luxury dogs are thus able to justify their existence by contributing to the comfort of our sick and wounded, for dogs' wool is collected by the Ladies Kennel Association for the purpose of turning it into socks, jerseys, and underclothing for the Red Cross Society.
>
> A Maltese contributed twenty pounds of wool the other day – the product of his short life. One dog lover sent the produce of her kennel during the last twelve months – twenty pounds of wool, which has been knitted into forty jerseys, the softness and warmth of which are remarkable.

Lloyd George was resolved on victory and he infused people with his own ruthless determination. But Lloyd George was in an exposed position, politically. He was not the Leader of the Liberal Party: Asquith was. And Asquith had neither forgotten nor forgiven the way in which he had been ousted. Suddenly, in May 1918, an issue arose which enabled Asquith to focus Parliament's wrath on the Lloyd George administration, to threaten the very existence of the Government and, in the end, to break the Liberal Party once and for all. The issue was the Maurice Letter.

*

Before dealing with General Maurice's correspondence it is necessary briefly to outline the military situation in the spring and early summer of 1918.

Russia, convulsed by revolution, was out of the war. This freed 100 German divisions for a final assault in the West before the American armies arrived. On 21 March these veteran divisions fell upon the tired and stretched British Fifth Army. The Germans attacked with great élan, using specially equipped storm troops to infiltrate the British position. The Fifth Army under General Sir Hubert Gough virtually disintegrated. All at once the Allies, after nearly four years of grinding unceasing struggle, were faced with a war of movement in which the enemy was back to his successful sweep of 1914. The Kaiser Schlacht (the Kaiser's battle, as it was named in honour of Wilhelm's presence alongside the two commanders of the German forces, Hindenburg and Ludendorff) was a series of assaults, each designed to wrong-foot the Allies and leave them in doubt as to where the next blow would fall.

So grave was the situation by late April that General Sir Douglas Haig, C-in-C of the British Armies in France, issued an order of the day demanding that every soldier stand and die at his post. This backs-to-the-Wall message struck the House of Commons like the knell of doom. Why was our army so weak? What had gone wrong? Who was to blame?

Into this sea of doubt and anxiety Major-General Sir Frederick Maurice, lately Director of Military Operations, threw a stone that threatened to swamp Lloyd George. For Sir Frederick claimed, in a letter to *The Times,* that the Prime Minister had misled House and country by saying there were more British troops in the line in France in 1918 than in fact there were, and that he had done this to cover up for the waste of British resources caused by his eastern strategy of keeping large Empire forces in the Middle East when they should have been on the Western Front.

Mr Asquith stepped in to place what amounted to a vote of censure on the Government for lying to the House and betraying the Army. The debate was held on 9 May, 1918, in an atmosphere of intense drama. The House was more crowded than at any time since Lloyd George had become Premier. The fate of the Government hung on the outcome and the fate of the war – with the Germans exerting every ounce of effort against the British front – could hang on the continuation of the Government. By a strange co-incidence the date, 9 May, was the same as that of the historic debate in 1940 which overthrew Chamberlain and brought Churchill to office.

This time however there was no change of Premiers. Lloyd George had a devastating answer to General Maurice. The figures of British troop strengths in the West had been supplied by Maurice's own office. If *they* were wrong then Maurice was to blame.*

---

* Many years later Lloyd George's personal secretary, Miss Stevenson disclosed that a memo from General Maurice *correcting* the original figures (i.e. those given by Lloyd George to the House) was discovered in the former Premier's private papers. The offending memo was burned.

Despite this crushing retort Lloyd George's critics, who were not so much interested in the merits of the case as in getting their own back on the man who had forced his way to the top by shouldering Asquith out of the way, mustered 106 votes. They were however overwhelmingly defeated, the Government mustering nearly 300 MPs. When the result was announced the manager of His Majesty's Theatre went to the front of the house during the interval of *Chu Chin Chow* to announce: 'England has won a great victory.' His words were received with prolonged applause.

So ended the Maurice debate. And so ended the Liberal Party. For those, mainly Liberals, who opposed Lloyd George were denied his endorsement when he went to the country in the General Election in December. The Liberal Party split in two: Asquithian and Lloyd Georgian and never again did it hold office.

But from the point of view of the Grand Alliance the vote was indeed an unqualified triumph, for if the British Government had fallen morale in the Army, fighting a desperate rearguard action, might have collapsed. The French would have been utterly dismayed at the disappearance of Lloyd George from the scene. At that juncture it could have been fatal. For the little Welshman, like his opposite number across the Channel, 'Tiger' Clemenceau, was an essential ingredient for victory.

Having survived the test Lloyd George presided majestically over the last phase. 'It is always darkest before the dawn' proved to be absolutely true of Allied fortunes. The German offensive petered out. The French began to counter-attack. On 8 August (described by Ludendorff as the black day of the German Army) 600 tanks rolled forward on the front of the British Fourth Army; bombers strafed enemy artillery while other aircraft dropped smoke to confuse the Germans. This was blitzkrieg – twenty years before Hitler.* Within hours six German divisions had ceased to exist. By the end of the day the British Fourth Army had advanced ten miles and taken 10,000 prisoners. The tank had become mistress of the battlefield.

It was not that machine's first appearance. Almost two years previously this paragraph appeared in the *Daily Express*:

The new type of heavy armoured car mentioned in the British official

---

* Twenty-two years later young British officers in 1918 were, as senior commanders in France, on the receiving end. The Germans had learned the lesson of that the British – inventors of the tank – had forgotten.

despatch as having been used for the first time is a formidable engine of war which should considerably reduce our casualty lists.

A large percentage of our casualties have been caused by the enemy machine guns, which are turned on the infantry when advancing after the initial bombardment is supposed to have shot away the trenches and wire entanglements. The new car completes the work of the artillery before the infantry advance.

Its chief work is to locate the German machine gunners and blow them out of their positions. This done, there is a clear course for the infantry to occupy the abandoned enemy positions.

Unfortunately the tank (called so to disguise its nature from the enemy should they intercept messages referring to this tracked monster) was used on the wrong terrain in penny numbers. A year after its brief appearance on the Somme, Percival Phillips, special correspondent, showed exceptional powers of prophecy when he reported on 22 November, 1917:

> An army of tanks helped to break the Hindenburg or Siegfried line.
> Creeping silently through the mist at dawn – unheralded by any of the usual portents of battle – these mobile fortresses drove squarely into the massive trench system of the enemy a few miles southwest of Cambrai and cracked it with contemptuous ease – cracked it and went through to the furthest side with exultant infantry following in their wake.
> This is an inadequate summary of the opening of what, I believe, may prove an historic day – a day that may stand out in the annals of this war as even more important than some of the harder-fought victories of the past.

Again the chance was let slip. There were not sufficient tanks to exploit the breakthrough at Cambrai. A year later tanks and infantry were in abundance. The German front caved in as the British, French and American forces rolled remorselessly forward. In three months the British Army alone took 180,000 prisoners. Bombs by the ton were hurled down on marshalling yards and munition factories inside Germany. As the First War came to an end the weapons of the Second were being forged.

CHAPTER EIGHT

Aftermath

At the eleventh hour of the eleventh day of the eleventh month of 1918 the armistice came into operation and the fighting ended. Now the British celebrated victory:

When the Premier, Mr Lloyd George, appeared he was at once the centre of a cheering, laughing gathering of friends. He tried to speak, but the cheers drowned his voice. He waved his hand above his head, and flags and handkerchiefs and hats answered his gesture. There was no happier smile in all London yesterday than the Premier's, and there was exultation and joy in his voice when he cried: 'It is over! They have signed! The war is won!'

At eleven o'clock the Union Jack was hoisted over Downing Street, maroons were set off, and the 'All Clear' sounded from the plinth of Nelson's Column and at other centres.

Until now it seemed as if the people were reluctant to believe, but as the crowds steadily moved towards Buckingham Palace a new and pleasant note of laughter, of assurance and of joy made itself felt.

Shortly before one the music of the Guards' Band was heard and expectancy ran high.

The band played 'Home, Sweet Home', and a sudden hush fell on the vast assembly. It was a most moving incident of a great occasion, and no person there but had a sad and tender thought for the boys who will never again see home but who have laid down their lives to make our homes secure. When the sweet tune ceased the silence remained unbroken until the marching song of the 'Old Contemptibles', the immortal 'Tipperary' with its haunting lilt and unforgettable memories, provoked an outburst of cheering that warmed the heart. This was followed by Elgar's 'Land of Hope and Glory', the crowds singing the fine triumphant hymn. France and her heroes were brought to mind by the crash of the 'Marseillaise'.

At home there was a general election on the theme, propounded by some, of 'Hang the Kaiser' and 'Squeeze Germany till the pips squeak'. The Conservatives in coalition with Lloyd George's Liberals won easily. Those Liberals who had opposed Lloyd George in the Maurice debate were denied the coalition 'coupon', or endorsement, and fared badly. They nursed their grievances and waited their chance for revenge.

Meanwhile the people counted the cost of winning 'the war to end war'. United Kingdom dead totalled 700,726. Empire losses exceeded a quarter of a million. The ratio of other ranks to officers was 7–1 : the highest ratio of officers to men of any belligerent and a testimony to the mortal peril of being first over the top.

But even those stark figures did not measure the full toll. Within a month of the Armistice this report appeared in the *Express* :

> Anxiety in connection with the war has driven many people to seek the false solace of drugs, but there is another side to this question. There is a regular and profitable and despicable traffic in drugs carried on by men and women whose object is sordid money gain at the expense of young lives.
>
> Drugs are hawked in London on the streets and in notorious cafes. Anybody who knows the ropes can buy heroin, cocaine, morphia, or any of the preparations known as 'chandoo' or 'pop'. Haschisch, the drug of the Assassins, the Canabis Indica of the pharmacopaeia, is available in cigarette form, in the compressed tablet, or in dark green treacly liquid.
>
> The dope fiends of London seek only one thing – the feeling of well-being, of exhilaration, the elimination of time and space. War has increased the nervous tension of the individual to an unheard-of degree. Men and women alike have craved for a change from the normal to the fantastic and rare.

And some of the 2,000,000 wounded were worse off than the dead.
From the *Sunday Express* of 15 August, 1920 :

> A distressing story was related at Willesden Police Court yesterday, when a blinded soldier wearing a Mons Star, appeared on a charge of being intoxicated.

He told the magistrate that he could not sleep unless he took drink, and added that he had practically been without sleep for six weeks, until he was on the point of madness. He had pleaded with the doctor to give him a sleeping draught, and was told to take stout. When he did so, however, 'a reaction immediately set in,' and he seemed to be 'back in the trenches waiting for the zero hour, and then over the top and in a bayonet charge.'

The magistrate, in fining him 5s., remarked that he was sorry for him, but he had far better leave drink alone.

The soldier: 'It's a pity the bullet did not go straight and finish me. I am only in the way.'

Well on into the twenties and thirties piteous stories of suffering, bravely borne, were recounted. Like this one from the *Sunday Express* on 25 January, 1925:

Trooper Samuel Rolfe, known all over the world as 'the man who lived in a hot bath,' has died.

A great number of people, including many representatives of public bodies, assembled to pay their last tribute to him.

Rolfe was taken for burial to Inverell from the Randwick Military Hospital in Sydney, where, in a bath of warm water, he had found his only relief from pain for the past five years.

He suffered from an illness, caused by mustard gas in the war, which removed all the skin from his body.

Every effort of the most eminent specialists both in Australia and London failed to make it grow again, and nothing except hot water could come in contact with his body without making him cry out in agony.

The doctors finally devised the treatment of a perpetual bath after it was found that he could not even bear to rest in pyjamas, which had been thickly covered with vaseline.

Rolfe actually slept in the water, being accommodated on a water bed, automatically raised by winding gear when the water rose too high. There were water-filled pillows for head and feet.

He was astonishingly 'bright and cheerful to the end,' laughing and chatting with friends as if his experience was nothing out of the common. Trooper Rolfe was thirty-five years old.

For others the mental strain of years of warfare was just too much. The following paragraph (from the newspaper of 11 January, 1920) was duplicated many times:

'I am down and out. God forgive me and have mercy on my soul.'

This was the note left by William Stanley Holman, aged twenty-eight, an ex-soldier, of Muswell Hill, who was found dead in a bathroom with the geyser gas turned on.

It was stated at the inquest at Hornsey yesterday that Holmes had been depressed since he left the Army because he could not find employment, and a brother-in-law said the Government was to blame.

The coroner, in recording a verdict of 'Suicide while of unsound mind' said that he was not an economical adviser and had only to certify the cause of death.

Everywhere there were signs of tension, strain and longing. Spiritualism had an enormous appeal for distraught mothers, wives and sweethearts, longing to get in touch with loved ones 'on the other side'. The *Express* decided to test the claims of mediums and offered £500 to any one who could 'prove' his, or her, claims. A masked woman, who insisted on remaining anonymous, offered to act in a private capacity without reward. An *Express* representative attended her seance and having sealed the doors and windows, bound the woman's arms and legs, admitted that 'The events produced a mental metamorphosis in the sceptic.' The masked lady then performed before a select committee of believers and non-believers – the believers including such notabilities as Sir Arthur Conan Doyle, creator of Sherlock Holmes, and Sir Henry Lunn, the holiday travel 'king'. The results were predictably inconclusive : nobody changed their minds.

Spiritualism's sweeping appeal was all of a part with the desire to experiment.

'Would you like to see your mother smoke?' asked Mr Joynson-Hicks MP answering his own question by remarking that he was old fashioned enough to object to smoking among women. At the same meeting in November 1918 Mr Bramwell Booth anticipated the anti-smoking propaganda of sixty years on by observing : 'I suppose we shall see the mothers of the future puffing smoke into the face of their babies.'

*

The world was out of kilter. The old restraints, the old taboos were breaking down. But there welled up in the consciousness of nations, victor and vanquished alike, the need to commemorate the dead before they picked up the threads of living again. The Germans had their haunting song 'I Had a Comrade', the French had the eternal flame.

Now Britain had the Unknown Warrior, buried with the utmost solemnity in Westminster Abbey and, in 1920, at the prompting of ex-servicemen the first Armistice Day was proclaimed to mark for ever the nation's homage to the Glorious Dead. On the first Armistice Day a particularly touching scene was added to the grandeur of Westminster Abbey:

By Herbert Thompson
(West Yorkshire Regiment, a blind inmate of St Dunstan's)
The ceremony in the Abbey left an indelible impression on my mind – a feeling of ineffable sadness and melancholy, yet there was a message of inspiration and hope. I felt as if the spirit of the Unknown Warrior had whispered in my ear, 'Courage, brother; hope on.'

I was one of the lucky three, chosen by ballot, from 170 blind inmates of St Dunstan's.

I understood all, even though every step and every movement was explained to me by an accompanying guide. The atmosphere was impregnated with meaning. The Great Alchemist by some miracle, vouchsafed to me a more powerful vision than those who had eyes to see. Clear-out pictures of France and Flanders rose up before me. The dread solemnity of the occasion stirred the most poignant memories. I felt with my comrades almost ashamed that I had given so little, while he who lay sleeping by us had given all.

I stood near the tomb of a mighty king. Not far away were the hundred VCs. I heard them limp to their places and knew who they were. The solemn rolling of the drama and the slow martial music of the massed bands meant more to me, perhaps, than to other people. When the long roll of the reveille echoed away in the distance I thought a cloud had passed over my head and had been chased away by the sunshine.

Then with my comrades I was granted a privilege denied to all others. Each of us had been given a chrysanthemum before we left St Dunstan's. Others had placed their wreaths at the foot of the coffin. A hand guided us, and we were allowed to bestow our tribute on the coffin itself. We spoke in the name of our blind comrades, and I felt a supreme emotion as my fingers brushed the resting place of the unknown hero. I came to the Abbey glad that I had been chosen from among so many. I went away sorrowing, but with the message of hope locked in my heart.

Memories were also kept fresh by visits to the battlefields: Thomas

Aftermath

Cook were early on the scene, organising package tours to the Somme, Arras and Vimy Ridge. Other memories were stirring too – of Germany's debt to 'outraged humanity'.

Allied occupation of the Rhineland, as laid down in the Armistice conditions, was described in newspaper reports and tended to strengthen a bitter remembrance. Percival Phillips, with the British Army wrote:

In Germany at last!

British lancers and dragoons, streaming through the high street of Malmedy, sabres drawn and pennons stiff in the winter wind: horse guns clattering past the cobble-stoned market place led by a great Union Jack, wagons and cyclists and staff cars passing through a silent, curious crowd; shaven heads bared reluctantly to the vanguard of the 'contemptible British Army'; furtive scowls partially countered by a few bleak smiles of conciliation; stern faces peering through half-drawn blinds; gleeful children chided by apprehensive women and sullen men glowering at the troopers from their doorways – such is my impression of our entry into the first Prussian town within the British zone of occupation.

The peace of Sunday morning was in no wise broken by this historic journey. People paused on their way to church to stare at the first two troopers riding with drawn sabres at either side of the valley road, and some of them waited until the first following squadron had passed before going their way. The life of Malmedy began as usual, and went on without a pause while the columns of khaki flowed through the town.

One could not help thinking of the contrast with that other advance more than fours years ago, when the occupation of a hostile town meant the seizure of hostages, ruthless oppression of defenceless citizens, and perhaps a massacre in the market place. I saw a memorial to such a tragedy on the road from Spa to Malmedy yesterday.

In a little roadside orchard, hardly five miles from the frontier where I crossed this morning, had been erected a rough, wooden sign, 'Here lie seventeen hostages shot by the Prussians.' I wonder if the people of Malmedy remembered the fate of their Belgian neighbours as they watched the British cavalry ride into their town today.

The surrender of the German Fleet at Scapa Flow in November 1918 should have signalled to the British public how complete was the victory, how absolute the deliverance. Here was the Kaiser's High Seas

Fleet, the standard bearer of the All Highest's ambitions to overthrow Britannia bending the knee in utter submission. The Germans had claimed a 'victory' at Jutland in 1916 (certainly they sank more British ships than they lost) but their navy had only dared to come out of its harbour once since then. To surrender. Could triumph be more overwhelming? Yet dread of German resurgence remained and when on 21 June, 1919, in defiance of the Armistice terms, the German sailors scuttled their ships at Scapa Flow fear of Germany, democratic or Imperial, was reinforced. Admiral Sir Percy Scott remarked: 'It serves us right for trusting the Huns.'

Gathered at Versailles for the final negotiations to produce a peace treaty, the Allied representatives reacted vehemently to what they regarded as German trickery, backsliding and prevarication and in a message to the German plenipotentiaries declared:

'The German delegates fail to understand the position in which Germany stands today. In the view of the Allied and Associated Powers, the war was the greatest crime against humanity and the freedom of peoples that any nation calling itself civilised has ever consciously committed. The rulers of Germany required that they should be able to dictate and tyrannise to a subservient Europe. They sought to sow hostility and suspicion instead of friendship between nations. They kept Europe in a ferment by threats of violence, and when they found that their neighbours were resolved to resist their arrogant will they determined to assist their predominance in Europe by force.

'The German revolution was stayed until the German armies had been defeated in the field and all hope of profiting by a war of conquest had vanished. Throughout the war the Germans supported it by vote and by money, and obeyed every order, however, savage, of their Government. They cannot now pretend, having changed their rulers after the war was lost, that it is justice that they should escape the consequences of their deeds.'

The Allies gave Germany five days to sign and rejected German claims to retain their colonies, a substantial navy and army and to be relieved of debts concerning those territories, i.e. Alsace-Lorraine and the Saar, that were being taken from the Reich. The Germans caved in. On 28 June, 1919, the anniversary of the assassination of Archduke Franz Ferdinand that sparked off the Great War, Germany signed the Treaty of Peace. Herren Muller and Bell of the new German Republic's

Foreign Office signed for Germany; Messrs Wilson, Clemenceau and Lloyd George for the three principal allies. But these signatures, in the Hall of Mirrors at Versailles – a scene that had witnessed the birth of the German Empire in 1871 – sowed bitter recriminations. A cartoon in the Labour *Daily Herald* showed the statesmen walking out of the council chamber while in the corner a baby cries. With prophetic insight the baby is captioned 'Class of 1940.' The implication was that the terms were too harsh, too 'reactionary'. That, naturally, was the German view too. Long before Adolf Hitler bellowed out his rage at the Versailles *Diktat* German Liberals were bewailing the betrayal of President Wilson's idealistic proposals which, claimed the Germans, had induced them to sign the Armistice in the first place.

President Wilson, who naively believed that nations – as distinct from individuals – possessed goodwill had thoughtfully produced 14 commandments to make the world safe. (Clemenceau remarked that God had been content with 10.) Among these 14 points were promises concerning armaments, colonies, self-determination which the Germans were at pains, after the Armistice, to emphasise and which the Allies blithely ignored. The core of the German complaint, echoed and re-echoed ever more loudly down the years, was that the Allies had wickedly seduced honest Germany : Berlin lost its colonies : the Allies kept theirs. Germany disarmed. France rearmed. German territory was torn away without reference to the wishes of the inhabitants.

This powerful argument had immense influence in England and America in the twenties and thirties even though it was founded on a lie. For Wilson produced his 14 points in January 1918 and the German armies launched their offensive on the Western Front in March 1918. It was only after that offensive had been broken and the German armies were in headlong retreat that the German Government agreed to open negotiations for peace. Yet it was the victorious Allies who were made to feel guilty and this feeling of guilt bred the widespread conviction that the Great War had been a terrible futility; that the sacrifices, so movingly commemorated on Remembrance Day, had been in vain. So when, ten years later these sacrifices were recounted in the play *Journey's End,* the *Evening Standard* recorded the experience of the principal actor, Colin Clive :

'I receive many letters from members of the audience. A large percentage are from the younger generation who were babies when the war broke out. The young women are mostly against war at any price and young men write too condemning it.'

When everyone condemns war all is well. When some condemn it and others prepare for it all is ill.

PART TWO

Intermission

CHAPTER NINE

Workers of the World, Unite!

A world turned upside down faced the statesmen and peoples of Europe at the end of the Great War. Never in history had there been such an upheaval. Never had so many men died in battle. Never had there been such a clattering fall of dynasties. Down came the Hohenzollerns of Germany with Kaiser Wilhelm II seeking refuge in neutral Holland. Down came the ancient Hapsburg throne, heir to the Holy Roman Empire, master of the polyglot Austro-Hungarian Empire. Down came the ramshackle Ottoman Empire with its Sultans and Caliphs and Viziers. In their place sprang up nations with unpronounceable names: Czechoslovakia and Yugoslavia (both carved out of the non-German elements of Austro-Hungary) and tiny states – Lithuania, Latvia, Estonia, which had wrenched themselves away from Russia.

Russia: there was the greatest fall of all. The Romanov dynasty had vanished and in its place peering out of the murk and chaos was a new breed of men, the Bolsheviks, followers of a new prophet, Karl Marx; men who rejoiced in the pseudonyms they had used to disguise themselves from the Czarist secret police: Ulyanov who used the alias Lenin; Lev Bronstein known as Trotsky; Joseph Vissarionovich Djugashvilli – otherwise Joseph Stalin.

These men preached the doctrine of world revolution as vouchsafed to them by the writings of Karl Marx, notably *Das Kapital* and the Communist manifesto, both published many years before the Russian revolution. They preached it with the fervour of converts to a faith mightier than nationalism and with a certainty that they had the key to scientific truth. Just as physics obeyed unalterable laws so, said the Bolsheviks (the name was Russian for the majority in a minor dispute within the old social democratic movement) did politics and economics. One class displaces another until, with capitalism, societies reach the penultimate stage when resources are increasingly concentrated in fewer and fewer hands – as competition eliminates the least successful. Finally the working classes, the industrial proletariat, realising their strength (for it is the surplus value of their labour – surplus, that is, to the subsistence wage paid them) overthrow their oppressors and usher in the age of communism when property is equally shared and the State with its organs of exploitation, police, army, etc. withers away.

Now Marxism was no visionary, utopian ideal but a hard, inevitable, irreversible process. It could not be short-circuited. Each society *must* go through the differing economic stages from feudalism to capitalism before the synthesising was complete. Only those societies in the final stages of intensive capitalism, where the urban masses far outnumber the peasantry and wealth is concentrated in a few hands as the bourgeoisie (the middle classes) are pauperised could be considered ripe for communists. There might be revolts elsewhere. There could only be communist revolution in the most advanced societies, of which the prime examples were Britain and Germany.

In theory, these countries should have reached the revolutionary stage by the late 1800's. That their people had not been driven to rebellion by grinding poverty was explained away by Lenin. Their rulers had embarked on imperialism and were grinding the faces of coloured workers so that the domestic proletariat in Britain and Germany could enjoy a living standard that, in communist eyes, ought to be far beyond their means. Imperialism, passing the buck of exploitation, so to say, was the only way of explaining the undoubted fact that the masses in Britain and Germany and in America, France and other advanced countries as well, were better off than ever before.

What Lenin couldn't explain was why Bolshevism should triumph in backward Russia: Russia, where the industrial proletariat was minimal, barely organised, politically naive, whose society was almost feudal and capitalism had barely taken off and the peasantry – considered non-revolutionary – formed the overwhelming bulk of the people.

Yet Lenin didn't feel the need to justify this fundamental departure from revealed truth. It was enough that he, Vladimir Ilyich Ulyanov, had succeeded to the role of maker of a new age; that he who had guarded the purity of the doctrine against those who had tried to water it down – or heat it up – should put it into action.

But Lenin did not make the Russian Revolution. He inherited it.

Workers of the World, Unite!

The Czar, Nicholas II, was not overthrown by the Bolsheviks; he was required to abdicate by members of the Russian *Duma,* or Parliament, for gross dereliction in the conduct of the war against Germany. The astounding news of the Czar's downfall was flashed to the world by Exchange Telegraph on Thursday, 15 March, 1917:

> The Czar has abdicated. His brother, the Grand Duke Michael, has been appointed Regent.
>
> A telegram received from Petrograd states officially that a revolution has broken out in Petrograd.
>
> The *Duma* refused to be dissolved, and an Executive Committee was formed with M. Rodzianko, the President of the *Duma,* as its head. The Committee, which is made up of twelve members, two days ago proclaimed itself as the Provisional Government, and issued the following proclamation:
>
> Owing to the difficult circumstances and the disorganisation of the interior of the country, for which the former Government is responsible, the Executive Committee of the *Duma* considers it necessary to take over the government of the country. Fully realising the importance of the decision come to, the committee feels sure that the population and the army will assist it in the difficult task of forming a new Government which will be in a position to fulfil the wishes of the people, and be ensured of public confidence.
>
> The revolutionists, supported by the populace of Petrograd, and by the whole garrison of 30,000 men, thereupon arrested all the members of the Cabinet, and declared the Cabinet to be non-existent.
>
> To-day, the third day of the revolution, Petrograd is quite calm, and there was no difficulty in maintaining order. A member of the *Duma,* Colonel Engelhardt, has been appointed commander in Petrograd.
>
> This evening the Committee issued a proclamation requesting the population and the banks and the railways to continue their industrial activities.

A week later the ex-Czar and Czarina and their family were placed under house arrest by the provisional government who relied wholly on the old Imperial Army to implement its order. For a while it seemed that Russia was about to become a twentieth-century-style democracy, fit partner for the Western Allies in their struggle against Prussian militarism.

David Lloyd George telegraphed the Russian Premier:

'I believe that the revolution whereby the Russian people have based their destinies on the sure foundation of freedom is the greatest service which they have yet made to the cause for which the Allied peoples have been fighting since August 1914.

'It reveals the fundamental truth that this is at bottom a struggle for popular government as well as for liberty. It shows that, through the war, the principle of liberty, which is the only safeguard of peace in the world has already won one resounding victory.'

What the Western Allies did not appreciate was that a parallel revolutionary organisation had grown up, owing nothing to the *Duma* but basing itself on *Soviets,* or committees of workers, soldiers and peasants which was, though not wholly, under the influence of the Leninists. These *Soviets* were to be used by Lenin to take Russia out of the war. How ignorant the West was of the true purpose of this parallel organisation is shown by a despatch published on 18 April, 1917:

The British and French Labour deputations now in Petrograd to-day paid a visit to the Congress of Workmen's and Soldiers' Delegates from all Russia, and were received with immense enthusiasm. They were accompanied by M. Plekhanoff, a famous refugee, who has returned to his native land.

M. Tcheidze, the president, in an address of welcome, said:

'Russia is now living the best days of her life, for she sees her best men coming back from exile. We have here with us our master, M. Plekhanoff, who had given his word never to return to Russia until Nicholas II had been arrested. His dream has come true.'

Mr J. O'Grady, one of the British Labour delegates, said:

'The British have for a long time been looking for their great ally to cast off the yoke of despotism, and are delighted to see Russia freed from it. We are convinced that the Russian revolution will find an echo throughout the world. Henceforth we shall fight side by side for the destruction of the oppressor of the world – William of Hohenzollern.'

Two days later the influence of Lenin was recorded and dimissed*:

The refusal of many of the extremists to support the fantastic anti-British policy of the returned exile Lenin has defeated the German

* So convinced was the Western Press that Lenin and Trotsky were German spies that their real names were originally given as Alderblum and Braunstein.

trick of facilitating the return of certain exiles from Switzerland in the hope of their pro-German peace proclivities creating disorganisation, discontent, and disruption here, out of which only Germany can profit. The exposure of the German design has been sufficient to turn the enthusiasm with which Lenin was at first received into contempt for his inability to perceive that he was a deluded German tool.

Reports of Germany's part in facilitating Lenin's return to Russia from exile in Switzerland (the sealed bacillus as Churchill called him) via a secret train were completely accurate. The German High Command had counted on revolution as the means of taking Russia out of the war. However the events of March had merely led to the overthrow of Czarism; the provisional Government of Russia was more determined than the Czar's rickety administration to prosecute the war against Germany.

A non-Marxist socialist, Alexander Kerensky, had emerged as the dominant figure in the Russian republic's provisional government. His position was Minister of Justice, his function that of inspirer-in-chief of Russia's continued resistance to Germany. On 24 April, 1917, he gave an interview to *Daily Express* correspondent, Herbert Bailey:

M. Kerensky pointed out that if Czarism and the old regime, of which throughout the interview he spoke with great bitterness, had continued in power at the moment Germany was preparing her spring offensive, the defeat of Russia would have been inevitable.

'In January men were intermittently deserting from their regiments,' he said. 'Instead of three weeks' food supply, the armies were only provided for two days. Many soldiers were starving. Of the blast furnaces only 70 per cent were working, owing to the shortage of fuel, while the output of minerals had fallen to one-quarter of the normal.

'The disorganisation which made such a state of affairs possible has now been replaced by an efficient organisation. The workmen are all striving to increase the output to the greatest limit and particular attention has been bestowed on the problem of transport to Vladivostok to secure American supplies.'

Despite Mr Kerensky's optimism – and a Russian summer offensive – the Russian soldier had had enough of war. It did not need the plotting, oratory and intrigue of Lenin, Trotsky and their adherents to bring tottering Russia to her knees. The official Russian communique of 31 August 1917 is eloquent testimony to the final collapse: 'A large proportion of the men occupying trenches in this sector [the Rumanian front] abandoned their positions and dispersed.'

Newly-raised women battalions, the so-called battalions of death, did their utmost to shame the men, but to no avail. Three days later a Russian officer reported to the Western press:

'Suddenly, the panic set in. Whole regiments mutinied and refused to advance. There was no means of dealing with the situation. Regiment after regiment threw down their arms and seized whatever means of transport there was.

'At that time I was with the car near the Rumanian frontier. We were told to attempt to hold up the enemy until order could be restored. Never shall I forget the scene on the roads. Thousands of men were struggling to get away. They seized motor transports bringing up food and equipment, and flinging these on the road, turned the wagons round and fought like men demented to get away.'

And days before the Bolshevik take-over, the redoubtable English suffragette, Mrs Pankhurst, retailed her impressions of Russia on the eve of dissolution:

'The people have had no training in democracy. The great majority cannot even read the posters continually displayed on the walls. They were never allowed to listen to speeches under the old regime. The consequence is that now they are mesmerised by speeches. Meetings are held on every possible occasion. The wounded men, for example, in a certain hospital met and voted whether they should take their pills. The convalescents had a meeting to decide whether they should get up or stay in bed!

'Liberty means to these people doing what they like. The soldiers in a train compelled the stationmaster to alter the signals that were against them and to permit them to go on.

'The women in the battalions of death are splendid. The leader, Mme Bochkeroya, is a peasant woman with a fine ideal of patriotic duty. The original idea of these women soldiers was to inspire the men to do their duty.

'The women's battalions have been followed by the men's battalions of death, made up of soldiers, wounded and discharged, who have volunteered for further service. It was pathetic to see these men, some with one leg, others with one arm, marching along the streets on their way to the station.

'It was curious to notice that as the discipline among the rank and file of the army grew less and less, the officers became more and more rigid in their observance of every detail of military etiquette.

'The Cossacks are in many respect the most attractive figures in revolutionary Russia. They are the antithesis of all that we in Great Britain have supposed them to be. They have always enjoyed a large measure of liberty and they realise that freedom entails obligations. They have a fine tradition. They are disciplined, courteous, educated and high minded.'

The last of these interminable conferences of 'democratic' Russia was held in Petrograd on 28 October, 1917. The report was headed simply:

NO RUSSIAN ARMY

The officers of the Petrograd garrison had held a meeting to discuss their role in the present situation in the army. After a long debate a resolution was adopted affirming the practical non-existence of the army as it is at present and the non-existence of any authority on the part of the chiefs.

The resolution concludes: 'We do not renounce our duty, but in answering for ourselves we do not answer for our men. We consider that the time has come to make this declaration openly in order that no one may be deceived or trust in vain illusions.'

Twelve days later the first order from the Red Army was issued under the seal of the Military Revolutionary Committee: in effect Leon Trotsky and his chief Lenin. Explicit threats of what would happen to those who disobeyed betokened the new order of things:

Petrograd, Thursday, Nov 8
To the Army Committees of the active Army, and to all the Soviets of Soldiers' Deputies:
The garrison and proletariat of Petrograd have deposed the Government of Kerensky. The change which resulted in the deposition of the Provisional Government was accomplished without bloodshed.

In announcing this to the army at the front the Revolutionary Committee calls upon the revolutionary soldiers to watch closely the conduct of the men in command. Officers who do not join the accomplished revolution immediately and openly must be arrested at once as enemies.

The Petrograd Soviet considers as the programme of the new authority :

The offer of an immediate Democratic Peace.

An immediate handing over of the large proprietorial lands to the peasants.

The transmission of all authority to the Soviets.

An honest convocation of the Constitutional Assembly.*

By March Russia was out of the Great War but not out of suffering. For two years civil war raged between Red and White armies. The Red triumphed. By the autumn of 1920 the Union of Socialist Soviet Republics was established and then the light of perpetual revolution shone in baleful glare from the Kremlin towers. Aware of what this phenomenon could mean to the peace and stability of the capitalist world Lord Beaverbrook, now sole proprietor of the *Daily Express,* asked H. G. Wells to interview Vladimir Ilyich Lenin, master of all the Russias, for his (Beaverbrook's) newly-launched *Sunday Express.* Wells was at the height of his powers and reputation. He was an inveterate believer in the perfectability of human nature. So was Lenin. Both died disillusioned. Lenin had got to know what Stalin had in mind. Wells, who died in 1946 after the first atomic bomb explosions, reckoned he had seen the future and it wasn't worth knowing. Nineteen-twenty, however, bade fair to be the springtime of humanity : Soviet man emerging from the holocaust :

The arangements leading up to my meeting with Lenin were tedious and irritating, but at last I found myself under way for the Kremlin.

The Kremlin, as I remembered it in 1914, was a very open place, open as much as Windsor Castle is, with a thin trickle of pilgrims and tourists in groups and couples flowing through it. But now it is closed up and difficult of access. There was a great pother with passes and permits before we could get through even the outer gates. And we were filtered and inspected through five or six rooms of clerks and sentinels before we got into the presence.

This may be necessary for the personal security of Lenin, but it puts him out of reach of Russia, and what is perhaps more serious,

* It was never assembled. The Bolsheviks were afraid they would lose the elections.

if there is to be an effectual dictatorship, it puts Russia out of his reach. If things must filter up to him, they must also filter down and they may undergo very considerable change in the process.

We got to Lenin at last, and found him, a little figure at a great desk in a well-lit room that looked out upon palatial spaces. I thought his desk was rather in a litter. I sat down on a chair at a corner of the desk, and the little man – his feet scarcely touch the ground as he sits on the edge of his chair – twisted round to talk to me, putting his arms round and over a pile of papers.

He spoke excellent English. I had come expecting to struggle with a doctrinaire Marxist. I found nothing of the sort. I had been told that Lenin lectured people: he certainly did not do so on this occasion.

Much had been made of his laugh in the descriptions; a laugh which is said to be pleasing at first and afterwards to become cynical. This laugh was not in evidence. His forehead reminded me of some one else – I could not remember who it was until the other evening I saw Mr Arthur Balfour sitting and talking under a shaded light. It is exactly the same domed, slightly one-sided cranium.

Lenin has a pleasant, quick-changing, brownish face, with a lively smile and a habit (due, perhaps, to some defect in focussing) of screwing up one eye as he pauses in his talk: he is not very like the photographs you see of him, because he is one of those people whose change of expression is more important than their features: he gesticulated a little with his hands over the heaped papers as he talked, and he talked quickly, very keen on his subject, without any posing or pretences or reservations, as a good scientific man will talk.

Our talk was threaded throughout and held together by two – what shall I call them? – motifs. One was from me to him: 'What do you think you are making of Russia? What is the state you are trying to create?' The other was from him to me: 'Why does not the social revolution begin in England? Why do you not work for social revolution? Why are you not destroying capitalism and establishing the Communist State?' These motifs interwove, reacted on each other, illuminated each other. The second brought back the first: 'But what are you making of the social revolution? Are you making a success of it?' And from that we got back to two again with: 'To make it a success the western world must join in. Why doesn't it?'

In the days before 1918 all the Marxist world thought of the social revolution as an end. The workers of the world were to unite, overthrow capitalism, and be happy ever afterwards. But in 1918 the Communists, to their own surprise, found themselves in control of Russia and challenged to produce their millenium.

The commonplace Communist simply loses his temper if you venture to doubt whether everything is being done in precisely the best and most intelligent way under the new regime. He is like a tetchy housewife who wants you to recognise that everything is in perfect order in the middle of an eviction. He is like one of those now forgotten suffragettes who used to promise us an earthly paradise as soon as we escaped from the tyranny of 'man-made laws'.

Lenin, on the other hand, whose frankness must at times leave his disciples breathless, has recently stripped off the last pretence that the Russian revolution is anything more than the inauguration of an age of limitless experiment.

Both Wells and Lenin agreed that capitalism was wicked but whereas Wells thought collectivism could be introduced by education and legislation, Lenin insisted that a revolution was essential. Lenin produced a book called *The Triumph of Nationalisation* and said it would be impossible for there to be both free enterprise and nationalised concerns in Britain. The capitalists wouldn't let you. Wells reluctantly agreed.

In his concluding article (the series proved so popular that queues formed at newsagents) Wells appealed for Western, particularly American, aid to save the Russian people from starvation. His, and other appeals, were answered. The following year saw a massive international campaign to feed Russia and Lenin himself responded by encouraging free enterprise food production in the Soviet Union and decreeing the right of individuals to own their own homes.

Yet these concessions could not alter the fact that, for the first time, a sixth of the earth's surface was held in the grip of fanatical zealots who desired nothing else than to visit their dogma on the remaining five-sixths. The triumph of Bolshevism in Russia meant that for decades every industrial dispute, every class fracas, every terrorist outrage – in Ireland, America, India, the Middle East – would appear to have in it the hand of Moscow.

No one was more implacable in his enmity to 'this foul baboonery' than Winston Churchill who had done his damndest to strangle the infant communism at birth by backing the Whites with interventionist Allied forces. He had finally been frustrated by a combination of ardent pro-Soviet trade unionists and coalition politicians who were well aware there were no votes in war.

His eloquence, however, was still at the service of anti-Communism. He replied to Mr Wells with a restatement of the classical case for economic freedom :

'The scientific apparatus which has rendered possible the great expansion of the populations of the world in modern times is the result of capitalist production by individual effort. And from much earlier times the power of men to form themselves into civilised communities depended upon the observance of laws which secured personal possessions of the fruits of work, enterprise, or thrift, which procured respect for contracts entered into between man and man, which gave greater prizes for greater efforts or for greater aptitudes.

'These conceptions were based upon the primary desire of man to seek his own benefit and that of his family. By harnessing this desire into laws, capable, no doubt, of indefinite improvement, the motive of material progress was obtained.

'The world at last, in the nineteenth century, had got rid of slavery and had liberated in every land the native energies of man.

'The demand of the French revolutionaries, *"la carrière ouverte aux talents,"* had been fully met. In Britain, on their merits, without any revolution, a private soldier became Chief of the Imperial General Staff, and a lad from a Welsh village became Prime Minister and the leading figure in Europe. In the United States the road is always open from the bottom to the top for brains and worth and leadership.

'However, in the underworld of the great cities of Europe and America there dwelt a sect of men to whom all these ideas, material or spiritual, were repulsive, who held, generation after generation, that property was a crime, patriotism a folly, and religion a delusion. The motive of their system of thought was not the well-being of the individual himself, but the denial of superior well-being to any other individual. The ideal that they pursued was that of an absolute and permanent equality. Better a world of equally hungry slaves than a world of unequally prosperous freemen : and the miseries as yet unrelieved and the wrongs as yet unredressed of large classes of the population, particularly in the great cities, lent a driving power to their doctrines.

'These beings, animated by the most ferocious hatreds that the human breast has ever contained, bided their time, and at last, when the loosely knit structure of the Russian Empire was shaken by the stress of the great war, their chance came. They attempted to thrust upon mankind universal slavery disguised as universal equality under the permanent dictatorship of their own sect.'

Wells riposted that Churchill was the last of the romantic adventurers 'who has a dread of the coming supremacy of justice, sanity and order throughout the world' and he forecast that in this rational universe 'Mr Churchill will never again hold office.'

In essence, the argument between Churchill and Wells echoed and re-echoed down the years. The Churchillian view was that Communist Russia attempted to divert attention from its own appalling tyranny and failure by stirring up class hatred and discord in the capitalist states. The Wellsian line was that collectivism – a kind of co-operative socialism-by-consent – was the only way to solve the contradictions of capitalism (over-production in the midst of shortage; unemployment).

Certainly Mr Churchill and his supporters did not lack evidence for their convictions about Soviet intrigue and oppression.

On 23 June 1923 the *Express* published documents from the Praesidium, or chief committee, of the International Communist Bureau in Moscow outlining the duties of the British Communist Party which, like all others, took its political 'line' from the Soviet Union. These duties included winning affiliation to the Labour Party – which was just about to come into office in Britain for the first time – for the purpose of exposing to the masses the 'bourgeois character' of the leaders of the Labour Party. Instructions were also sent to the Communists' lone Parliamentary representative, Comrade Newbold, to give preference to his revolutionary duties and to use his seat in Parliament to embarrass and hold up to ridicule the Labour Party moderates in the Commons. Comrade Kuusinen signed the letter on behalf of the Executive Committee of the Communist International.

More than a year later, an infinitely more notorious missive, the Zinoviev letter, was published by the *Daily Mail* while a minority Labour Government was in power and in the middle of a General Election campaign. The letter was an order to the British Communist Party to suborn soldiers from their duties and, as a legal case had already taken place over just such an attempt, the Zinoviev letter fanned fury over the traitorous goings-on of the Left. The Conservatives won the election of November 1924 at a canter, thus provoking the charge that they – or their agents – had forged the whole business.

Whether or not the Zinoviev letter was a fraud devised by Russian exiles is of minor importance. It can hardly have cost the Labour Party the election as it was the Labour Prime Minister, Ramsay MacDonald, who authorised its publication and the letter did not say anything confidentially that the Russian communists were not publicly proclaiming.

While taking aid from the West in massive quantities and using the profit motive to stimulate their own agricultural production the Marxists of the Kremlin maintained unchanged their declared resolve to destroy Western capitalism and to do so by any means.

Two-and-a-half years after the Zinoviev letter Scotland Yard raided the premises of the Soviet Trade Delegation at Arcos House, London. There, it was claimed, documents were discovered which proved that Arcos House was simply a spy centre. According to the Home Secretary, Sir William Joynson-Hicks, the Russian trade delegation were attempting to discover:

Listening devices (early asdic?) in regard to aircraft
Air cooling of airplane engines
Plans of new destroyers
Plans of directional wireless (early radar?) in our ships of war.

Considering the Soviet achievement in spying on the Nazis and on the West's atomic secrets, it would be surprising if the 'trade' delegates had not been engaged on espionage. All this, of course, confirmed Churchill's worst fears about Bolshevik duplicity and unrelenting struggle against democracy. His fear that Bolshevism would brutally oppress the Russian people also appeared to be vindicated.

When Lenin died in January 1924 – to widespread lamentations – an interregnum followed. No clear leader emerged. Trotsky, the obvious successor, had broken with the triumvirate of Stalin, (the Iron Man, the British press called him) Kamenev and Zinoviev, who had ruled Russia during Lenin's frequent illnesses. Trotsky was also out of countenance with other leading Soviet personalities because of his dogmatic assurance and abrasive tongue. Alexis Ivanovitch Rykov was chosen to succeed Lenin as President of the Council of Commissars, but that was clearly a titular apointment; the real power would lie with the man who could sway men and grasp hold of the Central Committee of the Communists Party, the true lever of authority. In the end Joseph Stalin (originally described in the overseas press as 'of Turkish descent'; actually he came from Georgia in South Russia) emerged the undisputed master. One by one his rivals were eliminated; mostly by execution, a few by 'accidents'. And once firmly in control Stalin applied measures in the tradition of Ivan the Terrible and, in their scale, well worthy of the twentieth century, which dwarfed Ivan's efforts.

Even as he was beginning to get his grip on the lever of Soviet power a Jewish anarchist leader, Miss Emma Goldman, reported on her second visit to the USSR in December 1925:

'The Soviet is carried on by a reign of terror more complete and horrifying than ever existed under the Romanoffs. Democracy in Russia is a complete farce – a tragic farce – for the illusion that the people rule is maintained by the imprisonment and death of all who disagree,' Miss Goldman declared.

'It is extremely hard to find out the truth about conditions. The Soviet leaders are very clever men and I myself was deceived at first.

'Communist Russia is maintained by a spirit of militarism antagonistic to every principle for which the people fought. Soldiers are a privileged class who are given the best of everything. They are pampered in every way in order that they may be ready to shoot down their fellow-workers at the bidding of the Communist leaders, whose only hope now lies in a reign of terror.

'A huge system of espionage has grown up. It is impossible to trust any one. Children are bribed or terrified into spying on their parents, the spies of the *Cheka* – the secret police – are everywhere.

'The prisons are full of peasants. Everywhere I went, when they discovered that I was a friend, I was told of dissatisfaction and of tyranny such as I hardly believed possible.

'The Bolsheviks, who at one time waxed so indignant at the mere thought of capital punishment, have now compiled a code of laws which comprises, among 200 articles on punishment, forty-two crimes punishable by death.

'Only those who really know Russia since the revolution know these things. The truth is not allowed to leak out. Persons who leave Russia have to sign a declaration that they will remain loyal to the Soviet before they are given passports. They must leave behind them two guarantors, who are liable to death should their friends publish outside the country anything antagonistic to the Soviet.'

In January 1931, C. J. Ketchum, special correspondent, was reporting on forced collectivisation of the peasantry – they were obliged to give up the small holdings granted them by Lenin – and conscripted labour:

The Government of the Soviet must stand exposed as the greatest employer of impressed labour the world has ever known.

For certainly it is no exaggeration to say that not only the major part of the work of the Five-Year Plan but the whole industrial system of the country is proceeding on a basic system of coercive, if not actual conscript, labour.

It is true, first, that under Russia's five-day week employment of labour has been increased by more than 40 per cent.

But this only partly settled the problem of the workless. The actual solution has been found in Stalin's sweeping abolition of the labour exchanges, of all the unions, and his latest decree, now broadcast up and down the land, that every man and woman who would eat must first surrender his labour to the State.

Work, no matter the nature of it, has become compulsory. It has become the nation's badge of citizenship. Without it you cannot exist.

Once absorbed in the factory, there is, of course, little escape for the worker under the trade union system of Communism. Here is how it operates.

Having already been enrolled and made a member of the union, he is summoned to its periodic meeting. There a resolution is passed that all members must remain at their posts until their particular State task has been completed.

There is a standing vote, and should any member, by any curious chance, remain seated, he is promptly asked for his union card.

This surrender automatically deprives him of his ration card, and, in turn, of every single privilege as a citizen of the State.

Ketchum recorded how doctors were sent to far-flung parts of the Soviet Empire on pain of being removed from the medical register and becoming unpersons. He reckoned that some 3,000,000 *kulaks* (yeoman farmers) had perished. Here indeed was tyranny on the grotesque scale.

But if Winston Churchill was upheld in his beliefs that the Bolsheviks would imprison their own people and threaten the life and liberty of others, H. G. Wells was also apparently justified in his warnings about the coming collapse of capitalism. For in the 1920's Britain, the first nation of capitalism, seemed ripe for Communist subversion, if not for revolution.

CHAPTER TEN

General Strike

Unemployment was no new feature of the capitalist system. It was regarded by economists, and accepted by most people, that unemployment was a factor in the wages equation. Push down wages low enough and work would be found for surplus labour – because employers would not reckon it worthwhile to install labour-saving machinery – while low wages would produce cheap goods, find more buyers, and create greater demand. This, in turn, would bring wages up again, until once more the process brought about its own correction.

Where the twenties (and the thirties) differed from previous decades was in the strength of the trade unions – who were determined *not* to allow wages to fall – and the total disruption of the delicate world-wide marketing system brought about by the war and by the existence of the Soviet alternative to capitalism: Marxism in practice, not just in theory.

Britain and Germany were the two most vulnerable nations. Both had highly advanced capitalist economies. Both highly organised labour movements, heavily impregnated with Marxist doctrine. France was still very much a nation of small farmers and the United States was so large that if work fell off in one area it was probable that jobs were available elsewhere. Moreover America had little in the way of a class structure and not much in the way of organised Labour or Marxism.

It was on Britain and Germany (whose experiences are dealt with in a later chapter) that Soviet Russia pinned its hopes and put its money. And it was the General Strike that was the chosen weapon of the revolutionaries.

As early as 1915 the leaders of the miners, railwaymen and dockers in Britain had formed the triple alliance to support each other in industrial disputes and so bring unendurable pressure on government and employers to concede. Clearly if such strikes were to be imposed for political, not merely financial ends, the authorities would be faced with the breakdown of social order.

What that could mean was shown by the strike of Liverpool policemen in August 1919:

> Thousands of pounds worth of jewellery, boots, drapery, sweets, and other articles were stolen from wrecked shops on Friday night, and in the absence of the police, a strong organised force of looters had things practically their own way. Shops were completely sacked and pavements covered with wreckage and property which the thieves were unable to carry off. 'It is worse than the anti-German riots after the sinking of the *Lusitania*,' is the general comment.
>
> The Liverpool authorities promptly sought the aid of the military after Friday night's outrages. Troops were sent in response to telephone calls, and 900 soldiers arrived from Crosby.
>
> They are now quartered in the city and patrolling with fixed bayonets the streets where looting has taken place, and guarding shops, the town halls, and other places. Special constables are being rapidly enrolled.
>
> The police strike spread to Birkenhead. Pickets of Liverpool strikers brought a large number of the local force out, and looting of jewellers' and pawnbrokers' shops followed inevitably.
>
> The handful of loyal police in Liverpool were roughly handled by the mob when they made baton charges and arrested men for theft.

Most police in other parts of the country refused to join the strike called by the Police Union, but with strikes on the railways, in the pits and at the mills breaking out daily the example of Liverpool was a potent recruiting factor for the Citizens' Guard, established in October:

> The Government's call for a citizen guard has met with an immediate and enthusiastic response all over the country.
>
> Prompt action has been taken by the Lord Mayor of London, Sir Horace Marshall, who yesterday appointed a committee of representative City men to consider what steps shall be taken.
>
> The Mayor of Kensington, Sir W. Davison, has already enrolled 500 volunteers, who are 'card-indexed' with regard to the following particulars:

Name and address
Telephone number
Special qualification.

'There has been no necessity for calling a citizens' meeting,' stated the mayor. 'The residents of Kensington have responded voluntarily, old and young.'

Sir Nevil Macready, Commissioner of the Metropolitan Police, explained to a *Sunday Express* representative yesterday exactly of what the scope and duties of the Citizen Guard will consist.

'Our idea,' said Sir Nevil, 'is to get a further form of protection to relieve the military. We want the Citizen Guard to take the place of the military in protecting railways, bridges and other points of importance.

'The members of the Guard will be sworn in like the special constables, but they will not be part of my organisation. They will be distinguished by a brassard, but will not wear uniform.'

'Will they be armed?'

'If they want arming,' replied Sir Nevil, 'they will have to go over to Field-Marshal Haig.'

A Home Office official said yesterday: 'There is no suggestion that the railwaymen are likely to depart from the peaceful methods which their leaders have declared to be the only method by which the dispute will be carried on. On the other hand, it is public knowledge that there have already been instances reported of sabotage and violence – the work of hangers-on of all such disputes. It is consequently felt that in the grave situation in which the country is placed there is urgent necessity for the formation of a Citizen Guard.'

The response in the country to the Government's appeal is encouraging as is shown by the following messages from *Sunday Express* correspondents:

CARDIFF – Since early yesterday morning numbers of prominent citizens, including demobilised soldiers, have called at the City Hall to enrol.

LIVERPOOL – Enrolments already approach 2,000.

MANCHESTER – Large response already. More than 1,000 'specials' – many of them with war service – enrolled.

LEEDS – Hearty co-operation. Lord Mayor to invite enrolments tomorrow.

NEWCASTLE-ON-TYNE – Every indication of a quick and generous response.

PLYMOUTH – A great many citizens have expressed their readiness, but the town is strongly garrisoned and it is felt that there is no immediate need for such a measure.

As the twenties wore on the certainty of a general strike sometime came to be accepted by unions, employers and Government. At the Socialist core of the Labour movement were activists – not all Communist by any means – who believed that the capitalist system would be brought down *at a stroke* by the use of the general strike. In its place there would arise a British variant of the Soviet system. The militants embracing such men as Arthur Cook, the miners' leader and Ernest Bevin, the dockers' spokesman, were not too concerned about how socialism would actually work in a highly competitve trading nation: what they wanted was to destroy the existing machinery.

Hatred of the 'capitalists' was very strong among men who were wholly patriotic Britons. Their sense of fairness was outraged by the casual treatment accorded workers who had toiled perhaps thirty years for one firm and suddenly found themselves, through circumstances entirely beyond their control, surplus to requirements. Unemployed. Trade union stalwarts and socialists refused to accept that wages were a factor in production which must move – up or down – according to demand for the products. Wages must not be cut. Hours must not be lengthened. Workers must not lose their jobs. The three 'Thou shalt nots' became the bedrock of labour faith at a time when the world economy was hopelessly out of kilter.

America had emerged from the Great War as the major creditor nation in place of Britain. But America was a self-sufficient giant not dependent on international trade and consequently not motivated towards outward investment to oil the wheels of commerce. Germany, another mighty economic engine, had all but ruined her economy by currency depreciation. Britain, striving to regain her pre-war pre-eminence, had valued the £ at its 1913 par with the dollar. As a result British exports were too costly and sales slumped. Add to that the virtual disappearance of Russia as a buyer of capital goods and fruitful recipient and repayer of Western investment and it is not difficult to understand why even enlightened capitalists could not cope with international competition, were they to be shackled to the inflexible commandments of the trade unions.

And not all capitalists were enlightened. F. E. Smith, the witty, brilliant and savagely anti-socialist Lord Chancellor, remarked: 'We [the Conservative Government] thought we could never meet with such bone-headed stubbornness as in the mineworkers – until we met the mine-owners.'

So the two sides of industry moved irreversibly to a showdown. On 3 September 1924, this report appeared in the press:

> A drastic resolution carried by a majority of more than three million votes established the general council of the Trades Union Congress as a general headquarters in all future disputes.
>
> The general council in the past had intervened in important strikes by request only. Now, and in future, it will do so in all disputes, and by right of its authority every union will have to inform the general council when a dispute of any kind is pending, and the council will be able to negotiate or take a fighting hand.
>
> The terrible weapon of a national general strike can be used if the council deems fit.
>
> Three years ago, when similar powers were proposed for the general council, the whole congress turned the suggestion down. The change in voting shows the unions' industrial war spirit.

The unions' weapon, tempered by the experience of six massive strikes in heavy industry in six years, was now ready. When the next challenge came the unions would move as one to replace the capitalist state with the workers' one. In reply the Conservative Government of Stanley Baldwin, a ruddy-complexioned squire-like figure who genuinely sought an accommodation with the unions, set in motion emergency measures – calling up reservists to buttress the armed forces and police, stockpiling essential food and materials; appointing civil commissioners to direct their distribution and categorise and regulate volunteers. The Government had already met previous attacks on its authority, notably the railway strikes of 1919 and 1920 and the triple alliances' test trial of strength in April 1921.

In that year the Coalition Government issued an appeal to Loyal Citizens:

> Loyal Citizens, on presenting themselves at a Territorial drill hall, will be informed of the conditions, and will then either be attested at once or asked to register their names and addresses so that they may be called out, should their services be required.
>
> Loyal Citizens are requested to bring with them, if possible, the following:

Uniforms (if in possession)
One day's food
Two blankets
One mug or cup
One knife
One fork
One spoon
Greatcoat or waterproof
Change of underclothing
Thick socks
Shaving and washing materials
Towel

Loyal Citizens who have previously served in His Majesty's Forces should bring papers of identification – such as A.B. 64 or protection or discharge certificates.

The response was so overwhelming – 'from dukes to dustmen' as a euphoric Home Secretary remarked – that the resolve of the strikers waned and vanished. The miners were left isolated and bitterly reproached the railwaymen for their timidity. 'Next time,' they vowed, 'things will be different.'

'Next time' arrived at the start of May 1926. Inevitably the miners were involved. The coal industry was in a nightmare situation. It employed 1,000,000 men in 2,000 pits but the old days of easy dominance were gone. Substitute fuels, notably oil, were eating into its market. New competitors, like Poland, had arrived on the scene offering cheaper coal from wider, more accessible seams. Labour relations were bad: not in every region but without exception in the poorer districts where coal was hard to come by and foreign buyers could pick and choose, adding a terrible uncertainty to jobs.

Mining communities were self-contained and usually remote from big towns and cities. This bred fierce loyalties – first of which was loyalty to the union and the Labour Party – but also created suspicion of people, including other unionists, from outside.

Coal mining was ripe for change, but change was the last thing the miners and the owners would accept.

So they stood pat on their demands. The owners said: 'Unless we increase hours and cut pay we cannot compete with foreign suppliers and we will go under.' The miners replied: 'Not a penny off our pay, not a minute on our day – and don't you dare try to set pit against pit, for we are solid. If you do go under the State will have to nationalise coal and that will bring us job security and higher wages.'

The Government, caught in the middle, provided a temporary subsidy to take the industry over the worst of its troubles. However, by May 1926 Mr Baldwin told the Miners' Federation and the Mining Association (the owners) that the country could not afford to contribute £40 million annually to keep coal in the circumstances to which it had become accustomed. A miners' strike leading to a General now loomed.

Representatives of 205 trade unions, comprising the 3,700,000 members of the TUC voted. By 75–1 (3,653,527 to 49,911) they voted to strike in support of the miners. The Labour Party mobilised 'the masses'. Over 100,000 men and women marched through Glasgow, in a procession two miles long. Astonished reporters recorded that 'many of the women wore silk stockings and even fur coats. Attractive girls distributed red rosettes.' Was the middle class becoming red? Was this the long dreaded revolution at last?

When the printers of the *Daily Mail* halted work in protest against a leading article denouncing the strike on the night of 4 May nightmare turned into reality. Everything stopped. And then most things started up again. The Government took over the principal parks to assemble lorries to distribute milk. RAF bombers undertook the delivery of mail (air line traffic was uninterrupted because the staffs were non-unionist). The power engineers' association announced:

'In view of the national emergency which has arisen and in the interests of public safety, the Electrical Power Engineers' Association hereby resolve:

'(1) The essential public services in connection with the supply of electrical energy should be maintained.

'(2) The association deprecates the entrance of voluntary workers in the industry, but in the present emergency the executive instructs its members to co-operate in the Government scheme for the maintenance of public services.'

A condition of the continuing provision of electricity was that power to strike-hit firms should be discontinued. The condition was impractical and was neither implemented nor insisted upon.

A short editorial in the *Express* before it closed down – until reappearing three days later as a news sheet – read:

FACE THE FACTS

A general strike is not a new experiment. It has been tried before and has always failed.

Those persons who suggest that the present situation is a parallel to that of August 1914 grossly distort the truth.

The crisis will pass – and will pass quickly.

The Government are completely competent to meet the situation. Keep calm and support the Government.

H. V. Morton, who was to make a famous name for himself as a travel writer, noted:

> The most anxious day and the most glorious weather of the year coincided yesterday; and the combination was a heady one.
>
> I walked up Whitehall – blue skies, a thundering breeze that whipped the flags on the Cenotaph, civil servants taking their lunch-hour constitutional, groups of cloth-capped men standing about silently, and a continuous stream of volunteers trickling into the Foreign Office quadrangle.
>
> Here they formed up in fours and entered their names in the temporary office in the wooden hutment, so reminiscent of the Army, that houses the Transport Control for the delivery of food in the London area.
>
> We were all calm, but we were all thrilled, and we were united, so far as I could gather from the talk about me, in the tragedy of it all.

A further article recalled the fearful disputes of the immediate pre-war era and the astronomic loss of working days in 1921: a total of 85 million (proportionally 20 times greater than the average for the 1970's.)

The public responded not only by volunteering to drive buses and lorries, act as bus conductors or engine drivers, but also, and very sensibly, by buying bicycles and wireless sets (the Government having commandeered the non-union BBC). Mr Eric Gamage of the noted London store stated that his firm had sold 50 bicycles by 9.30 a.m. on the first morning of the strike. Wireless and camp beds (for dedicated anti-strike office workers) had been in very big demand too.

For the first two days of the General Strike there was confusion. Road jams built up because the special constables were inexperienced in traffic control; coal was not moved and many factories were at a standstill. On the third day the situation began to change. Railwaymen started to drift back to work. The *British Gazette* – official organ of the Government published with immense gusto by Winston Churchill, Chancellor of the Exchequer, eagerly abetted by the Production Director of the *Express,* Sidney Long – recorded Stanley Baldwin's message to the people :

'Constitutional Government is being attacked. Let all good citizens whose livelihood and labour have thus been put in peril bear with fortitude and patience the hardships with which they have been so suddenly confronted. Stand behind the Government, who are doing their part, confident that you will co-operate in the measures they have undertaken to preserve the liberties and privileges of the people of these islands. The laws of England are the people's birthright. The laws are in your keeping. You have made Parliament their guardian. The general strike is a challenge to Parliament, and is the road to anarchy and ruin.'

The BBC, though strictly neutral in its news broadcasts, was available for official announcements so that wild rumours were swiftly quashed. All the report flooding into the command centres of the civil commissioners made it plain that the workers had no stomach for the strike, let alone the 'revolutionary situation' so ardently desired by the activists.

The idea that middle class students and upper class debutantes sabotaged the toilers does not conform with the facts. Three quarters of the country's workers were not members of the unions. And girl clerks who walked six miles to work and back were unquestionably members of the working class.

By 7 May single-page sheets of the press were on sale and the next day they published a legal opinion which was to pave the way for an end to the strike :

Sir John Simon, one of the foremost authorities on Industrial Law, speaking in debate in the House of Commons on the Emergency Regulations, said :

'The General Strike is not a strike at all. A strike properly understood is perfectly lawful but the decision of the Trades Union Congress to call out everybody regardless of contracts and without notice is not a lawful action at all. Every workman is bound by a contract to give notice before he leaves work and who in view of that decision has either chosen of his own free will or has felt compelled to come out without proper notice has broken the law if he had failed to give due notice to terminate the existing engagement of the men. Every railway man now out in disregard of his contract is himself personally liable to be sued in the County Court for damages. Every trade union leader who has advised and promoted that course course of action is liable in damages to the uttermost farthing of his personal possessions.'

Referring to clauses in the ordinary rules of the Trade Unions that workmen would forfeit their benefits if they repudiated the orders of the Executive, he said that no Court in this country would construe such a rule as to say that a man would forfeit his benefit if he were asked to do what was wrong and illegal.

Lenin once said of the Germans that if their workers ever decided to take over the country's railways they would first buy platform tickets! How much truer was this of the British. The strange majesty of the law exerted its influence on the strikers and their leaders. Instead of revolutionary battalions taking to the barricades, strikers and policemen played football while convoys of voluntary-driven lorries filled with food were driven from the docks to distribution centres:

A great crowd gathered at the Marble Arch yesterday afternoon to witness the arrival of a food convoy from the docks. A stream of 104 motor lorries more than two miles long passed through the gates to Hyde Park. Two or three soldiers in full service dress with steel helmets and carrying rifles were mounted on each vehicle and there were eleven armoured cars carrying machine guns in the procession. Earlier in the day two battalions of the Guards had been sent to take over the docks and 500 volunteers had also gone down to help unload a shipment of flour. The convoy was greeted with almost as much enthusiasm as a Lord Mayor's Show.

All was quiet in Regent's Park which had been converted into a parking ground for omnibuses. A field hospital had been erected in the grounds as well as a complete machine shop with sleeping quarters for volunteer drivers.

Stanley Baldwin, sensing that the railwaymen – and especially their leader J. H. Thomas – were looking for an honourable end to the strike broadcast this appeal:

'The Government is not fighting to lower the standard of living for miners, or of any other section of the workers.

'Anyone can approach the Government who is authorised and can parley with us, and it is our duty to parley with them.

'The Trades Union Congress have only to cancel the general strike and withdraw the challenge they have issued and we shall immediately begin attempts to put an end to the long laborious dispute which has been pursued for these many weeks.

'I am a man of peace. I am longing and working and praying for peace: but I will not surrender the safety and security of the British constitution.'

On Wednesday morning, 12 May, the single page newspapers carried another legal opinion, this time delivered in the High Court, by Mr Justice Astbury:

'The so-called general strike, called by the Trades Union Congress Council, is illegal and contrary to law, and those persons inciting or taking part in it are not protected by the Trades Dispute Act of 1906.

'No trade dispute has been alleged or shown to exist,' he added, 'in any of the Unions affected, except in the miners' case, and no trade dispute does or can exist between the Trade Union Congress on the one hand and the Government and the nation on the other.

'No trade unionist in this country can lose his trade union benefits by refusing to obey lawful orders, and the orders of the Trade Union Congress and the Unions who are acting in obedience thereto and bringing about so-called general strikes are unlawful orders.

'Trade Union funds are held in a fiduciary capacity, and cannot legally be depleted by paying strike pay to any member who illegally ceases to work and breaks his contract without justification in pursuance of orders which are unlawful.'

The Judge's important observations were made in confirming the temporary injunction, granted last Friday, against officials of the Tower Hill and Mersey branches of the National Sailors' and Firemens' Union restraining them from calling on members to strike.

The same issue carried the news that 5,000 trains were now running daily on the main line services: that increasing numbers of bus and tram staffs were returning: that Smithfield Market was operating almost normally. Thanks to volunteers, the Hyde Park canteen was offering hot sausages and mash for 4d, cheese for 2d, and a cup of tea for 1½d to strike-breakers. And the Earl of Meath, despite his 85 years, had been sworn in as a special constable at Chertsey. 'He says he is still able to tackle a man and has boxed every morning.'

Next day the news sheets carried the glad tidings: 'The strike is over.' Messrs Arthur Pugh and Walter Citrine, respectively chairman and secretary of the TUC General Council, accepted a face-saving formula presented to them by Sir Herbert Samuel, chairman of the Coal Commission, promising another temporary subsidy while a Royal Commission looked at the coal industry's structure. The TUC gladly endorsed this pallid 'solution', knowing full well that the miners would never accede to it but acknowledging that the other trades union chiefs had no intention of allowing their funds to become liable for damages in an illegal escapade and themselves to be at risk for leading members astray.

Revolutionary fire did not die out on 12 May 1926. It never took light. Apart from one or two violent incidents – the most notable being an unsuccessful attempt to derail the Edinburgh-Glasgow train – the nine-day wonder passed off entirely peacefully. Not a shot was fired, not a bayonet drawn.

Mr Baldwin remarked in the Commons that the swift ending of the strike (he forebore to say unconditional surrender of the TUC) was 'a victory for common sense'. The *Express* exulted. 'The British people have been magnificent.'

A news item in the same issue announced: 'The names for the infant daughter of the Duke and Duchess of York will be Mary Elizabeth Alexandra. She will be known as Princess Elizabeth.'

During the entire period of the strike the one page papers were at pains to carry the latest cricket scores.

The General Strike was over. The coal strike continued. With a bitterness to match their sacrifices, the Miners' Federation denounced the betrayal of their trades union comrades.

Arthur Cook, the miners' general secretary, at a meeting to gratefully acknowledge receipt of £274,000 from the Soviet Union, displayed his vengeful anguish:

'We have been fighting,' he said, 'not only against the Government and the owners, but against a number of Labour leaders, especially the political leaders, whose position has been compromised.

'I have had experience of being bullied, but never have we been bullied by the employers or the Government to the extent we were bullied by certain trade union leaders to accept a reduction of wages.

'The Labour Party made a last bid in the House of Commons,

crawling, and creeping, and begging. The speeches of MacDonald and Thomas are speeches that the working-class movement will read in future with shame.

'I say to the railwaymen that one of the greatest crimes that can be laid at door of their leaders is that they not only left the miners in the lurch and betrayed them, but they betrayed the railwaymen.

'They were prepared to call off the strike without securing adequate protection for their men, which was one of the dirtiest things ever done in the annals of working class struggles.'

Fear of 'betrayal' entered the soul of the Labour movement and made the Party in Parliament morbidly suspicious of collaboration with the bosses or their agents. A considerable degree of alienation was a consequence of the General Strike.

As for the miners, they continued with their dispute: more than ever determined to secure the implementation of the minority of the Sankey Commission of 1919 which recommended the nationalisation of the coal industry. 'No Surender' was the war cry of the miners' executive – and the suffering was borne for another six months.

Special correspondent C. J. Ketchum reported from the coal field of South Wales:

I have just made a tour of the two Rhondda valleys, where, in a populace of 180,000, more than 40,000 miners normally are employed.

Everywhere sullen crowds of idle mine workers, unshaven and dishevelled, fill the narrow streets while in the doorways of the endless rows of uniform cottages their womenfolk sit for hours staring sadly into space.

The plight of the women and children is pitiful. I am told, for example, that the Rhondda Urban District Council will require at least £1,500 a week in order to supply milk to expectant mothers and to babies up to the age of twelve months, in place of £150 which they are are present permitted to spend under the Ministry of Health regulations.

More than 40,000 applications for the relief of destitute persons have already been dealt with by the various stations set up by the board of guardians in the Pontypridd district alone. Twenty thousand of these applications were received in one day this week. The Feeding of Necessitous School Children Act has been brought into operation in the schools and in nearly all the elementary classes youngsters are lined up in food kitchens two or three times a day for their meals.

The *Express* and other newspapers denounced the owners' obdurate insistence on a return to the eight hour day, and their 'vendetta to the death' with the Miners' Federation.

In its turn, the union zealots showed no mercy towards miners who sought to relieve their families' plight by returning to work without permission as this report from Mansfield, Notts, in August 1926 made plain:

> Extraordinary scenes of intimidation have to-day prevented many hundreds of miners willing to work from going to the pits.
>
> Crowds of miners and women lined the roads to various collieries. Any worker who appeared was booed, and his name and address taken. Cases have occurred of workers being pulled off their bicycles and violently attacked as they rode to the pits, and one man was discovered lying in the roadway by a police patrol.
>
> Terror has been caused among the wives and children by mobs going from house to house and ordering men not to resume work.
>
> In one case today, a man endeavouring to go to work was pursued by a crowd of men and women. He fell on his knees before them and begged for mercy, and was allowed to go home on assuring the crowd that he would not attempt to work again.
>
> I made an extensive tour this afternoon. Pickets lined the roads leading to the collieries, and large detachments of police, in motor-cycles ready to carry them to the scene of any disorder, stood about. To-night the police are sleeping in some of the mining villages.

Finally in November the miners caved in. The era of the great strikes was over.

The next year Parliament passed the Trades Disputes Act. This Act outlawed sympathetic strikes, intimidation and the closed shop in local councils, forbade civil servants being members of unions affiliated to the TUC, declared strikes by employees of public authorities to be illegal; reversed the system whereby union members automatically paid a political levy and had to contract out for not paying it, into a system where they consciously had to contract in.

This curbing of union power was much acclaimed by the bulk of the public and provoked little reaction from a movement whose morale had been shattered by the failure of the General Strike. Baldwin's triumph was complete. But he was careful never to show the slightest sign of satisfaction.

A Conservative MP admirer of his wrote a poem to the tune of 'Danny Boy'. He called it Stanley Boy. It sounded like a hymn to tranquillity.

Now, perhaps, people could get to enjoy the twenties with its bright young things; old morality versus new; talking pictures, talking wireless and dancing, dancing, dancing.

CHAPTER ELEVEN

No Licence for Saxophones

Dance crazes from America had invaded Europe before the First World War: the Turkey Trot and the Bunny Hug had been duly performed and anathematized. What was different about the post-war dance craze was that it was a mass craze: something like 11,000 dance halls and night clubs were opened in the six years after 1918. There was a hectic flush about the whole thing, a desire to make up for those four hellish years, to enjoy life and if that meant shocking the older generation, so much the better.

That the older generation was shocked was made clear in frequent denunciations in the letter columns, although in sweeping condemnation of young womanhood none exceeded author James Douglas. Writing in the *Sunday Express* in June 1920 he thundered:

> What is the meaning of the riot of nudity into which the world of womanhood has plunged so frantically?
>
> The war has profoundly disturbed the feminine mind. Many millions of young males have been slaughtered, mutilated or deranged. The strange herd-soul of woman, moving in the mass, has taken fright at the sentence of celibacy which has been passed upon her. There are not enough men to go round.
>
> Before the war the rivalry of women was acute. Today it is frenzied. Instinctively the herd-soul of woman is doubling its allurements, trebling its wiles, quadrupling its baits.
>
> It has cast modesty to the winds. It has abandoned all its reserves and reticences.
>
> The vogue of the jazz dance is one symptom of this frenzy. The violent outbursts of vehement colours in feminine raiment is another.

The hysterical eccentricity of feminine attire is another. But the most alarming symptom is the absolutely brazen display of feminine charms.

The growth of feminine shamelessness has been so gradual that we have become inured to it. We can hardly remember the days before the war when decency was still practised in the public theatre and the public restaurant by respectable women. It is not easy to recall the era of the veiled calf.

But the climax in effrontery is the vogue of the bare back. The other night at a theatre the bare backs in the stalls suggested that the stage had ceased to compete with society. A man said to me that he felt inclined to go to the theatre in future armed with a rubber stamp. Before him sat a lady with nothing on her back, which was enamelled with some pink liquid. 'I should like,' he said, 'to brand her in red, with the words "Wet Paint".'

It is not pleasing to see a matron of forty or fifty summers with dyed hair, rouged lips, painted cheeks, blackened eyelids and eyelashes, brandishing her adipose back at a disgusted crowd.

And the tide of corruption flows more and more strongly every day. The decadent and degenerate poisons of Paris infect our fashions.

The remedy is the lash of public opinion. It ought to be applied without delay.

Dr O'Doherty, Bishop of Galway, was all for the direct approach. He told parents of wayward girls to 'lay the lash across their backs'.

'I lay the blame on the girls themselves,' he added. 'They are not innocent, and they are not misled. Some of our Irish girls are becoming regular devils, and are a source of disgrace to the countryside.

'If it were not for the purity of Irish boys there would be far more scandals than there are today. Parents should not allow their girls to wander along countryside roads at night and go to all-night dances where there is drinking.'

Maurice, described as a well-known society dancer, gave the professional view:

The low-necked dress has got lower and lower. Girls have vied with each other in extravagent decolletée, until today in many ballrooms you may see women whose backs are completely bare. The dress has grown so scanty that the whole back of it has disappeared.

No decent girl would adopt this exaggerated dress, which is often deliberately suggestive.

Those cranks who cry out that all dancing is a deadly sin are talking sheer nonsense. Dancing, quite apart from it being a most difficult art, is one of the greatest sources of innocent pleasure in the world.

When people are happy they like to dance.

But the joy of an innocent dance and the pleasure some derive from the modern jazz are far removed; they have nothing in common. To watch some couples jazzing is frequently to witness an exhibition of nastiness. Their looks, their attitudes, and their actions all betray sensuality. To see a girl being lifted high in the air by her partner's knee is not pretty.

There are two ways of jazzing – the right way and the wrong way. The jazz can be either an innocent, delightful dance or the reverse. In all cases it depends upon the dancers. It is exactly what the dancers make it. As a professional dancer I can only protest most emphatically against those couples who degrade the dance and make it loathsome.

Certain girls, who are regular habituées of the night clubs, and show far too much back, are most often to blame in this respect. The unfortunate thing is that quite nice girls see what goes on, and, thinking it smart, copy it.

The best way to bring improvement about is to ban the bare-back jazzer. Make it an offence for any woman to appear in a place that is licensed for public dancing unless she is decently dressed.

Edmonton Borough Council was not interested in improvement. It simply banned jazz in its town hall 'as jazzing is neither graceful nor dignified.' Wallasey was a mite more liberal, granting dance licences on the condition that the saxophone was not played.

Offspring of the upper middle classes (the middle-middle class being defined as 'those who dine in a dinner jacket every night for a fortnight at the seaside and put it away in moth balls for the rest of the year'),* were held to be chiefly responsible for declining moral standards. Headed:

---

* This same class gave fervid support to the bowler hat. Eight out of ten men wore it in the financial districts of Leeds and Glasgow.

FRIVOLITY IN
LENT

the Reverend Hugh Chapman, minister at the Royal Savoy Chapel chastised the Bright Young Things:

> 'It is most unfortunate that the spirit of Lent should be going out – if not already extinct – in what is called society.
>
> 'Lack of faith is not the cause. It is the lack of self-discipline, and the hatred of anything like dullness or self-examination. A wave is sweeping over not only England but the whole world, in which the sense of God and eternity is being engulfed.
>
> 'There seems to be no definite explanation, except that it is a great cycle of worldliness for which the rich and the well-placed are mainly responsible.
>
> 'If Lent were rigidly observed, without any slavishness or fear, the indignation of the labouring classes would be minimised. The word "Conservative" would have a truer meaning if it included the conservator of the principles of religion, and would be the only possible chance of avoiding the same collapse as has come to pass in Russia, which is entirely traceable to the utter selfishness and gross misuse of privilege which preceded it.'

Others tried to dim the dazzle. Mr F. A. Macquiston, MP, tabled amendments to the Criminal Law Amendment Act of 1922, to make girls of sixteen or under who 'bobbed' (closely cropped) their hair liable to heavy fines or possibly imprisonment.

> Every female of the age of sixteen or under that age shall wear the hair either loose or plaited and hanging down her back, and any female who is of the age of sixteen or under that age who shall wear her hair up shall be liable to the penalties of this Act, and on a third conviction shall be confined in a Borstal institution until she reaches the age of sixteen years.
>
> 'My proposal,' said Mr Macquiston, 'aims at protecting young men and young women. The method suggested is to my mind both simple and effective. It will safeguard girls against the worst type of man, and it will also provide some sort of protection to young fellows who are sometimes victimised and blackmailed by unscrupulous girls who no doubt act under the direction of women who use them as a means to extort money.'

Concern for the moral protection of young women led Wandsworth Council to forbid mixed tennis unless a chaperone was present. Oxford University did its best for morality by sending down graduettes – female students – for one single moral lapse. The rules then, in the early twenties, were that outside of certain excepted celebrations, undergraduates should not dance in public. Proctors (dons who had responsibility for discipline) scoured the town and if they found wayward students, fined the men and expelled the women. 'If,' said a male student in a letter to the *Express*, 'the average girl student seems dowdy and a man hater it is not really her fault. She is afraid to be anything else.'

The International Association of Masters of Dancing meeting in conclave at the Commodore Hotel, New York, vowed to ban all eccentric and suggestive ballroom dances. To no avail. The 'shimmy' and the 'shake' survived. And dancing went from strength to strength.

On 29 March 1925 H. V. Morton reported in the *Sunday Express*:

I went to Covent Garden Dance Hall the other night. Over that gloomy portico, beneath which police have marshalled the cars of royalty on nights when duchesses and people like that were as blackberries in September, there was a vast red electric sign that has never told about Caruso. It says that you can dance at Covent Garden (Opera House) for 2s 6d from seven-thirty till midnight, except on late nights, when you have to pay 3s 6d.

A girl in a box gave me a ticket. I was in the foyer, which in the old days looked like an illustrated edition of *Debrett* come to life. It was full of young men in spats.

I walked up that ornate Victorian staircase, and found myself in that which was once the grand tier! The boxes had gone. Round the gentle sweep of the opera house were tables at which sat hundreds of young men and girls drinking coffee and sucking lemonade through straws. Below stretched the dance floor, occupying the vanished stalls and stage. It was romantically dark. At the far end on a pinkly-lit platform an orchestra swayed and throbbed.

In a pen I observed the lacy, black-gowned maidens with whom you can dance for sixpence. Funny to watch a lone man pretending not to assess their charms before he nervously goes up and claims one!

Men dancers could also be hired and a 'paid partner' wrote of his experiences:

If you are a woman you may hire me for one dance at a cost of sixpence.

What do they feel, these women, as we swing them out on the floor? Those who keep their eyes lowered are kindest. We sense a humanity that goes far to discount the material side of the arrangement. Naturally, they are shy of speech; they have done much that once was unconventional in securing a man to dance with them at a price. They have not arrived yet at the stage of making sympathetic advances. Certainly we cannot do so – we are paid servants.

Some women let us know this only too well. With wide-opened eyes they survey us frankly, approving or disapproving of our appearance and our clothes. 'Well,' they seem to say, 'I have a fairly decent one this time. I might have done worse!' And if, obviously, they think they have done badly, we can only do our best to assume the character of the inferior piece of mechanism that they take us for. A sense of humour helps us here.

We can all dance well – we have to – but women seem never to consider us wholly as dancers. 'I don't like him,' I heard a woman say whom I had just taken back to her seat, 'but he dances so well that I simply must have him again.' And another: 'I love dancing with him because he looks so sad.'

When first I took my place in the 'pen', as we called our enclosure, I confess that I felt ashamed. Was this a man's job? It was not, and I have never thought it so, but we live in a state of civilisation so complex and artificial that men have been forced to turn their hands (and their feet) to work that primitive standards would condemn.

By 1927 the Charleston was all the rage. The effect of this particular dance was noted in trams and buses. 'Women,' it was reported, 'now turn in their toes instinctively as soon as they take their seats . . . others twitch their feet at intervals to the rhythm of the last-heard tune.'

But change was coming. On the very day of the Wall Street crash in October 1929, the dancing élite met, again in conclave (they seemed to have shared with the Vatican a passion for secrecy) and announced their findings:

Everywhere there are signs of the growing unpopularity of jazz rhythm, and instructors are facing the grim truth that dancing is dying.

The great Hammersmith Palais de Danse, 'London's Ballroom', has closed down as a dance hall, and is to become an ice rink.

Restaurants and clubs are daily favouring more cabaret turns and less dancing time.

There has never been so much unemployment among musicians as there is today. The talkies are largely responsible for stealing the public.

Jazz has spent itself. The tunes are merely well camouflaged versions of old-time melodies, the passion for 'kazoos' and 'hot' music has given an irritating sameness to the dance programme.

*

Aside from dancing, the nineteen twenties presented a tableau of conflict strikingly similar to the nineteen sixties. Women's liberation took the fashion world by storm. Bosoms were flattened out, waists disappeared; hair was shorn and women did their utmost to look like men. Unisex was not the prerogative of jeans and lumber shirts. Seventeen-year-old Lady Patricia Moore, daughter of the Earl of Drogheda, insisted on the removal of her pigtails before being presented at court. As she had already toured America, held long conversations with George Bernard Shaw, H. G. Wells and Arnold Bennett and had written a novel she could, legitimately, say that she was sufficiently grown up to do as she liked.

Yet the whole question of the liberated woman swung, pendulum fashion, during the twenties.

The term 'new morality' was not an invention of the sixties; it was used as early as 1922 by May Edington, co-authoress of *Secrets*. She wrote:

A little while ago a man who is wealthy and healthy and wise and outwardly conventional opened his heart, and said to me, 'If I marry I should like my wife to have some money of her own. And if she had none I would like to make some settlement on her, without her knowing about it. I would like to get a lawyer to arrange an anonymous legacy for her, or something like that.'

'But why?' I asked.

And he answered very sincerely: 'So that she could leave me any time if she wished. So that she could have free will.'

That statement, made by a man of ordinary conventions and decencies, meant much – it meant the new morality.

The sins of today pale before the sins of yesterday, just as the sins of to-morrow – since the world always goes forward and not backward – will pale before those of to-day*. The tragedies of less than a hundred years ago, for instance, were wholesale and national, and not confined mostly to a little over-dressing or under-dressing, a little dancing . . . They included, during a most religious epoch, the working of babies of eight years old in the coal mines.

The new morality demands, above all, honesty. It longs for truth. Grandmotherly lies are no longer venerated as texts in the home.

New Morality was taken several stages further in 1925 by Mrs Bertrand Russell, wife of the philosopher. She wrote a book *Hypatia,* described as the hand book of the New Morality. The *Express* waxed indignant:

> Mrs Russell dedicates her exposition of the New Morality to her daughter Kate. She is deliberately defiant and provocative. In her preface, she says that:
>
> Hypatia was a university lecturer denounced by Church dignitaries, and torn to pieces by Christians. Such will probably be the fate of this book; therefore, it bears her name. What I have written here I believe, and shall not retract or change for similar episcopal denunciations.
>
> Is there something wrong with the education of women, and, if so, what? I think we must judge that there is. The reason lies in the sense of inferiority bred in women by so much oppression, and the natural result that their chief aim was to prove that they were just as good as men. The second aim was to prove that they could jolly well do without them.
>
> Marriage brings a jealous, intolerant husband, children, prying and impertinent neighbours – degraded and humiliating slavery for the vast majority of women.
>
> As a Labour Minister is corrupted by Court dress, so is a free woman by the marriage contract.
>
> Build a trade union of lovers to conquer the world.

About the same time Dr Marie Stopes' book on birth control was exciting enormous attention. Sex and women's place in the world was being aired as never before.

The establishment moved into line. In March 1923 the House of Commons gave women equality on the grounds for obtaining a divorce. Under the previous law a man could gain a divorce merely by proving misconduct on the part of his wife while she had also to establish either cruelty or desertion on the part of her husband. For the (Tory) Govern-

---

* Miss Edington was writing some twenty years before Auschwitz.

ment Major Entwistle declaimed: 'The day is gone when a wife can be regarded as a husband's chattel and when marriage can be regarded as a purchase.'

In the year the flappers (women between 21 and 30) got the vote – 1928 – the Archbishop of Canterbury was moved to comment:

> 'We want to liberate the sex impulse – which is part of the heritage of humanity – from the impression that it is always to be surrounded by negative warnings and restraints, and to place it in its rightful place among the great and formative things of every healthy and joyous boy and girl.
>
> 'I would rather have all the risks which come from free discussion than the greater risks which we run by a conspiracy of silence.
>
> 'I rejoice to see that many of the old purely conventional and unreal restraints have broken down and that our young people meet together on terms of perfect frankness and equality.'

And in 1930 women successfully campaigned against licensing regulations which excluded them from going unattended to restaurants and pubs at night. They also won the right to continue in Civil Service employment after marriage.

However the traffic was not all one way. Conventional morality was frequently roused to counter-attack.

As early as February 1920 a correspondent in France was reporting:

> A league has been formed by a group of young women in the Grenoble region, the object of which is 'to combat by example immodest fashions and propaganda'. The young women have adopted as their creed the Lenten adjuration of the Bishop of Autun, which bids them avoid 'suggestive nudity, transparent lingerie, skirts which are too short or which exaggeratedly define the figure, which awaken passions and drag into vice.'

What Grenoble had begun Bradford continued:

> Bradford is much exercised over certain lingerie displays exhibited on the occasion of the local shopping week.
>
> They are the subject of a protest submitted to the chief constable by the Bradford Diocesan Lay Readers' Association, and a resolution passed by the Association says there is a tendency to indecency in certain window diplays, and takes special exception to lingerie

advertisements comprising, they assert, scantily garbed female figures.

It is understood that in deference to the lay readers' views certain modifications have been made in some of the displays.

The Courts sometimes took an old-fashioned, excessively chivalrous view of women's sensibilities:

'It will be necessary for the proper trial of this case that disgusting and offensive evidence be given. I do not think it will be right to expose women to evidence of that description.'

The dramatic dismissal of two women jurors by Mr Justice Darling in the High Court yesterday was the prelude to a libel action which concerned the relations of Dr Arthur William Wilson, of Tufnell Park-road, N., and Mrs Vidal, a young married woman, one of his patients.

Some parts of Society also clung to the old ways. The social columnists recorded in April 1924 that: 'The Countess of Carlisle will chaperone her twin sisters, the Hon Alison and Margaret Hore-Ruthven, at dances this season.'

For these women who strayed from the stern path of moral duty there was, occasionally, condign chastisement:

Mrs Beulah Johnston was taken from an hotel porch at Tenaha, Texas, by a dozen masked men clad in white, who took her by motor-car several miles into the country, stripped her, and coated her with tar and feathers. Mrs Johnston was afterwards arrested on a charge of bigamy.

And an echo from an earlier, more autocratic, day was heard in June 1923:

Miss Dorothy Hedges, of Bayswater, one of the witnesses before the Committee of Inquiry into Domestic Service, which continued its sittings yesterday, startled the assembly when she remarked that starvation might bring a certain type of domestic servant to her senses.

'This class of girl is pampered from childhood. Society women start these ridiculous clubs for them, at which they are encouraged to dance all night. Is it reasonable to expect them to go in for domestic service? If there were no dole, they would have to settle down.'

As late as 26 March 1933 unconventional attitudes were liable to provoke retribution:

> Two young women were mobbed on the front here to-day when they stepped out of their motor-car and started to walk along the promenade clad in the latest 'Hollywood trousers'.
> For twenty minutes they braved a following crowd. Once they were in danger of being arrested for causing an obstruction.
> They were screeched at by an old woman in a bonnet and shawl, and finally denounced in Biblical terms by a man carrying a text-banner in the gutter.
> In the end they gave up in despair, jumped into their motor car and drove away.

In America – outside the tarring and feathering deep South – women's opinions dominated legislation and theatrical criticism. The temperance movement was, overwhelmingly, a female creation, and in January 1920 the sale of alcohol was totally banned in the USA under the Prohibition Amendment to the Constitution. Women had long maintained that drink was the greatest cause of family breakdown.*

In the New World rampant feminism took the offensive, not only against the drink trade but against male lasciviousness. Dominant in the church, they prevailed upon the Methodists to proscribe 'dirty' shows from London. The Commissioners of the Methodist Episcopal Church reported on an English play *Lullaby* produced in New York:

> 'The play is packed with valuable suggestions for roues and their youthful imitators.
> 'The American stage has for the first time sunk to depths of indecency which must be characterised as alien. In years past there has been dirt on the American stage, but it has been American dirt. It has been foulness which Americans could understand, and which, while it represented what was lowest in American life, was still human and not beastly.
> 'At present "shows" are on the New York stage which are as foreign to America as anything which would be tolerated in Suez.

---

* Prohibition was abolished by Franklin Roosevelt's Administration in 1933.

'Two girl shows in particular are grossly indecent and lascivious. At one of these shows girls perform dances while practically naked.

'Never before have leading theatrical producers made such a public appeal to the physical side of sex emotion. What has heretofore been intimate and personal is dragged out in indecent display. It is not American. It never has been. It never will be American.'

Many English playwrights of the period – 1921–25 – were severely censured in the US. Apart from Mr Knoblock of *Lullaby* infamy, Frederick Lonsdale was castigated for elevating a fallen woman to moral superiority. Somerset Maugham was scourged for flaunting 'vice naked and unashamed through three acts of glittering immorality'. Noël Coward was damned for 'shovelling up ordure of an unprincipled smart set'. The three plays so flayed were: *Spring Cleaning; Our Betters;* and *The Vortex.*

Nemesis could descend on the avant garde. A Mr Avery Hopwood was jailed in November 1921 for producing a farce, *The Demi-Virgin.* The charge was 'promoting an immoral, impure play with an intentional appeal for box office profit to lustful, licentious, morbidly erotic, vulgar and disorderly minds.' The play was supposed to portray the doings of the movie colony in California.

The doings of the movie colony in California were indeed colourful. They were also the cynosure of the entire Western World. For 'the pictures' were to become the laudanum of the masses: the most marvellous escapism ever invented.

CHAPTER TWELVE

Lure of the Silver Screen

Silent films were well established before the First World War but, in the main, they were either terribly goody-goody (critics noted ten religious movies in the West End of London in Spring 1910) or rather tawdry two-reel shorts. They weren't much beyond the magic lantern stage. The Great War proved to be the catalyst for the movies as for so much else.

Hunger for entertainment, for a break in the tension, led to an enormous increase in film-making and Hollywood – with its eternal Californian sunshine, Jewish flair and money – acted as a magnet to acting talent all round the globe.

For nigh on forty years – until the advent of television and pop groups – Hollywood film stars were showered with adulation. They were dream people: none more so that Mary Pickford, dubbed 'the world's sweetheart'.

Six weeks before she married that dashing, and equally popular, Douglas Fairbanks in spring 1920, the *Sunday Express* carried this item:

> While the average screen star is content to receive about a hundred or so letters per week from his or her admirers, Mary Pickford says that she receives two thousand, of which the largest proportion, of course, consists of love letters. Mary says that most of this huge mail comes from South America, Japan, and Europe. 'Some of them fairly ooze with love,' she says, 'and the writers offer me everything under the sun – cattle ranches, plantations, silver mines, sometimes entire villages, if I will only consent to marry them. Some of the Japanese letters are couched in very flowery language.

'Here, for instance, is one from a young Japanese nobleman in Osaka. He says that if I will marry him he will make me the most wonderful flower of his flowery country. Quaint I call it! I am sorry to say that many of the love letters are not sincere. They flatter me, and on the next page ask a favour. Men fall in love in one line, and in the next tell me that I shall be committing a sin if I do not immediately help them buy a farm somewhere in Indiana or Alabama.'

Hannen Swaffer (one of the quaint characters who once peopled Fleet Street) went to interview Douglas and Mary at Beverly Heights, 'a paradise of palms'. According to Mr Swaffer the number of Miss Pickford's admirers had swollen to 9,000. That may have been the pardonable exaggeration of a journalist who never liked to be bettered in the excess stakes. But what was undeniable was the worshipful atmosphere surrounding these two stars who, along with Charlie Chaplin (the three had just formed United Artists) were the first super-stars of the silver screen.

Swaffer recorded:

'Would you have known me if I had met you in the street?' she asked me, directly I met her for the first time.

I looked at Mary Pickford very carefully. I was gazing for the first time at a face I had seen thousands of times on the screen. Then I said: 'No; your curls aren't down.'

When you meet Mary Pickford at tea, as I did, her curls are fastened up under a hat. Her eyes smile at you under a wide brim, and she strikes you at first as being merely a very pretty girl whose face reminds you of somebody you have seen somewhere.

'I want to go to England this summer,' she told me, 'but I can't stand being mobbed. I had enough of that during the Liberty Loan Drive, when I raised $50,000,000 in a few days, and was made the Little Sister of the Navy and Queen of the Air Service. But it is awful being made such a show of even in a good cause.'

She read me a telegram from a London newspaper promising her a triumphal procession down the Strand. She shuddered at the idea.

'What I really want is a quiet life.'

A quiet life would be a change, for wherever she goes in America Mary Pickford is followed by admiring crowds. If she goes shopping in Los Angeles hundreds wait outside the shop to catch a glimpse of her; inside, the counter at which she is purchasing something is mobbed; every detail of her life is discussed; she gets 9,000 letters a week from admirers – Fairbanks told me he only gets three thousand – and her secretaries answer every one, enclosing Mary's favourite photograph with her signature carefully printed on it to look real.

Directly I met Mary Pickford I knew why California is so wonderful. When Mary smiles the sun comes out. . . .

Douglas Fairbanks is a human dynamo – a restless, palpitating force, a vital dominating personality. He is a god with a nickname; his colleagues and employees all worship him, but they all call him 'Dug'.

First, I was struck by his charm; then by his shortness. Looking at a film, you imagine him to be a giant. Really he is not much over 5 ft 9 ins. We drove to the wonderful house, Beverly Heights, where Fairbanks was living with his horses, his dogs, his motor-cars – and Charlie Chaplin.

'When I was poor I yearned for a bedroom,' he said, 'which would be so big that one window would look on the city, one on the sea, one on the mountains. Well, there it is' – we were sitting in a gorgeous bedchamber worthy of a French king – 'and now that I've got it Charlie Chaplin insists on sleeping here, and I have to go into one of the guest rooms.'

'We are a funny trio – Fairbanks, Chaplin and I,' Mary said. 'There are 16,000 picture theatres in the United States and one or other of us is always playing on one out of every two.

'You ought to come to one of our board meetings. They are as funny as *Shoulder Arms* itself. You wouldn't think so, but I am the business end. I have to be. Solemn financiers sit round and add up figures, and technical advisers argue about all sorts of details that you would think were Greek. And there are Charlie Chaplin and Doug Fairbanks, millionaires both of them playing tag in the corridor, while I have to sit down and wrestle with the business.'*

Such reporting was the essence of dryness compared with the normal line of unqualified awe and admiration that flowed from the pens of hundreds of movie scribes.

Well aware of the universal and growing appeal of 'the pictures' – 50,000 cinemas were in operation world-wide by 1920 – the newly-born *Sunday Express* launched a competition 'search for a film star'.

---

* Pickford and Fairbanks' joint income was £50,000 a year – about £6 million by the value of the 1970s.

Thousands of young women sent in their photographs and a committee of figures experienced in the movie business selected twenty they considered worthy of a screen test at Stoll's Studio at Kew Gardens. Mr Jeffrey Barnard, a director of Stoll and a judge, announced that he hoped to find 'a star' among the twenty. In fact he found two – June and Miss Majorie Hume. Both however were already established names in the theatre and withdrew. Their places were taken by others and the fortunate twenty embarked on a three-day outing which, as much as anything, evokes the atmosphere of the carefree summer immediately after the Great War:

Passers-by in Oxford-street on Monday morning were enthralled to see a bevy of beautiful girls sauntering along to where a four-horsed brake stood awaiting their pleasure. The legend 'Stoll Film Co' hung above the building near by, gave the answer to those who wished to know whence and for what purpose came such a pretty assembly.

It was a remarkable fact that these girls – strangers to each other – became at once so friendly and cordial to one another that the absence of men was never noticed.

'This is splendidly original!' one declared. 'Ripping' was the response.

The first test seemed simple enough – to the onlooker. Each competitor was asked to walk down a few steps, turn towards the camera, smile a 'how d'you do?' then to express a sudden overwhelming grief, and finally to assume a recovery to the first expression.

There were some to whom this test would have been unfitted – such as the girl with the laughing eyes. For these the producer had prepared other kinds of tests. One girl had to run on and exclaim, 'Hulloa! You want me? Yes! Well, I don't want you!' and she did this very well indeed.

Another, with a Madonna-like face, simply had to repose in thought, while others were given a letter-writing test.

A sumptuous tea – patisseries, strawberries and cream, cream buns, ices! – was provided at the studio by the Stoll Company, and the journey home began.

By the time Hammersmith Broadway was reached, the workaday world was hastening to catch omnibuses and tramcars for home. The spectacle of a brake-load of beauties, however, arrested the stream, and again the girls came in for a deal of eulogistic comment.

An excellent dinner was served in the Oak Room at the Trocadero,

Women's March Past

Women flocked to fill the ranks ... delicately reared women rushed to train as nurses.... the suffragette movement switched overnight from an agency of rebellion into a weapon of war. Women celebrate victory — and the vote.

Suzanne Lenglen
A favourite of the crowds at Wimbledon. Her dress would surely have won the approval of the councillors of nearby Wandsworth who forbade mixed tennis without a chaperone.

and the party left for the Coliseum, where an enjoyable evening was spent. Three motor-cars conveyed the party to their hotels and home.

The climax of their happiness was when the company went flying at the Avro Co's aerodrome at Hounslow.

It was understood that there was to be no stunting, but the girls showed the undaunted courage said to be a qualification for screen acting by unitedly declaring that unless they were allowed to 'loop the loop' it would be no fun.

So in pairs the *Sunday Express* cinema competitors flew high up over Hounslow, looping the loop, nose-diving, banking and doing every conceivable air stunt. They each vied with the other in breaking records. Some went up twice, others three times.

The Trocadero . . . Frascati's . . . driving in motor-cars, looping the loop and getting a screen test. It was the modern girl's idea of heaven. Those who were already there (i.e. in the heaven of movie stardom) had to make sure they remained there. For this purpose publicity was vital. A sceptical report of April 1921 read:

New York, 17 April*
Bebe Daniels, a cinema star, has discovered a new way to publicity by going to gaol on a ten days' sentence for exceeding the speed limit while motoring at Los Angeles. She could have appealed, and the sentence of imprisonment would probably have been reversed, but she declined, saying: 'Since I have been found guilty by a jury I have decided to be a good sport and go to gaol rather than try to obtain delays through legal technicalities.'

The actress' adventure is printed on the front page of newspapers throughout the country this morning.

Publicity of another kind shocked the anything-goes Hollywood of the twenties and sent producers, directors and cinema owners scurrying for cover.

Roscoe (Fatty) Arbuckle was one of the outstanding comedians of the early cinema. He weighed 19 stone and was described by Charlie Chaplin as 'a bundle of good nature'. On 12 September 1921 the press reported that Fatty Arbuckle had been arrested on a charge of murder. The killing was alleged to have taken place at an orgy in Arbuckle's

---

* Bebe Daniels and Ben Lyon, her husband, earned the gratitude of the British public by remaining in England to broadcast comedy shows during the Blitz and indeed throughout World War II.

suite at the St Francis Hotel, San Francisco. The victim was Virginia Rappe, a 23-year-old brunette and a chirpy light comedienne, also in films. A post-mortem examination disclosed that she had died of peritonitis but the doctors reported there was considerable bruising on her body.

Arbuckle's story, issued as a statement by his lawyers, was:

'While I was at the St Francis Hotel on Monday, Miss Rappe, Mrs Delmont and Mr A. L. Seminacher, Miss Rappe's manager, came to my room to have a few drinks. I have been acquainted with Mr Seminacher for ten years, and with Miss Rappe for five. I was clad in pyjamas, bath robe, and bedroom slippers, and was having breakfast when the trio entered. We had a few drinks and talked over matters that concerned us.

'Shortly after Miss Rappe had taken a few drinks she became hysterical, complained that she could not breathe, and started to tear off her clothes. I requested two girls present at the time to take care of Miss Rappe. She was disrobed and placed in a bathtub to be revived. The immersion did not benefit her. I telephoned to the hotel manager a request that she should be given a room.

Mrs Delmont however claimed there was a great deal of drinking at the party (this at breakfast time), and that Miss Rappe seemed overcome after three gins and orange juice, whereupon Mr Arbuckle carried her into his room and remained there for 15 minutes. Mrs Delmont kicked on the door, was refused admittance and sent for the manager. He opened the door to disclose Mr Arbuckle in pyjamas and Miss Rappe lying on the bed with torn clothes screaming: 'I'm dying. Arbuckle done it.'

Things looked black for Arbuckle as the Grand Jury began considering the testimony on September 14, especially as Miss Rappe's fiancé, Mr Harry Lehrman, Fatty Arbuckle's first director, condemned the actor in startling terms:

'The tragedy is the direct result of taking people like him [Arbuckle had been a barman] into the cinema world, paying them huge salaries, and placing them on a pedestal to bask in popularity and public esteem.

'Virginia worked in pictures with him, but always disliked him because of his vulgarity. Her friends were decent people. She would not have gone to Arbuckle's room without good reason. Mrs Delmont told me over the long-distance telephone that Arbuckle called up Virginia on the telephone and said that he wanted to see her in connection with some pictures. She was afraid to go alone, and got Mrs Delmont to go with her.

'I want to see justice done, and believe that it will be done. I am glad that Virginia died as she died. She died fighting.'

However the case against Arbuckle began to come apart when Mrs Delmont, the key witness, admitted she had had ten whiskies before the bedroom fracas and that she had possibly been mistaken in thinking she'd heard Virginia Rappe cry out: 'Arbuckle did it.' The charge of murder was reduced to manslaughter, but Arbuckle was finished.

Women's clubs in San Francisco began the agitation for a clean up of the firm world's morals. Movie houses moved quickly into line. New York's Theatre Owners' Chamber of Commerce passed a resolution barring Arbuckle's films from every cinema in New York. Other cities followed. Producers caught on and Arbuckle's existing contracts were cancelled. His place was taken by Will Rogers, a natural wit who began his stage career as a rope twister and won fame with his side-of-mouth quips. Rogers went on to win screen immortality. Arbuckle, after being acquitted, vanished into obscurity, producing a number of films under the pseudonym of William B. Goodrich and dying in 1933, aged 52.

Miss Rappe enjoyed a short-lived reputation as a sacrifice to male lust and bestiality. Seven thousand women attended her lying in state, many leaving flowers. The numbers however were minimal compared with the mighty female lamentation that arose on the death of womanhood's dream man: Rudolph Valentino.

Not until Beatlemania swept teenage-dom in the 1960's did anything in entertainment equal the impact of Rudolph Valentino. He seemed to women the essence of male virility (whether he was or not is neither here nor there; as befits the screen, the shadow was all).

He was operated on for appendicitis, developed pleurisy and died within 48 hours. It was 23 August 1926, and the silent movie was at the peak of its popularity. Next day, Tuesday, the body was transferred from the undertaker's parlour to a front room on Broadway. Then it began:

A great crowd which gathered in the street, in spite of a downpour of rain, exerted so solid a pressure that a large window in the undertaker's establishment was broken. A girl who had taken up her position at eight o'clock this morning refused to relinquish it, although her hands were cut by the glass, until she was taken inside to view the dead actor's body. More than a dozen other people were injured, including a woman of seventy.

The figure of Valentino, embalmed by the process which preserved the body of Caruso, the famous tenor, lies in a silver and bronze casket, with an unbreakable glass top, clothed in a dinner suit. The crowd waiting to see the body swelled to ten thousand this evening.

A political twist was given to the proceedings when the crowds gathered the following morning:

Twelve Fascisti in black shirts stood guard in watches throughout the night over the body of Valentino* in his glass-topped coffin near which at midnight there was placed a wreath with a card inscribed 'From Benito Mussolini'.

Albeit infrequently, politics and social issues *did* raise their heads in the movie business. Idealism blended neatly with popular appeal in a 1920 film sponsored by the League of Nations Union. Entitled *Auction of Souls* – a somewhat erotic touch – it portrayed the suffering of Armenians under the Turks. The film was launched at the Royal Albert Hall and was accompanied by a full symphony orchestra and choir of soloists.

At this juncture the cinema was regarded as the 'Esperanto† of the eye'. D. W. Griffiths, the most outstanding of America's early film producers, wanted to make movies that would 'strengthen international solidarity and make the world safe for democracy'. Too often, however, international dissensions were aggravated by films.

American insularity was entrenched by official attitudes. As early as January 1920 Franklin D. Lane, Secretary for the Interior, told representatives of the US motion picture industry: 'You should show nothing but 100 per cent Americanism on the screens . . . Your job is to counter the Bolshevistic and ultra-radical tendencies which endanger the very fabric of American institutions.' At the close of the conference a resolution was passed promising that the industry would do all in its power 'to upbuild and strengthen the spirit of Americanisation'.

Anything offending this code was deemed unsuitable. Thus the

---

* He was born in Italy in 1895 and emigrated to America in 1913.
† An international language which never quite caught on.

Exhibition Trade Review of New York issued a statement: 'This publication will hereafter accept neither advertising nor publicity concerning any picture dealing with venereal disease or sex hygiene.' Films dealing with drug abuse were shown only as propaganda against the vice – such as *Human Wreckage* sponsored by Mrs William Reid whose actor-husband had died from drug-taking.

Much concern was expressed in 1927 when the anti-war film *What Price Glory?* permitted actors to mouth obscenities, and so by-pass the sub-titles which were always clean and wholesome.

By and large, the cinema of the twenties *was* clean and wholesome. Here is a selection, chosen at random from scores of like columns, of film criticism presented by the *Sunday Express*. This is one for 20 March 1920:

THE BOND OF FEAR   Belle Bennett
American film

Sensational story of a girl who learns by bitter experience to prefer the rough but golden-hearted devotion of a cowboy to the most sophisticated attentions of a tender-foot. Lovers of strong 'Western' drama will get full value for their money out of this thrilling production.

*

RULING PASSIONS   Julia Dean
American film

Hectic story of an embittered banker, whose scheme of revenge against perfidious associates are brought to naught by the healing touch of love. A stirring combination of pictorial and dramatic art, heightened by very good photography.

*

THE SEA WAIF   Louise Huff
American film

Melodramatic story of a smuggler's daughter who marries a matinee idol sent to the seaside for his health. Good acting and fine coastal settings, beautifully photographed.

*

THE GATES OF DUTY   Bertram Burleigh
British film

Melodramatic and unconvincing story, with a war flavour, which roams from England to Northern Greece and Cairo and back to England again. Hero is a British officer and the heroine a nurse, but as he is already married nothing is left for her but to inspire him to become a Member of Parliament. Picturesque story, and good, but not very truthful settings, with some competent acting.

*

   THE CASTLE OF DREAMS Mary Odette, etc
      British film

Pretty, but far-fetched story of an unsophisticated maiden, offspring of a May and December union, who is wooed by a sturdy farmer and a young gallant from town. The farmer secures his bride by knocking the gallant into a pond. Excellent photography, and some polished acting by a long and talented cast.

*

   PECK'S BAD GIRL Mabel Normand
     American film

Excellent story, in which the delightful Mabel, starting as the 'bad girl of the town', ends by being acclaimed as the 'nicest'. A sparkling production, full of good comedy and American characterisations, with appropriate settings and photography.

*

A further eight films were featured as month by month and year by year the number of pictures grew: first at the expense of the music hall, then of the traditional theatre and of almost every other form of entertainment. Yet as early as 1923 a new threat arose to the silent cinema as well as the stage: 'It is going to be war to the knife between the entertainment industry and broadcasting,' declared Mr Andre Charlot, the producer. Films had to talk or die. They talked.

*

Although experiments in synchronising talk with screen movements had been tried on both sides of the Atlantic prior to World War I and after, the big breakthrough came with Al Jolson's *The Jazz Singer*. The talking – and singing! – film was here to stay. Or was it?

  Bernard Jacot, a distinguished critic of the period, was not sure how British audiences would react to 100 per cent Yankee accents. American producers were likewise wary. A hugely expensive tutorial system was launched to train the worst speakers in 'talking Limey'.

English elocution teachers enjoyed a golden harvest. So did English actors whose voices were so much more suitable to love and tenderness than the brash accents of the Bronx.

Until 1930 the arguments raged between advocates of silence ('dumb pictures', according to their opponents) and champions of sound.

Cosmo Hamilton, the author, wrote to the *Daily Express* in April 1929 that:

> Sound, however well rendered, talk however good, will quickly become nauseating in a film. The public ear will demand again natural, uncanned music, and go back to the theatre for the human voice.
>
> By that time, too, the public will have realised the obvious fact that the talkies have taken away their right to imagination, their innate gift to supply far more realistically to the little film the sounds the talkies make. They will clamour for the eloquent silence of Charlie Chaplin and Emil Jannings.

Mr Hamilton was mistaken. The silent films departed. The talkies really were here to stay. And while the world spiralled down into the slump the earnings of film stars rose and rose. As far back as 1925 Gloria Swanson was earning £500 a day, or £4 for every second's work (about £50 by the seventies' values.)

Film stardom had everything. When the French actress Annabella, of the glorious accent, visited London in 1932 her interviewer (anonymous) went over the top:

> I went along. Annabella was alone. Oh, Annabella!
>
> Annabella is twenty and looks sixteen. Her hair is neither dark nor fair, but what the French call *chatain clair*. Her eyes are so brown that when they are shadowed they look black. Annabella had on a simple little beige frock that you can buy in the shops for a few guineas. And she wore no rings.
>
> She loves eating and drinking, and dancing and reading, and music and flowers. She loves compliments and being in love, and not being in love. She loves everything.
>
> Most of all she loves work. 'I am never blasée,' she told me. 'Life is such fun. I want all it can give me.'

To balance the bright lights there was the shadow. In the same year, 1932, a news item on 18 August recorded:

> A penniless eighteen-year-old girl, 'discovered' and brought to

England in the hope that she might be starred as the screen rival of Greta Garbo and Marlene Dietrich, lies gravely ill in hospital while the greatest chance of her life is on the verge of slipping by.

Amelia Nielsen, a slender creature of cold and overpowering beauty, was found some days ago 'walking on' for a few shillings a week in the crowd scenes at a French film studio.

She had recently been ill from undernourishment, but had to go on working.

Mr Sam Morris saw her, seized her, gave her a square meal and brought her to England. Mr Morris is vice-president and general manager of Warner Brothers.

Warner Brothers had been searching Europe for months for a girl whom they could star in opposition to the famous actresses of their two powerful competitors.

Metro-Goldwyn produced Greta Garbo. Paramount Pictures produced Marlene Dietrich.

On Monday Mr Morris arrived in England with his find.

Two hours later the unknown beauty was in a West-end hotel, listening to plans for a try-out in the English studios, when pain seized her.

Half an hour later she was in hospital, unconscious, while surgeons hovered over her.

She cannot leave the hospital ward for a fortnight.

And within a week Mr Sam Morris, the arbiter of her fate, must sail for America.

For every Amelia Nielson there were a hundred other hopefuls who never even got walking on parts. Yet the dream of stardom was really only for the few. For the great mass of people the twenties had other excitements.

CHAPTER THIRTEEN

Towards the Good Life

Much has been made by dour sociologists of the giddiness of the twenties, of its tinsel brightness against the sombre backcloth of slump, industrial unrest, unemployment, poverty and the approach of war. In point of fact the twenties witnessed broadening prosperity to a degree unequalled by any decade until the fifties.

Unemployment there was: it never fell below 1,000,000 – but rarely rose above it and there were thirteen people in work for every one idle. The slump and mass unemployment belonged to the thirties, as did the growing fear of war.

Poverty there was – as will be shown in a later chapter.

Industrial unrest there was (see Chapter IX), but it reached its climax well before the decade's end and the last three years were comparatively tranquil.

What the twenties had in abundance was a taste for the good things of life: home ownership, motoring, foreign travel which had previously been the preserve of the well-off came within the purchasing power of the lower middle and upper working class: the £300 a year man. Talking pictures, the wireless and a host of consumer products were within the grasp of much humbler-paid folk. A survey in Glasgow towards the close of the decade revealed a large number of wireless sets in homes subject to a Means Test for social security.

Immediately after the Great War prices rocketed. Returning servicemen were spending their gratuities, munition workers were celebrating, demand far outran supply, prices soared and a short, sharp, unnatural boom ensued. Within eighteen months the bubble burst; there was a severe recession to be followed shortly after by a more even tenor of costs and prices.

So let us take examples from a full page advertisement from Barkers, the London store, offering Christmas gifts in December 1923. Converted from £ s d to pounds and pence :

Leather bag with top opening in real Morocco or Crocodile Calf leather ....10/- [50p]
Glass salad bowls of good quality glass ....2/1½ [11p]
Table cutlery, best quality stainless steel with square or round ivoried handles. Table knives per half doz. ....18/6 [92½p]
Manicure Set in roll-up crocodile case fitted with imitation Shell fittings ....14/6 [22½p]
Very handsome Cut Glass Smelling Salts perfectly fitting stoppers ....5/- [25p]
Leather Gauntlet Gloves, Fleece-lined and very warm. Price per pair ....12/11 [65p]
Cake or Fruit Basket. Sheffield Silver-plated on Nickel Silver. 25-year quality ....25/- [£1.25]
China tea service, fine quality china decorated with coloured roses and green foliage. Finished with neat green edge 21 pieces ....10/6 [52½p]
Copper Table heater or hot plate. Best quality and British made ....42/6 [£2.12½p]
Electric Irons ....12/6 [62½p]
Embroidered Lawn Handkerchiefs. 6 different designs. Box of 6 ....1/11½ [10p]
Reversible Electric Toaster. Toasts two pieces at one time and reverses the toast without being touched by hand ...37/6 [87½p]
Oak table of Jacobean design, fitted with two drawers, well constructed of seasoned timber and finished a rich antique shade ....29/6 [£1.47½p]
Motor Foot Muffs, made of cloth. Fur inside and out 18/6 [92½p]
Home Cinematograph, fitted with powerful oil lamp. Complete in attractive box with 3 films and 6 long slides 21/- [£1.05p]
The Mascot Safety Chair. Constructed of selected birch. Hand polished. In a natural or Walnut colour. Large detachable tray. Upholstered in moquette or velvet. Silent rubber-tyred wheels. 45/- [£2.25]
Boys' and Men's Leather Folding Slippers in leather case 3/9 [19p]
Pocket Theatre and Sports Glass. Aluminium construction, finish Black, covered leather ....15/- [75p]

Hall-marked Silver Cigarette Box, lined cedar wood. London made. To hold 25 cigarettes ....30/– [£1.50p]
*Decalion Gramophone. Jacobean model fitted with patent alloy cast 'Transmitter' 'Tripletone sounding boards
14 gns [£14.70p]
Floor Pouffs in Black striped poplina with Black and Gold stripes ....11/9 [59p]
Trolley Wagon in solid Oak on brass wheels and rubber tyres
69/6 [£3.46½p]
*Real English Velours of excellent lustre and soft finish, made from selected quality fur ....15/6 [77½p]

About the same time Harrods were offering ladies all-wool combinations at 73p. While for the 'east enders' the fashion editor reported on Easter outfits:

Every East End girl schemes to buy a new hat and dress for the Bank Holiday outing to Hampstead Heath. Hats and blouses are manufactured to pattern by the hundred, and frocks by the dozen, in all the brightest colours imaginable – vivid salmon pink, sky blue, or emerald green. The beads and silk embroideries are just as highly coloured. A hat that is worn morning, noon and night in the East End is the quaint French onion man's cap in cloth. This can be bought for 1s 0½d [5p] in brown and navy blue. A swagger version in black velveteen with a tassel costs 1s 11½d [10p].

Men's wear prices in 1926 – with costs and wages about exactly where they were five years before – may be gauged from this selection of bargains proffered by Pontings:

Smartly Tailored Suits. Two Styles. Superior quality Saxony and finished Tweeds ....50/– [£2.50p]
Plus Four Suits, made in Scotch Tweeds of the finest quality
63/– [£3.15p]
Double-breasted Blue Blazer ....22/6 [£1.07½p]
Men's Cream shade real English Balbriggan underwear
2/– [10p]
Tweed Sports Jackets ....18/6 [92½p]

* Gramophones were still something of a novelty, hence their relatively high cost. 'Velours' were men's homburg-style hats.

Lightweight Mackintosh for Men. A feather-weight mackintosh which can be folded small enough to carry in the pocket and weighs only 19 ozs .... 16/6 [82½p]
Grey Flannel Trousers .... 9/6 [45p]
White Oxford Shirts .... 5/– [25p]
Men's Taffeta pyjamas .... 7/9 [28p]
Cream Wool Socks .... 1/– [5p]

By April 1929, with the consumer revolution really rolling, bargains by post were enticing the customer with sewing machines at £3, three-piece suites for £7, baby prams for £2, boys' grey flannel suits for 52½ pence, vacuum cleaners for £5, bicycles for £3.25p.

Holidays abroad were gaining popularity, not surprisingly when 'a woman traveller' could report in December 1926:

Poor though I be, directly after Christmas I am going to the Riviera to rest and retrench for a couple of months.

If sunshine, abundant, well-cooked food, exquisite scenery, and cheap wine – all at a cost of about 2s 6d a day – appeal, then join me at 11 am at Victoria.

The second-class return fare to Marseilles, via Calais, is £7 1s 0d. Via Dieppe with the longest sea voyage, it is £5 16s 0d.

Nowhere, however, was the changing life-style so much in evidence as with the central feature of the family: the Home.

Before the First World War a mere 11 per cent of the people owned their own homes. Nearly 90 per cent rented them from landlords – council housing did not start until 1919. Between the wars home ownership rose dramatically to total more than one-third of the country's families. The South-East of England had the fastest growth.

Here is a selection of advertisements from the Modern Homes Guide for 30 June, 1923:

WELWYN GARDEN CITY, Hertfordshire.
Each home is connected with main drainage, Company's water, electric light and gas – wired throughout for electric light. The accommodation includes Kitchen, Scullery, Larder and fuel store.
3 bedrooms, bathroom W.C., 2 sitting-rooms, usual offices   £775

A BUNGALOW RESIDENCE. Wraysbury-on-Thames.
Built to your own requirements without delay and on easy terms.

2 bedrooms, living room, kitchen, bath (h and c), large verandah, every modern convenience, electric light available. £530 to £550 brick: £380 asbestos, mortgages arranged.

LIVE AT SOUTHEND. Travel daily by excellent service. From Liverpool Street. 1 hour from sea.

SEASON TICKETS

1st		3rd
£1 10s 0d	1 week	18s 6d
£2 13s 0d	2 weeks	£1 11s 6d
£3 9s 6d	1 month	£2 1s 6d
£9 9s 0d	3 months	£5 12s 0d

*

This was the peak period of the speculative builder and numerous advertisements offered land to 'speculators', a perfectly acceptable title in an era when 'buyer beware' was routine business practice. Most of the houses on the market in 1923 were designed to appeal to professional people and businessmen. By 1931 wages, raw materials and building costs had, due to the world-wide trade slump, fallen below 1914 levels. The stage was set for the greatest boom in housebuilding for owner-occupation ever seen. This is how prices and houses looked then, to a market that was beginning to attract the skilled worker as well as the senior clerk:

YOUR OWN FREEHOLD HOUSE FOR ONLY 15/11

Total Deposit £25 or £550 Cash.

Best Value ever offered. Just imagine a large sunny house, fitted with all the latest labour-saving devices for only £25 down and 15/11 per week. No extras. Clean concrete roads. No road charges. No legal costs.* The opportunity is too good to miss.

All Edward houses are sturdy and well built. The Estate is close to the Underground, and a park and Council school are on the Estate. Good shopping centre. Co-operative stores and all leading multiple stores.**

Edwards (South Harrow) Ltd

*

* These were paid by developers eager to sell their houses.
** Shops were built in anticipation of selling the house. They were let at very low rents and multiples such as Tesco were able to develop their chains in this way.

HORSENDEN HILL, Greenford, Middlesex.

You can buy a delightful modern house on Sudbury Hill Estate for 22/6 per week [£1.12½p].

3 bedrooms and bath, sitting room, living room, kitchen, food cooler, dry store, gas copper and point for cooker. Linen Cupboard. Gas fires. Fireplaces to choice. Modern sanitary arrangements.

*

LAINGS FAMOUS HOMES. Every House a Palace.

Golders Green. Well laid-out Estate. 10 minutes station. Adjoining Public Gardens and Park. Shops on Estate. Houses have 3 or 4 bedrooms. £875 to £1,700. Golders Green Estate, Hendon Way and the Vale, Golders Green.

Within a few years small terraced houses on the outskirts of Glasgow, Leeds and Manchester were selling for £300, each with pocket-size gardens back and front.

Domestic help was still abundant and the proud new house-owners could probably stretch their expenditure to pay about £40 a year to a general maid in the London area. Girls in the country could expect a good deal less. One 'domestic help wanted' advertisement from Trowbridge – fairly typical of Wiltshire and the West Country – read: 'Strong girl, housework, with business people, good home 1s [5p] a day, chance can earn extra in business.'

Domestic service was far and away the biggest source of female employment – close to 2,000,000 – but it was no longer the natural order for girls to go into service, let alone remain a lifetime with one household, as was the case before 1914. The pull of the dance floor and the 'flicks' were powerful factors in making young women prefer the factory, shop or office jobs with fixed hours and free evenings to the demands of a house-proud mistress. The one countervailing force to gadding about was the radio, or the wireless as it was invariably known.

Radio for entertainment, rather than commerce or war, dated from 1919 and was widespread in the USA by 1921. However it was not until November 1922 that the British Broadcasting Company went on the air, known by its code sign 2LO and operating from Marconi House, London. The company was formed to promote the sale of civilian radio receivers: there not being much point in owning a wireless set unless one could hear something enjoyable on it.

In 1923 a six-valve Marconi set retailed at £83.38p,* about half the annual wage of an unskilled labourer. Crystal sets, the ubiquitous 'cat's whisker', consisted of a tube with coil and metal detector. The price for one of these very basic and unreliable receivers was 75p plus £1.38 for the headphones.

A sample of the programmes available to wireless enthusiasts is taken from the newspaper of 9 January, 1923:

London (on a 369 metres wave-length) – 5 pm to 5.45 pm, Children's Stories and Music; 6.30 pm, Music; 7 pm, News; 7.30 pm Music; 8.25 pm, Dance Music; 9 pm, Music; 9.30 pm, News; 9.50 to 10.30 pm, Music.

Writtle (Essex) – 8 to 8.30 pm, Music.

Birmingham (on 420 metres wave-length) – 6.30 pm, Children's Stories; 7 pm, Concert; 7.30 pm, News; 7.45 to 8.30 pm, Concert; 9 pm, Concert; 9.45 pm, News; 10 pm, Final Announcements.

Manchester (on a 385 metres wave-length) – 5.55 pm, Call Up; 6 pm to 9.45 pm, News, Music, Lecture and Children's Stories; 9.45 pm, Dance Music.

Those who were not enamoured of music or children's stories presumably contented themselves with reading.

A week after that January programme list a news item appeared, emphasising America's lead in the new wonder of radio transmission:

'Hello, London. We had a snowstorm here this afternoon. I wonder what kind of weather you are having?'

These laconic but clearly audible words marked another milestone in the history of wireless telephony yesterday, when for the first time a Transatlantic interview was carried out from London. British journalists chatted with Mr H. B. Thayer of the American Telephone and Telegraph Company, in his office on Broadway, New York.

The wonder was achieved by the American Telephone and Telegraph Company (who control the Bell system) in co-operation with the Radio Corporation of America. The reception of the message in this country was organised by the International Western Electric Company.

---

* By 1934 the cheapest set on electricity mains cost £6; a high quality set £11.55p and a super-de-luxe £25. I am indebted to Mr Gordon Bussy of Philips for the information on radios.

Then on 29 April came the first SOS to be broadcast:

A dramatic call to a wife, to hurry from the country to the bedside of her husband, who lies critically ill in a London hospital, was sent out during the wireless broadcasting performance from the London station last night.

The thrill came at the end of a song, 'Son of Mine'. The last notes of the song had hardly died away before a clear, deliberate voice said:

HELP!

'Here is an appeal from the Middlesex Hospital.

'If any one is listening in from Ampthill, Bedfordshire, will he please inform Mrs Carr, of Thinnings, Flitwick, that her husband is very ill at the Middlesex Hospital? Will she please come at once.'

The SOS had an almost magical result. Hundreds of listeners-in round Ampthill started to pass on the urgent message to Mrs Carr. Some even set out from the far-off town of Bedford.

Many people cycled.

So blasé were people becoming that the prophecy of a French authority, Mr Edouard Belin, in 1923 that television would be with the public in a twelve-month period elicited a mere single laconic paragraph. Mr Belin was twelve years out in his forecast.

The day's broadcasting for Glasgow on 12 December, 1923, shows small advance on content over the start of the year, although by this time the UK had eight broadcasting stations (the US had hundreds upon hundreds):

GLASGOW (call 5 S C; 415 metres)
3.30 – Wireless Quarter. 4.30-5 – Interval. 5 – Talk to Women. 5.30 Children's corner. 6 – Weather report for farmers. 6.10-7 – Interval.
7.00 – News. Mr John Strachey (BBC Literary critic). Local news and weather. 7.30 – Symphony programme. 9.10 – Lieut F. W. Kealey. 9.30 – News. 9.45 – Continuation of symphony concert. 10.30 – Announcements. Close down.

Mr John Strachey, later a Labour Minister, was the Company's book reviewer. Kealey was the secretary of a scientific exploration to the Pacific.

Oxford Bags
A perfect example of a twenties 'silly season' extravaganza: the wide bottomed Oxford bags which pleased the wags but were spurned by the fashion conscious.

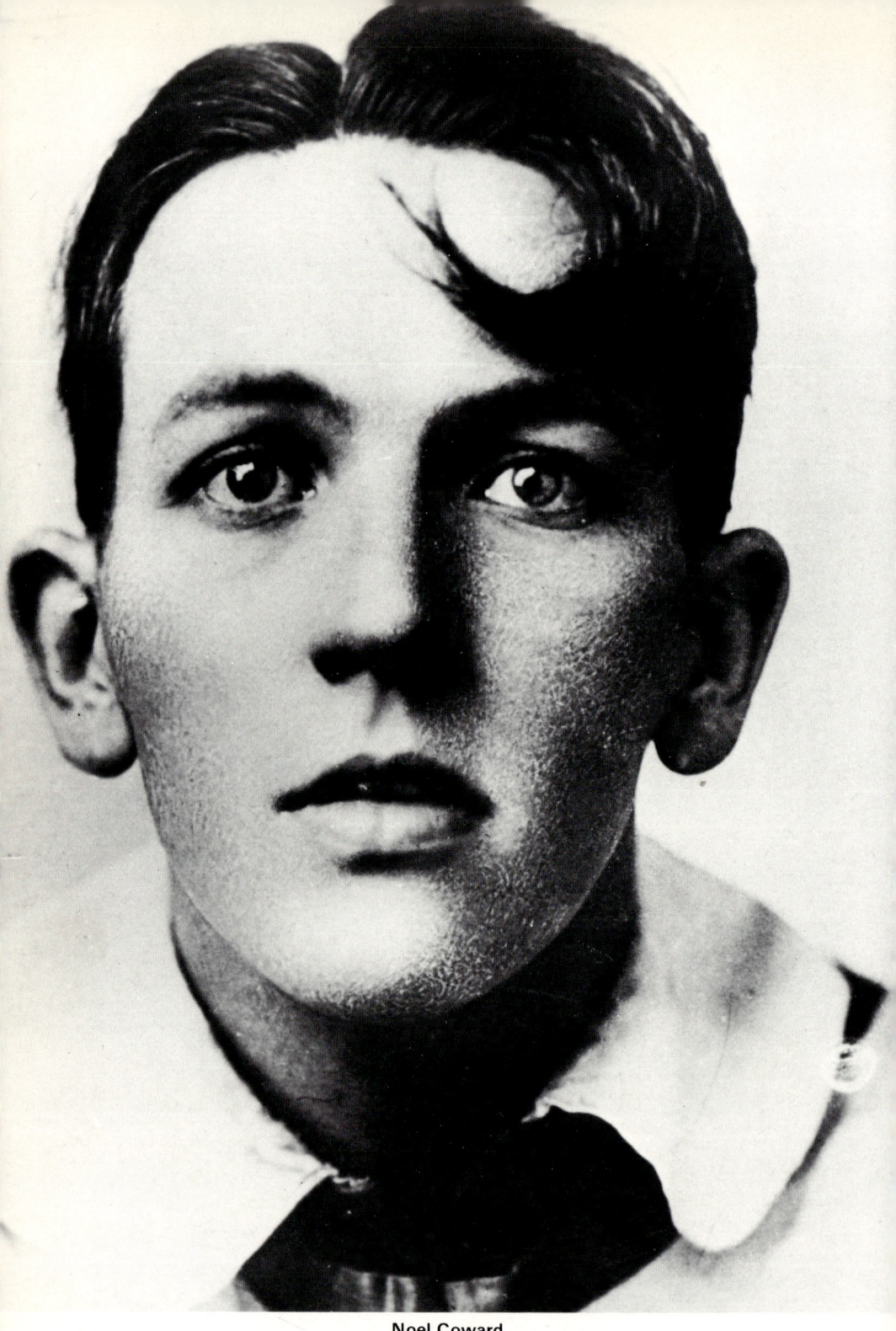

Noel Coward
The young Noel Coward was damned in the American press for "shovelling up ordure of an unprincipled smart set." One of the plays so flayed was ironically named *Our Betters*.

When, some days later, the Company went beyond talks and music and offered one act from a play *Little Nellie Kelly* it was frustrated by the theatre managements who refused to give permission. 'Provincial managers,' said Mr C. B. Cochran, the impresario, 'have arranged not to book any attraction which has been broadcast'. Fear of the impact of the wireless was widespread: for years some newspapers refused to carry radio programmes on the grounds that they would simply be cutting their own throats.

They really had little to worry about in the way of direct competition. Three years after the establishment of 2LO a typical day's 'listening-in' consisted of:

LONDON (call 2 L O; 365 metres)
1-2 – Time Signal from Greenwich. The week's Concert of new gramophone records. 4-5 – Time signal from Greenwich: Concert: The 2 L O Trio. A talk on Fashion, by Nora Shandon. Lily Lawrence (soprano). Careers for Women: the Art Illustrator, by Mary Stewart. 6-6.45 – Children's Corner. Aunt Hilda at the Piano. Miss Nobody's Special. *The Wind in the Willows,* by Kenneth Grahame. A trip across the world – Innsbruck. 6.45-6.55 – Scout and Guide News: The All England Troop, Copenhagen. 7 – Time Signal. Weather and News. Percy Scholes: the Fortnight's Music. Talk by the Radio Society of Great Britain. 7.55-8 – Interval. 8 – Faust.

More bizarre than the programmes was what happened to some listeners in these cat's-whiskers-and-headset days:

Gold and silver net caps are being bought by women wireless enthusiasts who object to the disarrangement of their coiffures caused by the ear-pieces.

The nets were originally designed for evening wear on the way to parties and dances. Now they are sold almost exclusively for 'wireless' wear.

*

A pair of spectacles, acting as a connecting link between a faulty electric lamp and a wireless set is now understood to have caused the death of Mrs Violet Rainford, aged fifty-nine, who was found dead in bed at her Sudbury home with the headphones still on her ears.

*

No motor-car silence has been more effective in its action than the loudspeaker and the headphones of wireless in the homes of England.

In thousands of houses people sit together for hours without exchanging more than half-a-dozen sentences.

Radio came of age for state occasions when King George V's speech opening the Wembley Empire Exhibition in 1924 was broadcast far and wide. But the British Broadcasting *Company* was nearing the end of its life. Competing commercial interests and overcrowded air waves led to the creation of the British Broadcasting Corporation, the BBC established by Act of Parliament; financed by licensing fees collected by the Post Office; governed by a board of independent governors and – for its first thirteen years anyway – moulded and motivated by a huge, beetle-browed Scotsman, John Reith, the Director-General.

Broadcasting's demure image became positively strait-laced under the unrelenting integrity of Reith. He boasted that he would use 'the brute monopoly of broadcasting' to raise cultural standards. He did. The *Daily Express* was almost guilty of *lèse majesté* when in August 1932 it printed this story:

> Here is something which the 4,800,000 radio licence-holders of this country are forbidden to know –
>
> The truth about the mysterious BBC announcers.
>
> For years a barrier of secrecy has been built up round these men's identity. They are the least-known men in Britain.
>
> I am going to throw over the barriers here and now.
>
> And – you are quite right – the voice you hear is generally the voice of Oxford. Five of the six graduated there.
>
> But – the five Oxford men are 'bossed' by a man from Cambridge. Meet the secret six. They are: Stuart Hibberd, chief announcer. He is the Cambridge man, and was enlisted because of his good microphone singing voice.
>
> John Snagge – In the last Boat-race he was the expert commentator, for he used to row at Oxford for his college, Pembroke. His father is Judge Snagge, the London county court judge.
>
> Freddie Grisewood – He was at Magdalen, and was a distinguished member of the Oxford University Dramatic Society. Mr Grisewood is a good baritone singer.
>
> Jack Cowper – was Uncle Jacko in the Midland Regional programmes.

T. C. L. Farrar – He is Uncle Ajax of the Children's Hour, and is a gifted singer.
Good morning, everybody.

Far from spending money on broadcasting sport, the BBC reckoned it was doing football a favour by reporting the Cup Final. When, in the late twenties, the Football Association tentatively suggested a fee the BBC broadcast excerpts of the match from outside Wembley, using a relay of messengers. In 1930 the BBC *did* agree to a fee but demanded that it should decide how the FA should spend the money, and the *Radio Times*, the Corporation's official periodical, carried this statement:

> It is a dismal prospect when the governing body of a sport originated, built up, and entirely supported by amateurs should be captured by professionals whose whole interest apparently is commercial.

Such comment was true to type. The BBC represented standards of decency set by John Reith and those whom he employed or who, theoretically, had authority over him. The conventional ruled. And the conventional was respect for people – (a minute's silence at the end of Children's Hour was observed for the death, in 1933, of John Kettlewell, the programme's organiser); for tradition (announcers and most performers wore dinner jackets and formal dress out of deference to their unseen audience) and institutions. In conforming to this pattern the BBC was reflecting the views of King George V and Queen Mary. John Reith would have asked for no better examples.

*

In the swirling uncertainties of post-war England King George and Queen Mary were the certainties to which millions looked. The Queen's dress – uncompromisingly Edwardian amidst bobbed hair, flattened bosoms and rising hemlines – was a reassurance in itself. The King's gruff no-nonsense attitude, Navy style, accorded exactly with that of fathers more than a little concerned that their offspring were 'not what they were in my youth'.

In recent years well-documented biographies have told how demanding George was as a father and how lacking in sympathy and understanding for her children was Mary as a mother. What is indisputable – and is confirmed by the biographies and other studies – is the sense of duty which animated King George and Queen Mary.

They stood for God, Service, Country and Empire. They were, of course, conservative – but with a small 'c'. The waves of social anger broke against them in vain. On the eve of election victory, in June 1923, the Labour Party conference rejected a resolution declaring that 'the Royal Family is no longer necessary as part of the British Constitution'. To be sure the man who defended monarchy did so with faint praise. Mr George Lansbury, a dedicated pacifist and future party leader, asked conference to oppose the motion for expediency's sake:

'Why should we fool about with a question which is of no earthly importance, and which will be settled whenever the economic conditions are settled?

'Years ago I used to think that the monarchy and the nobility were those who made people poor, but William Morris and H. M. Hyndman taught me that it is the capitalist system that makes them poor.

'I sat at the same table with a prince when I was a member of the Social Democratic Federation. I have sat at table with a queen and behind two princes at a football match, and you may take my word for it they are just ordinary common clay, like anybody else.

'They eat like you do, they talk like you do, only a little worse occasionally, and do everything just like you.

'When you have won the social revolution you may be sure what you will be able to do with the King, Queen, President, or any one else.'

However, if Mr Lansbury was tepid, not to say downright cool, Mrs Philip Snowden, wife of the ice-clear little cripple charged with carving out the financial revolution for Socialism, was hotly zealous in her championship of monarchy:

'The suggestion that the Royal House does not do any work is just absolute nonsense. I consider they are the hardest-worked people in the country. Only sheer ignorance could lead any person to make such a stupid and untrue statement.'

Mrs Snowden was replying to criticism of Royalty fired off by the ferocious Clydeside Red, Mr David Kirkwood. Mr Kirkwood later became Lord Kirkwood of Bearsden.

The public, including Labour voters, were in no way concerned about political anguish over the place of royalty. They revelled in it.

When the Sovereign's daughter, Princess Mary, was married to Lord

Lascelles in February 1922, the papers lavished attention on every detail of the preparations:

> The names of the firms who are supplying Princess Mary's trousseau were issued from Buckingham Palace last night.
>
> Afternoon dress, coat and skirt, tea gown: Mme Hayward, New Bond-street.
>
> Wedding Dress, evening dresses, tea gown: Messrs Reville and Rossiter, Hanover Square.
>
> Evening dresses, going away dress, afternoon dress: Mme Handley-Seymour, New Bond-street.
>
> Jumpers: Officers' Families Industries, Beauchamp Place, SW.
>
> Handkerchiefs, cushion covers: Messrs Robinson and Cleaver, Regent-street.
>
> Hats: Millicent, Conduit-street, and Mme Angrave, Queen's-road.

No fewer than nine concerns provided the lingerie. The little Shropshire town of Shifnal near where the couple were to spend their honeymoon (at Weston Hall) was bedecked with flags and the portion of the station platform on which Princess Mary was to tread was carpeted with Kidderminster fleur-de-lys.

Five months later, enormous crowds gathered outside Westminster Abbey to greet Miss Edwina Ashley who was marrying Lord Louis Mountbatten RN. The reason for the crowds was the presence of the King and Queen – they signed the register – and other members of the Royal Family.

By far the greatest outpouring of joy concerning a wedding at this period occurred in 1923 when Lady Elizabeth Bowes-Lyon married the Duke of York. For once a Court Circular mirrored the real, intense feelings of the Sovereigns as it proclaimed:

> 'It is with the greatest pleasure that the King and Queen announce the betrothal of their beloved son, the Duke of York, to the Lady Elizabeth Bowes-Lyon, daughter of the Earl and Countess of Strathmore and Kingbourne, to which union the King has gladly given his consent.'

The tale of the romance was recounted:

> Lady Elizabeth, a winsome, dark-eyed, vivacious beauty, found herself, when she had barely reached her twenty-first birthday, faced by

the heavy manifold responsibility of hostess during a royal visit to Glamis Castle, her father's seat.

The visitors were the Queen, Princess Mary, and the Duke of York. Lady Strathmore was ill. Lady Elizabeth was her deputy chatelaine. To her fell the duty of showing the castle to Princess Mary and the Duke of York.

Lady Elizabeth's charm won her more than she knew.

She is devoted to music and poetry, and a hard worker in the Girl Guide movement.

The engagement is a true love match, and is popular with all the members of the Royal Family.

Glamis, where Macbeth murdered Duncan, holds among many relics of Scottish history the sword of Claverhouse, bearing the inscription 'God Save King James VIII, prosperitie to Scotland, and no union'.

The King's shy second son was also given a write-up:

The Duke of York pays many private visits to factories, mines, mills, and all kinds of works, and enjoys discussing problems of work and wages with both employers and workmen.

He is a zealous president of the Industrial Welfare Society, and never misses one of its meetings. He keeps in touch with Labour leaders.

For two years the duke has held a 'Play the game' summer camp near New Romney for boys from factories and public schools – from Eton and Harrow, Poplar and Glasgow. All meet on an equality, and the camp has been a splendid success.

The Duke was brought up in the Navy, and was in the Collingwood at the Battle of Jutland. He afterwards transferred to the Royal Air Force, and won his wings as a pilot.

It may have sounded sycophantic at the time. It was true.

In bringing Elizabeth Bowes-Lyon and Albert, Duke of York, together Providence played Britain and the Empire a trump card. But no one that April day thought there was the remotest possibility of them coming to the throne when the *Express* reported:

The Duchess of York will long be known as the smiling bride.

She smiled a little wistfully yesterday as she drove to Westminster Abbey for her wedding. She smiled radiantly as she left the Abbey for Buckingham Palace. She smiled from the balcony of the Palace on a hundred thousand cheering people.

Her happiness infected everyone, and happiest of all was the bridegroom.

How King George and Queen Mary must have wished that their eldest son would find someone like Elizabeth Bowes-Lyon. For on his shoulders rested the responsibility of representing his father at many great State and Empire occasions. On him was lavished admiration amounting to adoration. Edward, Prince of Wales, was indeed Prince Charming and a modern one to boot: The very model of a Twenties' Hero.

*

Edward, Prince of Wales, was probably the most popular man in the world. He was certainly the most photographed and most envied. Blessed with boyish good looks, an encyclopaedic memory – he could recall names and append them to the correct faces with a facility that evoked wonderment from professional politicians – physical courage and a flair for getting on with people from all walks of life, the heir to the throne seemed tailor-made to adapt monarchy to the hectic pace of the 1920s. Until the fatal flaw of petty selfishness was revealed in his later years, Edward fulfilled the role in which fate cast him with marvellous ease. It seemed he could do no wrong.

His Empire trips, made in the comradely after-glow of shared sacrifice in the 1914-18 war, won him the adulation of tens of millions. This brave, shining, golden youth (although he was nearing thirty he looked eternally young) brought Canadians and Australians and ex-colonialists such as Americans to their feet in roaring enthusiasm.

So he went to India in 1921 in the aftermath of the Amritsar Killings (see Chapter XV) when nationalist, anti-Raj sentiment was at its height and his life could have been taken at any time. He triumphed. At only one place – Ahmedabad – did the Indian Congress call for a *hartel*, a day of mourning, have any effect. Elsewhere the welcome was tumultuous as this account of the reception in Bombay by Sir Percival Phillips – one of the few journalists of that period to have been knighted – makes plain:

> It was a wonderful picture as the barge drew alongside the quay, while the fleet on the silver sea, wreathed in smoke, united in a salute to the slender figure in white naval uniform and helmet, leaning forward to greet the Viceroy on the threshold of India.

Three scarlet attendants preceded him and his suite across the quay to the Crown Pavilion, the open arches of which were hung with garlands of green.

Here, seated on a golden throne on a carpet of Delhi brocade, with the Viceroy and the Governor of Bombay beside him, he read the King's moving message to his Empire. He read in a loud, clear voice, with great dignity and composure.

Volleys of cheers started him off on his journey of nearly five miles to Government House. All windows, balconies, and lofty buildings overlooking the amphitheatre before the throne were packed with spectators. The native population pressed eagerly behind the cordon of troops to acclaim him.

When he returned in June 1922 London went mad. He had to stand at the salute for more than five minutes while the masses cheered him to the echo. King George – not one of the Prince's fans – issued a special message:

'The Queen and I were deeply touched by to-day's remarkable demonstration. Our joy in welcoming our dear son was increased by the affection and enthusiasm of his reception from the vast crowds assembled to greet him. He has safely returned from a long and responsible tour, and I am confident that my people share in our humble thanks to God for this happy and memorable day.'

A winning schoolboy essay, submitted to an *Express* competition by pupil Francis Lauvreys, thirteen, of Winton and Moordown Council Boys' School, Bournemouth, described Edward thus:

Frank and kind, handsome and athletic, he stands as a type of the best the Motherland can produce . . . the Prince of Wales in tightening the bonds of friendship helps to keep the Empire together.

Edward's life was highly regulated. Take the month 12 November to 12 December, 1923. His major engagements included:

A royal wedding (Princess Maud's); address the Coal Trade Benevolent Fund; guest of honour at the National Film League luncheon; address the Electrical Manufacturers and the Great Ormond Street Hospital; open the Provincial Police orphanage; open extensions to the Royal Northern Hospital; preside at a dinner for the Home for Incurables; open the Fat Stock Show at Edinburgh; address the

Farmers' Club dinner; preside at the annual dinner of the Royal Society of Medicine; open another hospital extension.

In one day Edward could change clothes seven times to fit each appointment. And in those days dress could be *very* formal.

Regulations for a new court dress worn by Privy Councillors detailed these alterations to existing uniform: 'embroidered edging to be wavy and to be worked with rough purls; width of the embroidery, exclusive of the edging, to 4½ inches instead of 5; the hat to have treble gold bullion loop and tassels without hangers.' Fortunately Edward was a keen student of fashion. He needed to be.

He was also, like his youngr brother the Duke of York, deeply concerned with industrial relations. The early twenties were (see Chapter IX) years of bitter strikes. The coal mines were in a state of constant turmoil. With his princely title, Edward felt a special sense of responsibility to the men in the Welsh pits. He recalled too that the miners had been among the most numerous volunteers in 1914 and one constant in Edwards' career was solicitude for ex-servicemen. Consequently he devoted time and effort to the Coalfields Distress Fund. So effective was he as a fund raiser that A. J. Cook, the fiery-red leader of the miners, was moved to comment in April 1929:

'We owe to the Prince a real measure of thanks. His whole-hearted enthusiasm on the miners' behalf in this matter has brought the throne quite close to the populace.

'His conduct and his attitude have shown that all mankind have great qualities in common. He has proved to the miner and his children at a moment of great suffering and distress that they are not forgotten.'

The Communist Party denounced Cook for 'nauseating slavishness to the typical representative of the class which has battened on the workers', but the Miners' Secretary went on to reveal that the Prince had contributed to the Miners' Relief Fund, set up immediately after the failure of the 1926 General Strike, and that Edward had done more than anyone else to publicise the sufferings of the miners. The Patriot Prince reputation dimmed and vanished in later years but its luminous appeal to all his people in the 1920s was real and important.

Everywhere he went he received accolades; every trivial incident or action on his part was blazoned far and wide.

A news item of 9 March, 1921:

There was an extraordinary scene of enthusiasm at the Glasgow Industries Fair yesterday when the Prince of Wales arrived. He was 'mobbed' by thousands of women, and gifts descended on him in showers. He tried on a cap with the aid of a mirror, and asked that it might be sent to him.

From another of 16 February, 1927:

The Prince of Wales, during a visit to the slums of Hoxton last night, visited a fried fish shop.

Great secrecy had been observed about his intentions, even to the extent of withdrawing policemen in order not to call attention to the streets that he visited.

In spite of these precautions, hundreds of men and women surrounded his motor-car, some of them clambering on the foot-boards and hanging on the back.

Earlier in the day he visited Hackney, where he chatted with Enid Page, the nine-year-old daughter of an ex-service man.

'How do you do, your Royal Highness, and how are you?' was her greeting as she danced up to the Prince and held out her hand.

'I'm very well, and how are you?' replied the Prince, smiling, and he immediately started chatting to her.

Recognition of a different sort came from Mr Arthur Murray, of dance school fame and director of the National Institute of Social Dancing, who announced that the Prince of Wales had been voted 'the premier dancer of the world'. A new foxtrot was named after him. This was not so appallingly servile as it sounds. Edward was a first-class dancer (he had plenty of practice) and there must have been many girls 'who danced with the man who'd danced with the girl who'd danced with the Prince of Wales'.

Dancing was not the only pursuit publicised by the Prince of Wales. He was an inveterate cigarette smoker, a devotee of motor cars – the faster the better – and an advocate of mass air travel. All three were hallmarks of the twenties.

World War I gave a tremendous fillip to cigarette smoking: 'While you've a lucifer to light your fag, smile boys, that's the style.'* The

---

* 'Pack Up Your Troubles'.

Willie Woodbine was as much part of the war's lore as Old Bill and Mademoiselle from Armentiers. This item from 4 July, 1920 shows how socially acceptable smoking had become:

> Does smoking help the worker to do more work?
> Messrs Dick, Kerr, the famous Preston firm of electrical engineers, have found that it does. Three months ago their men were granted permission to smoke during fifteen minutes in the morning and fifteen minutes in the afternoon. The innovation has proved very popular with the men and such good business from the firm's point of view that it has resulted in increased output.
> The management has now decided to extend their experiment by allowing the men to smoke during ninety minutes each morning and evening from 9.00 to 10.30 am and from 3 to 4.30 pm.

John McCormack, the Irish tenor, endorsed Kensitas cigarettes. 'The only enjoyable cigarettes he can smoke without the slightest risk of irritating his throat and voice.' Kensitas drew from these remarks the conclusion that 'your own throat is just as important to you — start smoking Kensitas to-day'.

Kensitas were a rather superior smoke (it carried a butler on the package) and cost 5p for 20. Less redoubtable brands retailed at 4½p and the small cigarettes cost a mere 2p for 10.

Tobacco manufacturers were large advertisers and just to remind other trades that it paid to advertise, the press told this sad story in 1923:

> The business of Day and Martin whose blacking was used by Sam Weller to polish Mr Pickwick's boots is, after more than a century and a half, to pass into other hands.
> 'I am perfectly convinced that if only Day and Martin's had advertised their wares during the last quarter of a century the old firm would not be in the plight that it is today.'
> This statement was made by Mr Burlison, manager for the once famous house.
> 'How many people are aware that Day and Martin's has ever manufactured anything but the blacking which went partly out of use in 1896 when chrome leather was adapted for footwear?
> 'Famous literary men in the past century were not shy of advertising Day and Martin in their books. Dickens loved to refer to

it whenever possible because he hated the firm of Warren, where he worked when a boy. Carlyle, George Eliot, Hood and Bret Harte all immortalised the firm's name.

'We have never altered, although we have improved the recipe of the founder, a Doncaster hairdresser. Molasses, treacle, vinegar, and many other queer ingredients are contained in the famous blacking.'

Motor manufacturers certainly could not be faulted for failing to advertise. Starting with the Motor Show of 1922 they used advertising as their competitive battlefield.

Mr Vernon-Hunt reported from the exhibition of that year:

> Many people who can no longer afford the upkeep of a large chauffeur-driven car are eagerly waiting to inspect the new models of moderate horse-power that will be on view at the Motor Show.
>
> That the manufacturers are alive to this demand is shown by the large number who are now marketing models that range between 12 and 15 horsepower.
>
> The latest firm to announce a 12 hp model is the Daimler Company. It is a chassis that is eminently suitable for miniature, closed coachwork and makes an ideal inexpensive town carriage as a landaulette or coupe.
>
> It has high-grade coachwork of distinction, and although the price of £775 for the four-seater all-weather is not exactly cheap, the quality of a Daimler production must not be forgotten.
>
> The new 14 hp Wolseley is another car of high quality and low price that is the outcome of the growing demand for economy, and is sure to interest those who have £525 to spend and a family for whom to provide accommodation.

Sums of £525 and £775 represented two to three years gross wages for a senior clerk or experienced teacher. Within two years, however, mass production of cars was to produce the same kind of results as mass production was later to achieve with radio.

The *Express* motoring reporter noted on 3 April, 1924:

> I have just been reading a booklet, published by a northern firm, which proves that motoring costs less than walking! Here are the figures:
>
> Re-soling and heeling twice in 200 miles, 16s [80p]; depreciation

of footware, approximately 40 per cent, 12s [60p]; two pairs of good woollen socks, 8s [40p]. Total £1 16s [£1.80p].

Now for the motoring costs. The car costs £157 10s; interest on outlay at 5 per cent per annum, £23 12s 6d [£23.62½p]; insurance, £12; annual tax, £12. You may, say, motor 10,000 miles in a year at an upkeep or overhead cost of £53 10s.

Now for the actual road-running expenditure. The percentage of overhead for 200 miles, taken from the above figures, is £1 1s 5d [£1.07½p]; five gallons of petrol, at 40 miles per gallon, 7s 6d [35½p]; oil at 1,300 miles per gallon, 1s 2d [6p]; tyres at 15,000 miles per set, 2s [10p] – total £1 12s 1d [£1.60p].

Supposing three people are taken as well as the driver, the comparative costs with walking show a positive saving of £5 11s 11d [£5.60p] over 200 miles, or more than 6½d [3p] per mile.

To reassure the well-off that they could still do things in style the correspondent added that:

The Prince of Wales has bought a new seven-seater interior-drive saloon-limousine Crossley. The body is painted in the royal colours, maroon with a heavy maroon line.

The interior is upholstered in blue Bedford cloth and the fittings are in mahogany.

By 1926 Ford were offering open, five-seater cars for £125 and in the early 30s Morris had the Bull Morris and the baby Austin on the road for £100. With such prices and instalment payments, reasonably cheap motoring became a fact of life.

Adventure of the open road was still maintained however. Willys-Knight used an 8,000 mile journey from Manchester to Calcutta in 80 days as an advertisement for their 20 horse-power tourer, price £375. The advertisement showed two fearsome natives with guns peering over rocks at the peerless Mr Drader, driver of the Willys-Knight.

If Mr Drader needed nerves of steel, so did air travellers of the twenties. Hints for the growing number of lady passengers were given in the women's page of 15 January, 1927:

A good many women now travel to and from the Continent in the regular airway service. One only needs to be at Croydon on two or three occasions to watch the woe-begone appearance to realise that commonsense fashions for flying have not yet been appreciated.

The greatest point is to be certain that the feet and legs are perfectly warm. Ordinary silk stockings are inadequate, as are also light walking shoes.

Woollen stockings slipped over silk ones and a foot muff are practical and useful, and Russian boots certainly do justify their existence on a cross-Channel trip. An ordinary fur or leather coat is a blessing, but the greatest point is to avoid chilly feet and legs, and warm undergarments finished with elastics at the knee are advisable.

A broad flannel belt is very helpful. It exerts a steadying pressure on the abdominal wall and nerves.

It is not necessary to wear a leather helmet, as there is no exposure to the outside air in the big air liners; but the noise of the engine is a disturbing thing. The best way to minimise this is to plug the ears with cottonwool dipped in glycerine.

Air sickness is even more distressing than ordinary sea sickness. The only way to avoid it is to prepare some days beforehand, and to take a very light diet for two days before travelling.

Trans-Atlantic flying started when the British pilots Alcock and Brown crossed from Newfoundland to Ireland in 1919. Charles Lindbergh accomplished the first solo eight years later and in 1932 Jim Mollison, casually chatted to his equally famous pilot wife, Amy Johnson, over the Transatlantic telephone after flying through dreadful weather to St John, New Brunswick. Aircraft were in sight of reducing the Atlantic to a pond.

But while the twenties' people revelled in speed, speed and more speed, the older generation shook its head and muttered a popular doggerel:

> In greedy haste, on pleasure bent
> What need is there for sentiment?

Yet sentiment – virtuous and vicious – was far from dead. In Parliament, in the courts, in life generally, it erupted again and again.

CHAPTER FOURTEEN

Morality: Old and New

In many respects the twenties bore an uncommon resemblance to the sixties. They shared that curious blend of soft-option idealism on public issues with a desire to slough off responsibilities in the private sphere. Literature and the stage mirrored some of these attitudes – witness the works of Somerset Maugham and Noël Coward. But the war generation contained far more genuine sentiment, the blood-bound loyalty of the trenches, than did the trend-setters of the sixties, whose knowledge of the horrors of war came from the movies.

Among those who wanted to make the country a better place, if hardly the Home Fit for Heroes of Lloyd George's fervid imaginings, were young officers who sought entry into the Commons in the election of 1918. Most of them chose the Conservatives – though it is said of Walter Eliot that on receiving a telegram in Flanders asking him to stand as candidate he replied: 'Yes. Which party? . . .' – because the Conservatives lauded themselves as the patriotic party of King, Country and Empire. The rising Labour Party had too many conscientious objectors in it for the liking of ex-servicemen.

However following the boom-and-bust economic mishandling of the immediate post-war period some disillusioned former officers, now MPs, started to look at the Labour Opposition as a possible haven for talents and urge for reform. One such former officer was Mr Oswald Mosley, MP.

Mosley, an aristocrat, was disgusted with what he regarded as the crass commercialism of the Conservative-dominated coalition. The streak of romantic young Englandism was very strong in him; he leaned towards a paternalistic view of society and away from the laissez-faire policy of most of his fellow Tories. So this product of Winchester and Sandhurst, son-in-law of the Marquis of Curzon ('that most superior person') joined the Labour Party observing that he was joining 'the forces of progress, sanity and conscience'.

Conscience certainly flowed abundantly in Socialist veins. To give point to Mr Mosley's comment, Mr Lloyd Davies, Labour MP for the University of Wales* resigned on 31 March 1924, the very day Mosley applied for party membership:

> The circumstances of Mr Davies' resignation are unusual. He has discovered that through no fault of his own an irregularity of £2 occurred in his election expenses. He had been advised that it can be overlooked. But he has decided that he cannot overlook it, and that he must resign.

Conscience of a far different kind drove the newly-elected left-wing MPs who had come storming into the Commons in 1922. The most violent of them were the Scots, known as the Red Clydesiders. When Comrade Newbold gained an industrial town near Glasgow for Communism he cabled Lenin: 'Motherwell is won for Moscow.' It was lost to Moscow shortly afterwards. The Red Clydesiders evinced a disdain and contempt for Parliament. 'We will smash all this. We will give you tranquillity [The Tory election slogan].' These rough, tough men were going to have none of the foppery and outworn traditions of the past. They were the wave of the future, the revolutionary way, the Russian way.

The Red Clydesiders were members of the Independent Labour Party who objected to the link between the trade unions and the official Labour Party. In fact the ILP was an inseparable part of the labour movement – the sharp tip.

Again and again they launched themselves, sometimes physically, at what they saw as the 'smug ruddy-faced legions; the hard faced men who have done well out of the war.' Here is a typical Commons debate – or brawl – of the early twenties as described by a Parliamentary sketch writer:

> Four Scottish Socialists suspended. Shouts of 'Murderers' flung viciously across a taut and almost alarmed House of Commons. More shouts of 'Dirty dogs', 'White livered cowards', and other angry epithets.

* University graduates elected 12 MPs. The University seats were abolished in 1949.

Fatty Arbuckle
A fine comedian and "bundle of good nature" whose career was ruined by the 'moral revulsion' of American film-goers.

Mary Pickford
She received thousands of letters a week, many of them offering cattle ranches or plantations if she would marry the writer.

Then processions through the lobbies as MPs voted for the temporary expulsion of the quartet of Labour men.

The supended four were:

Mr Maxton. He was imprisoned during the war for a seditious speech.

Mr Wheatley. A Glasgow book publisher and magistrate.

Mr Buchanan. A one-time messenger boy, and then an engineer.

The Rev Campbell Stephen. A minister of the United Free Church of Scotland who afterwards became a science master.

The cause of the rumpus was an economy cut in the estimates for Scottish social services. Maxton and Wheatley said that anyone who supported the cut was a murderer of children and they named a Tory MP, Sir Frederick Banbury as the principal murderer. They also cast doubt on the impartiality of the Chair.

James Maxton's flaring rage was explained by a story the following day, 29 June, 1923, in the *Express*:

Mr and Mrs Maxton lived in a slum. The husband was a teacher. They struggled for many months to keep the child alive. They had difficulty in obtaining suitable food for the child.

In the end their efforts were rewarded, and the child lived, but the months of incessant care took Mrs Maxton to an early grave. Mr Maxton ever since has fought for child welfare with an almost fanatic zeal. It is a pathetic story, which shows once more how personal affliction may warp a man's judgment and obsess his mind.

It is doubtful if Mr Maxton was as poor as this story makes out. He was a graduate of Glasgow University – where he was a Conservative – and as a teacher there was no need for him to live in a slum. He may have chosen to do so in order to identify himself as closely as possible with his future constituents. Doubtless he witnessed genuine hardship which aggravated his own sad experience. He remained a zealot until the end of his days (he died in 1946), increasingly alienated from his fellow Labour MPs on policy though always warmly admired personally by members on both sides of the House.

Passion was very much in evidence in the House at this period and not just of the class variety.

The headline on 16 December, 1927 proclaimed: 'Protestantism Saved.'

The reason for this exuberant quote from an MP was the Commons rejection of a new Prayer Book sponsored by the Archbishops of York and Canterbury, blessed by lay and church authorities alike and blasted out of the Chamber by impassioned speeches from comparatively minor back benchers who saw the spectre of Rome and conjured up the traditional fears which have never quite left the English since Elizabeth I's time.

Actually it was a Scotsman, Rosslyn Mitchell, a Labour solicitor, who did most to swing opinion away from change and against revision. Until his intervention it appeared certain that the measure would be accepted with a majority of at least 100. It was rejected by 42. The majority ranged from Winston Churchill to the Communist Mr Saklatvala. Party ties were snapped. Conscience was all.

The burden of the opponents' case was that the proposed alterations in the form of service would promote Roman Catholic dogma. The highlight was Mitchell's speech of fire:

A more stirring and impassioned outburst has rarely been heard in the four walls of Westminster. His neat figure seemed to vibrate with his own eloquence. The House hung on his voice as he raised it in denunciation or dropped it to trembling appeal. He seemed to re-create the presence of a John Knox.

His words hissed as he described with Presbyterian horror the observance of Mass – a belief that human materials of bread and wine could recreate in themselves the blood and flesh of the Saviour.

'That is transubstantiation,' he cried; 'that is the deciding line between the Church of Rome and the Church of England. If the Church of England thinks that' – there was a loathing accent on 'that' – 'let her have it and God be with her. But if she does not want it she cannot pass this book. With this one book you can swing over all the children of England from the Protestant faith.

'The Church of England cannot permanently endure if half Reformist and half Roman. If the Church so chooses, I, for one, convinced in my Protestantism, thanking God from my heart, can do nothing but vote against this Bill.'

He paused and dropped his voice to a whisper. 'I do not want to do it, but I can do no other. So help me God.'

He did not seem to sit down so much as to be swept from his feet with applause.

Following the vote Archbishop Davidson left the House in tears and resigned. The 'Good Old Cause' as the upholders of the Protestant

Morality: Old and New

Act of Settlement liked to view their beliefs had triumphed. Cranmer's Prayer Book endured.

Elsewhere entrenched prejudices were under attack. Folkestone Corporation was astounded at the public uproar when its Cemetery Committee proposed that graves in a new final resting place should be officially classified: first, second and third class. The proposal was withdrawn.

Public indignation was aroused in June 1932 when it was discovered that a sports special had been nigh wrecked, with windows shattered and pictures ripped from their frames. The 'special' was one taking 400 Eton boys to the cricket match against Winchester. The headmaster thrashed the culprits.

On 24 May, Empire Day, 1926, a formidable social barrier came tumbling down:

> Amateurs and professionals of the England cricket team against Australia will use the same dressing-rooms at Lord's during the second Test match, and will come on the playing field through the same central gate of the pavilion.
>
> So dies the old social distinction between 'gentlemen' and 'players'.
>
> Because of the constitution of the MCC there has always been a rigid line drawn between the amateur and professional cricketer. Lord's is the only ground where amateurs and professionals use a different gate in coming out to field or going in to bat. Other grounds use the one gate to the field, although the ordinary dressing-rooms are separate.

Any idea that the Americans were much less class conscious than the English was dissipated by the decision, in 1928, of the American Lawn Tennis Association to bar 'Big Bill' Tilden from their Davis Cup match against France for infringing his amateur status. He had written newspaper articles like a common journalist. The ban was withdrawn following furious French and American protests.

Despite the apparent break-up of the old order – a million acres of land were offered for sale in one week in 1924 as death duties killed off one great estate after another – old attitudes persisted. Some good; some not so good.

A little item in December 1925 highlighted the chivalry that lingered on:

> 'I did not see the vehicle coming. The driver is not to blame,' said

James Snow, forty-six, a warehouse packer who was knocked down and fatally injured by a royal mail van in Fore-street, City.

Mr Johnson, a solicitor, who represented the owners of the van at the inquest yesterday, commented on this speech as 'the very gallant act of a perfect Englishman'.

The coroner recorded a verdict of 'Accidental Death' and exonerated the van-driver from blame.

Respect for women could be occasionally carried rather far. Mr John de Lyon was fined £2 for annoying women in Hyde Park. His crime? He deliberately went into the Park in the evening to raise his hat to the ladies!

Gambling still provoked magistrates to stern outbursts. A Mr James Charles Vincent was fined £75 and his son £50 for circulating football pool coupons; the prosecutor remarking that 'betting on football is becoming the curse of the country . . . it is the prostitution of a noble sport.'

The demure game of whist roused the ire of one magistrate in August 1921:

> The Liverpool stipendiary magistrate had two hundred and forty people brought before him to-day in consequence of a dramatic police raid on a whist drive party.
>
> The drive was advertised to take place in a large public hall, and play had not started when the police rushed into the place and took all those present into custody.
>
> Many protested, and some tried to escape but the street entrances were guarded by uniformed men. Street traffic was held up while police vans came to the hall and removed the players.
>
> It was stated on behalf of the prosecution that there were from seventy to eighty tables for solo whist, and that the stakes varied from a few pence to sovereigns.
>
> Forty-four respectable women were pushed and crowded into prison vans, and several of them fainted.

Dislike of impudent foreigners prompted another magistrate, Mr Frederick Mead of Marlborough Street, to observe in 1929 of a Japanese in the dock: 'You have come to this country to work in competition with Englishmen. I consider this objectionable. I shall recommend your deportation. Next case.'

Of course colour may have had something to do with Mr Mead's strictures. Racial prejudice was strong, even though there were comparatively few coloured people in the UK in those days.

When Frank Wilson, an American Negro, came to London with his all black cast to play *Porgy* the hotel management required them to have their meals in the basement. That was in 1929. In the same year Paul Robeson, the negro singer, recounted his experience at a London hotel:

'A friend of mine, white and an Englishman, invited my wife and me to meet him at the grill room at midnight for a drink and a chat. On arriving, the waiter, who knows me, informed me that he was sorry but that he would not allow me to enter.

'Both my wife and I haved dined at the hotel and in the grill room many times. I sent for the manager, who informed me that I could not enter the grill room nor the dining-room, because I was a negro, and the management did not permit negroes to enter the rooms any longer.'*

Robeson's experience, and that of another black American artist Mr Abbott who was refused entry to 20 hotels, led to protest meetings. But the call for change was muted. The right of hotel owners to run their premises as they pleased was largely unquestioned. The old ways ruled. As they did in the High Court where the admonition 'Crime brings retribution' was absolute.

*

'I am determined that young ruffians like you shall know, and know in the only way they can feel, that we protect our citizens, especially our women. You will go to prison with hard labour for nine months and also receive 20 strokes of the cat.'

With such words in December 1922 the Recorder at the Old Bailey sentenced a 25-year-old miner, Roderick Davis, for assaulting an elderly woman shopkeeper with intent to rob her. Davis would be marked for life and those who knew about such matters – among them Percy Hoskins, crime reporter for the *Express* – reckoned that a man who had suffered the cat o'nine tails never risked it again. Sentences like this were being handed out regularly as the judiciary struggled to contain the post-war crime wave. By the end of 1923 Mr Justice McCardle, surveying the calendar of trials at Durham Assizes, was able to declare: 'It is a great solace to know that the tide of crime in this country is slowly but surely decreasing.'

---

* Rich American guests objected to the presence of coloured people.

Harsh treatment played no small part in deterring the miscreant, but it fell too, with vindictive force, on the pitiful as well as the criminal, the minor wrongdoers as well as the irredeemable villains. Here are three examples from 1925, 1931 and 1933:

A motorist jailed for speeding for one month in the 'second division' (lenient treatment) described his experience in a letter to the press:

> At Wandsworth I, a first offender and second divisioner, was taken to a department of the prison known as 'The Reception'. I sat in a corridor in a line of prisoners from other courts. After a long wait two convicts came along; one handed me a lump of preserved meat and a hunk of bread, the other handed me a pint of cocoa in a tin mug.
>
> I could not stand the sight of the food, and declined it – but it was not long neglected, as some of my fellow 'criminals' soon accepted it.
>
> Subsequently I found I had made a dreadful error – I had declined what is really a prison banquet. For this is the menu given to second division prisoners: Brek, a pint of tea, a plate of porridge, 8 ozs of bread; supper, bread 8 ozs, one pint of cocoa, $\frac{1}{2}$ oz margarine – including Christmas day.
>
> The only difference between this and penal servitude is that for the first fourteen days the latter are deprived of their morning tea and get only water.
>
> The prison routine is the same for all classes of prisoner. No privileges are allowed, no matter under what qualification you enter prison until you have served thirty days.

*

Mrs Catherine Cunningham, aged forty-three, mother of fourteen children, of Marsh-road, Middlesborough, was sentenced to three months' imprisonment by the stipendiary magistrate here on a charge of attempted suicide.

It was stated in court that Mrs Cunningham had tried to commit suicide by gas poisoning, and her plea was, 'There's no money coming in. I've tried to keep up appearances and keep the home tidy for the children. There are three county court summonses in and nothing but trouble.'

On being sentenced she collapsed in the dock and had to be carried to the cells.

*

A sentence of two months' hard labour was passed on a man who gave the wrong age of his dog.

The man sentenced was Samuel Thomas Lewis, aged thirty-five, of Eastgate, Aberystwyth.

Lewis was sentenced at the recent Carmarthenshire Assizes for making the false statement in a dog licence case.

It was pleaded in his defence that Lewis had a wife and five children, and was in poor circumstances.

The dog was six months old in December, and he thought it hard that he should have to take out a licence then and another in January.

'A great deal too much perjury is committed in these small matters,' said Mr Justice Goddard, passing sentence, 'and it is time that it is understood that people committing perjury on their own behalf are committing crime, just as much as if they were doing so when called as a witness for somebody else.'

It is understood that this was Lewis' first offence.

It would be quite wrong to assume that these cases were typical. They represented the law at its most abrasive and against this excessive sternness must be set the fact that London was the safest city in the world. In 1928, for instance, the capital had only 12 murders: and every guilty person was caught. Had public opinion polls then been in vogue, there can be small doubt they would have shown overwhelming support for retribution over redemption. The protection of innocent victims was rated far above the welfare of convicted felons.

Yet it was during the twenties that there occurred a case which crystallised the clash between the old morality and the new and, probably more than any other single event, influenced the campaign to abolish capital punishment.

The case concerned Frederick Edward Francis Bywaters and Edith Jessie Thompson. They were jointly charged with the wilful murder of Edith's husband, Percy Thompson, early on the morning of 4 October, 1922.

When the trial opened Edith Thompson was 28. Her lover, Frederick Bywaters, was 20. The prosecution alleged that while Bywaters wielded the dagger that stabbed Percy Thompson to death in Ilford, Essex, Edith Thompson was the dominating influence urging him on.

Bywaters did not deny killing Percy Thompson but pleaded 'Not Guilty' to wilful murder, claiming that he had wielded the knife in self-defence. Edith Thompson admitted that she was Bywater's lover and had long ceased to have affection for her husband but she utterly denied inciting Bywaters to murder him. What was not in dispute was that

Percy Thompson, while in the company of his wife, had died from multiple stab wounds shortly after midnight on 4 October as they were returning from a theatre show. Bywaters had inflicted the wounds because, he said, when he tried to persuade Thompson to release his wife, Thompson had lunged at him and in instant reaction to protect himself he had used the knife.

There was never much doubt that Bywaters was guilty of murder. The burden of the prosecution's case was that he and Edith Thompson had plotted the husband's death for many months and that the killing, far from being a spasm of emotion by the desperate and frustrated lover, was the culmination of joint planning.

'The jury,' declared Thomas Inskip, the Solicitor General, 'will have to consider whether the hand that struck the blow was moved to the crime by Mrs Thompson.' The gist of his argument that Edith Thompson's was the hand that moved the dagger was the bundle of letters she had written over a period of sixteen months to Bywaters.

These letters had been discovered in Bywaters' lodgings. They were damning.

Thus, on 26 November 1921, Mrs Thompson had written:

> I had the wrong porridge today, but I do not suppose it will matter. You will probably say I am careless but I do not care either way.

Wrong porridge? The curious phrase of one guilty lover to another is made clearer in a passage from a letter dated 9 February 1922, enclosing cuttings concerning the poisoning of a curate and ground glass being delivered in a box of chocolates to a university don. The letter declared: 'I suppose dear, it is not possible for you to send it to me. I do chafe at wasting time, darling.'

The next letter, in April, after merchant seaman Bywaters had sailed for the Middle East was more explicit:

> Don't keep this piece. I am not going to try any more until you come back. He was telling his mother the circumstances of my Sunday morning escapade, and he put great stress on the fact of the tea tasting bitter as if something had been put in it. Now I think whatever else I try at any time again will taste bitter. He will recognise it and be more suspicious still, and if the quantity is still not successful it will injure another chance I may have of trying when you come home. . . . He says to his people he fought and fought with himself to keep conscious. 'I will never die except naturally. I am like a cat with nine lives,' he said. He detailed to them an occasion when he was young and nearly suffocated by gas fumes. I wish we had not got electric

light. It would be easy. I am going to try the glass again occasionally when it is safe. I have an electric light globe this time.

She followed that with another saying: 'I used the light bulb three times; the first time he found a piece, so I have given it up until you come home.'

In June she wrote once more to her lover:

On Thursday he was on the ottoman at the foot of the bed and said he was dying, and wanted to — he had another heart attack through me. Darling, I had to laugh at this because I knew it could not be a heart attack. When he saw this had no effect on me, he got up and stormed, I said exactly what you told me to, and he replied that he knew that was what I wanted and he was not going to give it to me. It would make things far too easy for both of us, especially you.

Inskip thrust to the heart of the matter by showing how Edith Thompson's pleas to Bywaters to take her away from a life that had become impossible grew more and more clamorous until finally, after two tea-room meetings at the beginning of October, he acquiesed and Percy Thompson's fate was sealed.

Edith Thompson was defended by Sir Henry Curtis Bennett KC, an outstanding counsel of his day. Bennett's case was that Edith Thompson was a romantic dreamer who fantasised about killing her husband without ever intending to do any such thing. She read wildly melodramatic books, *Belladonna* and *The Fruitful Vine!* by Robert Hitchens, and conceived a grand passion complex which was played out on her letters to Bywaters. Her lover, knowing he had little chance and still deeply adoring, dovetailed his evidence with her case, repeatedly declaring that her talk of poisoning her husband was nonsense and that she had no knowledge of his attempt to browbeat Thompson into giving her up. Edith Thompson's father confirmed that his daughter often wrote absurd imaginings.

Mrs Thompson helped her counsel's argument by sometimes appearing almost to be living in another world. She would gaze lifelessly at the court, never glancing at Bywaters, leaning helplessly on two wardresses for support on leaving the dock. Then, all at once, the mood would change and she would spring to her feet and lean over the dock rail to consult her solicitor.

And while some passages of her writing were filled with passionate endearments and possibly with make-believe others were pungently straightforward and notably lacking in sentiment.

> Yesterday I met a woman who had lost three husbands in 11 years. Two were drowned and one committed suicide; and some people I know cannot lose one.

Was Edith Thompson play-acting to save her life? That in essence was what the jury had to decide. James Douglas, author and reporter, vividly drew the last scenes at the Old Bailey, two and a quarter hours after the jury had retired to consider its verdict:

> There is a stir in the court. Every eye is fixed on the jury doorway. One by one, very slowly and sadly, the members of the jury file in. They are all pale.
> The verdict of guilty can be discerned in their strained eyes and mournful features. The woman comes in last. She is white to the lips. As they sit down in their places they look inexpressibly grave and grieved.
> Bywaters appears. His face is blanched, but he walks steadily to the front of the dock and gazes steadfastly at the judge.
> Slowly up the stairs comes Edith Thompson, supported by the wardress nurses who have been ministering to her for five days. She totters rather than walks to the dock-edge. She is barely able to stand. Her features are chalk white and her eyes are glassy.

Following the verdict of guilty on both defendants:

> There is a dreadful stillness while the black cap is placed on the judge's head. It is awry and askew, and under it the ascetic features of the judge are as gray as his moustache. He says no word of his own. He does not trust his memory. The awful words of the sentence of death are before him, and he reads them in a low, grave, but clear voice that is charged with controlled emotion.
> The pale, worn woman collapses in her chair. Every eye is fixed on her as she seems to swoon in agony.

From that moment on all attention was fixed on Edith Thompson. No one believed she would hang – it was fifteen years since a woman had last been executed – but the days wore on to the appointed day, 9 January 1923, without any sign that the Home Secretary meant to reprieve her. Despite public agitation, Viscount Bridgeman, the Conservative Government's hard man, informed Mrs Thompson's solicitor on the 8th:

'The Home Secretary states that, after full consideration of all the representations made to him, he regrets that he finds no grounds for departing from his decision in the cases of F. E. Bywaters and Edith Thompson.'

While Bywaters met his end stoically – eating a fair breakfast of boiled fish, bread, butter and tea, wearing his navy blue suit and patent leather shoes and marching briskly from his cell to the scaffold – a harrowing tale was told of Edith Thompson:*

It is learned that Mrs Thompson was prostrate nearly all night and was continually under the doctor's care. At five o'clock she was unconscious, and when the hour for the execution arrived she was in a dazed state, only partially conscious, and unable to walk, so that she had to be carried. The doctor was in attendance almost up to the time of the execution. In moments of consciousness she asked for Bywaters.

All the women officials who have been engaged in watching Mrs Thompson have felt the strain acutely. Many of them declare they could never again carry out the duty imposed on them yesterday.

Shortly thereafter a campaign opened to abolish the death penalty. Liberal MPs were canvassed to support abolition and J. R. Davies, the Under-Secretary at the Home Office in the minority Labour Government of 1924, promised to do away with capital punishment (he didn't).

About this time the law was greatly eased towards the crime of infanticide. Emma Temple, a 19-year-old domestic servant, was the first to benefit. She killed her newly-born child, pleading she didn't know what she was doing. The Crown accepted the plea and Mr Justice Lush, sentencing her to a nominal four months in jail, remarked: 'This Act is a wise and humane piece of legislation . . . a fresh step in the improvement of the criminal law.'

But what was sympathetically granted to young girls mentally disturbed by giving birth (and it was a Conservative legislature that did this) was sternly denied to women who had plotted murder.

The significance of the Thompson-Bywaters case was that it polarised views, not simply on crime and punishment but in society.

Those who tended to make Edith Thompson a martyr to injustice also tended to equate leniency with fair play and decent behaviour.

* The rope had to be altered to deal with her inert body.

They felt Edith Thompson was a passion flower crushed by the insensitive forces of law and order. In no small measure they spoke for all who believed in the perefectability of human nature and the supremacy of soulful emotion. They would later become pacifists.

Those who supported Thompson's execution argued that the one to pity was the victim, her husband Percy. He had been done to death by his wife's evil plotting and, in a sense, her paramour Frederick Bywaters was another of her victims, for he had been ensnared and induced to commit murder on her behalf. Reason demanded that the full penalty of the law should be exacted lest others be tempted to follow in Edith Thompson's footsteps, relying on soft sentimentality to save them from retribution.

These two strands in the English character were in violent collision over a matter infinitely greater in scale and tragedy: Ireland.

CHAPTER FIFTEEN

A Distressful Land

Three Irishmen personified their country's anguished destiny between 1914 and 1934: Roger Casement, Michael Collins and Eamon De Valera. Of these only one, Michael Collins, was wholly Irish – and he was assassinated by fellow Irishmen. The paradox is Ireland's deepest tragedy.

Long before the 'Troubles' of the twenties, fear and hatred poisoned Anglo-Irish relations. Going back no further than Tudor times, Elizabethan England went in mortal terror of Irish support for Catholic Spain, at the crisis of the Armada. Protestant Parliamentarians roused the country to a panic at the prospect of Charles I raising an army of wild Catholic Irishmen to secure the throne for absolutism and the Stuarts. The extraordinary amalgam of religious zeal and racial bigotry brought forth two characteristic war cries from theCromellians as they brought Ireland to heel: 'Jesus Christ and no quarter.' 'To hell or Connaught' – the latter being the bleak westernmost province to which all Irish Catholics should be consigned.

When Britain staggered under the onslaught of revolutionary France, the Irish, true to the aphorism: 'England's misfortune is Ireland's opportunity,' rose in revolt. Thirty thousand died in that 'Year of Freedom', 1798. Two years later the local Dublin Parliament was abrogated, Ireland was absorbed into the United Kingdom, her colours were stitched into the Union Jack and the whole country became, in name, a part of Britain. *In name only,* for when Arthur Wellesley, later Duke of Wellington, toured the land he described it as 'enemy country'. Yet the Irish provided magnificent fighting material for Britain's Armies, as they continued to do for a century and a half.

Here was the dichotomy. While small political-cultural societies kept the flame of Irish revolution burning, the mass of the people remained apathetic, emigrated or joined the British Army! There was an additional complication. Protestant Scots and English farmers, workers and manufacturers had poured into Ulster, the northern part of the island, to build up farming, shipbuilding and the linen trade. The unsuccessful siege of Londonderry by the Catholic James II in 1689-90 had given the Protestants a victorious rallying cry and, memories being what they are in Ireland, one that echoed Protestant supremacy down the centuries. Actually religion had little to do with the struggle – the Pope congratulated the Protestant victor William of Orange – but myth maketh man. From the late seventeenth century on the Protestant North regarded itself as apart from the rest of Ireland and far closer to England and Scotland. Belfast looked to Glasgow as its big brother and viewed Dublin as a foreign city: fun to visit, but never 'Home'.

Tension between North and South reached breaking point a month or two before the outbreak of World War I when Germany supplied arms both to theNational Volunteers of the South – seeking separation from Britain – and the Ulster Unionists who vowed to remain forever part of the UK. The declaration of war on 4 August, 1914 alone prevented civil war, but the reckoning was merely postponed.

Initially the Irish nationalists in the Commons pledged themselves to a united front with the Conservatives, Liberals and Labour to struggle for Belgium, freedom and resistance to German militarism. Gradually, however, the fanatics in Southern Ireland banded together to outbid the Nationalists. Once more the old slogan was whispered: 'England's misfortune is Ireland's opportunity – yesterday Napoleon, today the Kaiser.'

Throughout 1915 and early 1916 conspiracy was afoot. The Germans were naturally interested in anything to embarrass and weaken England. Whether they knew exactly all the details of the Irish Republicans' plans to stage an uprising at Easter, they nonetheless released their most potent weapon, Sir Roger Casement, on Ireland a mere two days before the Rising.

On 23 April, 1916, the British public was astounded to read this Admiralty communique:

> During the period between pm 20 April and pm 21 April, an attempt to land arms and ammunition in Ireland was made by a vessel under the guise of a neutral merchant ship, but in reality a German auxiliary, in conjunction with a German submarine.

The auxiliary sank, and a number of prisoners were made, among whom was Sir Roger Casement.

There followed a description of Casement, naturally weighted heavily against one who gave succour to the King's foes:

> Sir Roger Casement, who is fifty-one, was a distinguished British public servant before he became a renegade. What turned him into a traitor can only be surmised. Sir Arthur Conan Doyle, who knew him well, suggests that his mind was affected by tropical hardships. At any rate, his pro-German sentiments existed long before the war.
>
> He was first in the service of the Niger Company: in 1898 he went to the Congo as Consul. He undertook special service at Capetown during the Boer War, but in 1901 he returned to the Congo and began the investigation which culminated in the publication of his famous 'red rubber' report.
>
> From the Congo he was transferred in 1905 to South America, and two years later he became Consul at Rio de Janeiro. He was appointed a special commissioner to investigate the Putumayo rubber atrocities, and his report, published in 1912, caused a wave of horror throughout the country.
>
> He was knighted on the occasion of the coronation in 1911, and retired in 1913 on a pension of £400 a year.
>
> Even before this time he had traitorous leanings. During the year in which he was knighted he wrote a series of articles for private publication, holding up Germany as the champion of Irish and European interests.
>
> On his retirement, although a Protestant, he threw himself into the National Volunteer movement.
>
> When war broke out he was endeavouring to convert American audiences to the plan of freeing Ireland by force.
>
> A chance, which he eagerly seized, came when a large number of captured Irish soldiers were assembled in Limburg Camp. He promised them Home Rule for Ireland, a German farm, a German wife, and 3s a day for life for each man, or a free passage to America after the war, with a grant of £20 and assured employment. Then he asked them to forswear their allegiance to King George and join the 'German Irish Brigade'.
>
> The men heard him in silence. At the close of his speech a great storm of hooting arose, followed by the singing of 'God Save the King'. His specious promises obtained exactly three recruits.

At his trial three weeks later his counsel, Serjeant Sullivan, parried the accusations of wounded exchanged Irish soldiers who had actually heard Casement call for volunteers by saying that they were to be recruited to fight for Ireland not for Germany. The whole Casement case, taking place as it did within days of the Easter rebellion, became inextricably mixed up with Irish nationalism so that – in Ireland at any rate – his undoubted treason to Britain was entirely forgotten.

In court, touches of a more chivalrous age were noted, such as Sir Roger bowing to the ladies of his acquaintance. Despite his knighthood and his counsel's oratory, however, nothing could save Casement from the hangman. With just a suggestion of acerbity the *Express* reported:

> Until a few years ago traitors were sentenced to be publicly hanged, drawn and quartered, but this extreme penalty has been moderated, and Casement will be hanged privately in a London prison.

Casement entered the pantheon of Irish 'martyrs' with his concluding address in which he slyly accused his accuser, the English Conservative Attorney-General F. E. Smith: 'He chose a path that he thought would lead him to the Woolsack (the Lord Chancellorship), I chose a path I knew must lead to the dock and events proved we were both right. . . . What I did was to ask Irishmen to fight for their rights. If I did wrong in making that appeal to Irishmen, by Irishmen I should be judged. They alone are competent to decide my guilt or innocence.'*

In its romantic defiance of England, Casement's last speech matched the Republican manifesto issued by the Irish rebels who had seized the General Post Office and other public buildings in Dublin and were desperately trying to get a country-wide revolution under way.

> 'Irishmen and Irishwomen: in the name of God and of the dead generations from which she receives her old traditions of nationhood, Ireland, through us, summons her children to her flag and strikes for her freedom.
>
> 'Having organised and trained her manhood through her secret revolutionary organisation, the Irish Republican Brotherhood, and

---

* Excerpts of Casement's diaries were leaked by the authorities. The press reported: It is common knowledge that Casement is a man with no sense of honour or decency. His diaries are the monument of a foul private life. He is a moral degenerate.

Casement was a homosexual. His remains were buried in the grounds of the jail and were returned to Ireland in 1965.

Gloria Swanson
As far back as 1925 Gloria Swanson was earning £500 a day or £4 for every second's work.

Thompson/Bywaters
Edith Thompson with her husband and lover, Frederick Bywaters, six years her junior. Was she a passion flower crushed by the insensitive forces of law and order — or did reason demand the death penalty?

A Distressful Land

through her open military organisations, the Irish Volunteers and the Irish Citizen Army; having patiently perfected her discipline, having resolutely waited for the right moment to reveal itself, she now seizes that moment, and supported by her exiled children in America and by gallant allies in Europe, but relying in the first place on her own strength, she strikes in full confidence of victory. We declare the right of the people of Ireland to the ownership of Ireland and to the unfettered control of Irish destinies to be sovereign and indefeasible.

'Signed on behalf of the Provisional Government:

'Thomas J. Clarke, Sean MacDiarmads, Thomas MacDonagh, J. H. Pearse, Eamonn Ceannt, James Connolly, Joseph Plunkett.'

Whether the rising was meant to coincide with Casement's landing is unclear. A car from Limerick containing two Sinn Fein members (Irish nationalist extremists) did crash into the sea near where Casement landed. Were they liaison officers? What does seem beyond argument was that the Dublin rising went off prematurely and was not co-ordinated with revolts in the South and West.

On Friday, 28 April, four days after the Rising had begun, a business man returned from Dublin, described the scene:

'A feature of the manoeuvring of the Sinn Feiners was their holding of roofs from which they fired on people below. I understand they obtained possession of roofs by knocking at the doors of houses, and when a servant or other person answered the knock, held a revolver to her head, and demanded to be conducted upstairs to the roof. There was no help for it and the roofs were gained.

'The insurgents entrenched themselves on St Stephen's Green. The celebrated Shelbourne Hotel looks down on the green. The manager of the hotel was soon informed by the Sinn Feiners that any one in uniform who entered or left the building would be shot.

'A man was in front of the hotel with a lorry. The Sinn Feiners said they wanted the vehicle, and the driver replied that he would not give it to them. They shot him dead.'

Even in the midst of blood and misery, comedy and humour intervened:

'When an armed squad of green-clad Sinn Feiners entered a Dublin hotel, and ordered everybody to clear out, one of the guests went to rouse a friend who was still between the blankets.

' "Get up, Jimmy," he said, "you have only five minutes to leave the hotel."

' "Who says so?" inquired the startled Jimmy.

' "I don't know who the deuce he is," was the reply, "but he had a gun."

' "In that case," said Jimmy, "I suppose I had better be going but do you think he would lend us the gun while we are paying the bill?" '

On 1 May, the rebels surrendered unconditionally. The rising had not spread like a fire; it died with barely a whimper. The people of Dublin, said a report, 'watched the rebel prisoners pass without any demonstration save that an old woman spat on them.' The prisoners numbered 1,000 or so. Fifty times that number of Southern Irishmen were fighting on the Western Front and Ulstermen of the 36th Division were shortly to give an immortal account of themselves on the Somme.

Many of the troops who suppressed the revolt under the command of General Sir John Maxwell were Catholic Irish and some were nationalists: this was especially so in Galway where the troops in barracks were largely locals. Their foes, armed with scythes, pikes and shotguns, were known to them. Happily there were few casualties: 1 policeman and 3 rebels out of an 'army' of 800.

Within twelve days of the outbreak Ireland was tranquil again. Then began the executions. One after another the men who signed the proclamation of independence were shot. Other ringleaders also fell. The number assigned as necessary to teach the fanatics a lesson — fortunately a handful — stopped short of one who was to play a very long part in Ireland's story: Eamon De Valera.

Born in New York of a Spanish father and Irish mother, De Valera was among the first to join the Irish Volunteers on its foundation in 1913. He was then thirty-one, older than most of his fellow recruits. A commandant in Dublin at the Easter Rising he was sentenced to death, but reprieved. It was thought at the time that American pressure had been brought to bear in Whitehall to spare his life. But it was common practice in the aftermath of the revolt to sentence rebel leaders to death and then commute the sentence to life imprisonment. 'Dev' was no different from scores of others. He was, however, fairly high-placed and was lucky that the execution quota was filled before his number came up.

Released in the general amnesty of June 1917, De Valera plunged back into revolutionary politics. He was elected Sinn Fein MP for East Clare, pledged to immediate and total independence for the whole of —

Ireland – including Ulster. This pen portrait of De Valera and his country comes from the *Express* of 12 November, 1917, reporting events at Waterford:

> The police and soldiers politely ignored Sinn Fein flags hanging here and there, and girls with pigtails did a good business in Sinn Fein buttonholes with persons returning from Mass.
>
> There were about a thousand persons gathered. Two or three hundred young men were drawn up in a double line. They were not mere boys, but young men who might well claim to represent Young Ireland. They were the local Volunteers.
>
> Mr De Valera came up escorted by a band playing 'God Save Ireland'. He was greeted with cheer after cheer and the indescribable Irish yell.
>
> I think it is about time English people understood that Mr De Valera is neither a wild impossibilist nor a masequerading Mexican charlatan. He is, so far as I can judge, a shrewd, honest, able and determined man, as anxious for a real enduring peace in Ireland as anyone and as Irish as Paddy's pig.
>
> He spoke first in fluent Irish. Then he spoke in English with a brogue you could cut with a knife. He seems a very masterful man, and if he is not the Parnell of to-day he is not far from it. Now that he is the leader of the Sinn Fein movement, I think he means to keep a firm grip and he will be a leader who leads. He will be difficult to unseat.
>
> Mr De Valera is a tall, thin man with a clean-shaven and slightly ascetic face. He has a sense of humour, and although he is not an orator he is a trenchant and telling speaker.

Mr Eamon De Valera may have sounded reasonable but he was, in truth, an irreconcilable who was prepared to bide his time but make no real concessions to the British.

The moment the Great War ended Sinn Fein displayed its strength. It made a virtually clean sweep of Southern Ireland in the December 1918 elections and when the Government in London showed no inclination to recognise Sinn Fein's right to represent Ireland in Dublin, not Westminster, the Feiners declared all-out rebellion.

A Parliament of the Irish Republic was opened in January 1919 in the Round Room of the Mansion House, officially the residence of Dublin's Lord Mayor. Only 29 MPs were present: the Northern MPs were Unionist and had no intention of recognising the Dublin Assembly, and a number of Sinn Fein MPs were in jail, for an armed uprising against British troops and police was already under way. One of the jailed MPs – held at Lincoln – was De Valera. He was not in prison for long.

His dramatic escape helped build him into a legend and to perpetuate his leadership. Even British readers were entranced by the romantic aspects of his get-away:

> One Sinn Feiner started work on a garden plot of which there were several near the prison. He attracted De Valera's attention one day by singing a Sinn Fein song in Irish, in which he told the leader of the attempt to be made to rescue him. The warders' suspicions were not aroused, because it was not uncommon for Irish workers to be about the prison.
>
> The sentries about the rear of the prison were a grave menace to the plans. The committee tried to find girls in the neighbourhood who could be employed to influence the guards, but they did not know any, so finally they telegraphed to Dublin for two handsome young women, both highly cultured university graduates, who dressed themselves as shop girls and crossed the Channel.
>
> These girls deliberately set out to flirt with the soldier guards, and soon came to know most of them. They diverted them from the gate through which De Valera escaped.

Once free, De Valera promptly assumed the Presidency of the 'Irish Republic' and waged unceasing war against the 'enemy'. It became a brutal, unrelenting struggle, horribly reminiscent of earlier and later conflicts.

Police and soldiers were gunned down. Terror provoked counter terror as the Government recruited ruthless auxiliaries, some of whom were known as the Black and Tans from their dark slouch hats and fawn raincoats.

The catalogue of horror ran like this:

19 March, 1920: Constable murdered on the quayside at Cork.

20 March, 1920: Alderman McCurtain, Lord Mayor of Cork and ardent Sinn Feiner, shot to death at his home in front of his wife.

18 April, 1920: 'We, the jury (composed of Irish nationalists) find that the late Alderman Thomas McCurtain, Lord Mayor of Cork, died from shock and haemorrhage caused by bullet wounds, and that he was wilfully murdered.

'And we return a verdict of wilful murder against David Lloyd

George, Prime Minister of England; Lord French, Lord Lieutenant of Ireland.

In the same month H. J. Greenwell, special correspondent of the *Sunday Express*, reported:

> *Dublin, Saturday night.*
>
> This time last week I was with the British Army of Occupation on the Rhine. To-day I am with the British Army of Occupation in Ireland.
>
> In Cologne, the Tommies mix freely with the people, and blue-eyed, fair-haired Gretchens do not disdain to walk and talk with the Tommies. But here it is a totally different pair of shoes. Tommies on pass walk alone or in twos or threes. They promenade through Grafton-street, glancing at the blue-eyed, dark-haired Eileens who pass them by and heed them not.

Irish jockeys who had failed to volunteer for the British Army during the war were forbidden to ride by the Jockey Club, and the National Hunt Committee. The Sinn Fein Government held their own courts and elected councillors in what was, in effect, a parallel state.

Premier Lloyd George, a one-time supporter of Irish Home Rule, a champion – as befitted a Welshman – of the rights of small nations, delivered himself of a stinging rebuke to Irish terrorists in a speech on 9 October, 1920:

> 'I think during the year 283 policemen have been shot in Ireland, 109 of them shot dead. Something like 100 soldiers, I think have been shot, and many more have been fired at.
>
> 'I think about sixty-seven court houses have been burned down, and there have been attacks on police barracks.
>
> 'The police endured this state of things. There is no doubt that, at last, their patience has given way and there has been some severe hitting back.
>
> 'Now that men attempt to escape and refuse to stop then undoubtedly the police fire. Can we complain of that? We must restore order there by methods, however stern.
>
> 'We know how Ireland assisted the German submarine campaign. We can never agree to Ireland being given such an opportunity again, while we should trust to luck in our next war.
>
> 'I am taking no risks for the future. Ireland cannot be trusted with self-independence.'

Then there followed a hideous succession of events.

31 October: Terence McSwiney, who had followed his fellow Sinn Feiner MacCurtain as Mayor of Cork starved himself to death in prison in protest against the British occupation. His funeral further inflamed feeling.

1 November: Kevin Barry, 19, was executed for his part in the murder of three soldiers. The Irish pleaded for his life on the grounds of age. It was pointed out that one of the troopers who had died was 19. A patriot song was composed about Barry's hanging.

On the same day six policemen were murdered in different parts of Ireland.

21 November: morning: Fourteen military and legal officers in charge of courts martial murdered in their beds by armed gangs.

21 November: afternoon: Troops fire on Sinn Fein crowds attending a football match between Dublin and Tipperary.

10 December: Sixteen auxiliary cadets massacred by Irish rebels posing as British soldiers.

11 December: Viscount French, Governor-General, places most of Southern Ireland under martial law.

Although tentative suggestions for a truce came from No 10 Downing Street to Arthur Griffith, acting President of the 'Irish Republic' in the absence of De Valera who was raising funds among the Irish in America, the killings went on.

Two typical examples, one from each side: 7 April, 1921:

> One of the most cold-blooded crimes of the reign of terror in Ireland was enacted at Limerick in the early hours of the morning when Alderman Clancy, the Sinn Fein mayor and Mr O'Callaghan were killed.
>
> At a quarter past one o'clock this morning a knock was heard at Mr O'Callaghan's door, and he and his wife came downstairs. They asked who was there, and a voice outside replied it was a search party. 'Are there officers?' asked Mr O'Callaghan, and the reply was, 'Yes, two officers.'
>
> Mrs O'Callaghan then opened the door, and two men in civilian attire entered. One wore smoked goggles and the other clear goggles. Mrs O'Callaghan went to her husband's assistance, and was thrown down in the hall, and the men then poured a volley of shots into Mr O'Callaghan, who died within a quarter of an hour.
>
> The men appear to have walked straight to the house of the mayor. When the door was opened and the men stepped into the

hall, Mrs Clancy became suspicious and struggled with them. A shot was fired and she fell wounded. The men then turned on the mayor and riddled him with bullets. He died within an hour.

April 14, 1921 :

Sir Arthur Vicars, who was Ulster King of Arms at the time of the disappearance of the Irish Crown Jewels, was assassinated early today in the grounds of his home, Kilmorna House, Listowel, Co. Kerry.

Thirty men attacked his house, and dragged him from his bed in his dressing gown. Several shots were fired at him as he was brought to the front door, and a label was tied round his neck bearing the words :
Spy. Informers Beware
IRA Never Forgets

The assassins then set fire to the house, which, with its contents, was completely destroyed.

An event which may be connected with the present tragedy occurred in May 1920. Sir Arthur Vicars' residence was raided by about a hundred men in search of arms. Sir Arthur boldly faced the rebel raiders and refused to give up the key of the strong-room where the arms were stored.

The men levelled double-barrelled guns at him and asked if he was ready to die, to which he replied : 'Yes, a great deal better than you.' The men's courage failed and they gave up the raid.

By the summer of 1921 the security forces were gaining the upper hand. In a single day six convicted members of the IRA were executed in Mountjoy Prison under the Restoration of Order Act.

The guerrilla war had exacted a fearful toll of Ireland spiritually and materially and had only been sustained by the zeal of the core leadership of the Irish volunteers and the organising genius of one man : Michael Collins.

Collins, a mere twenty-six at the Easter Rising, youngest child of a poor farming family, wholly lacking the education of De Valera, advanced rapidly to command the rebels' military forces and be their chief fund raiser in Ireland.

He was the Robin Hood of the movement. His intelligence service was uncanny, penetrating even the most secret meetings of the British

Headquarters in Dublin Castle. He melted into thin air – a considerable feat as he was six foot, broadly built and known as 'The Big Fella' – whenever security forces thought they had him. Frequently it was assumed he was dead, for months would pass without sight or sound of him. Then suddenly he would strike at the point where he was least expected. He explained his ability to elude capture thus: 'I always watch for the fellow instead of letting him watch me. I make a point of keeping the other fellow on the run, instead of being on the run myself.'

Collins performed miracles of improvisation in smuggling arms from abroad, and stealing them from the troops and constabulary, but he realised in mid-1921 that Sinn Fein was losing the struggle. At this decisive psychological moment King George V, who was opening the loyalist Parliament in Belfast, resolved to try to break the deadlock as he had done once before over Ireland in 1914. Addressing the first session of Northern Ireland's separate assembly, Stormont, he declared:

'I appeal to all Irishmen to pause, to stretch out the hand of forbearance and conciliation, to forgive and forget, and join in making for the land which they love a new era of peace, contentment and good will.'

Several days before he was reported to have had the following exchange with Lloyd George:

King George: 'Are you going to shoot all the people in Ireland.'
'No, your Majesty,' the Premier replied.
'Well, then,' said King George, 'you must come to some agreement with them. This thing cannot go on. I cannot have my people killed in this manner.'

The King's private promptings and public appeal led the Prime Minister to address an invitation to Eamon De Valera, President of the illegal Dail Eireann (the Republican Parliament of the South) to talk about ending the strife.

Now came the fatal division. De Valera replied:

'We most earnestly desire to help in bringing about a lasting peace between the peoples of these two islands, but see no avenue by which it can be reached if you deny Ireland's essential unity and set aside the principle of national self-government.'

In effect, De Valera was dissociating himself from any agreement about future Home Rule for Ireland which excluded the Protestant North. He was prepared only to consult with the Belfast administration on how the Protestant interests could best be protected, *within the framework of a single Irish nation*. The Northern leaders, Sir James Craig, Lord Middleton and the formidable Edward Carson, would have none of it. They would hear no talk of a united Ireland. They wanted a united British Isles and if they couldn't have that they intended to keep the six counties of Ulster, where there was a large Protestant majority, part and parcel of the United Kingdom.

Months of negotiation followed the Lloyd George invitation on 11 July, 1921. Finally a conference was arranged and the Dail elected five delegates, including Arthur Griffith and Michael Collins to attend a conference in London 'with a view to ascertaining how the association of Ireland with the community of nations known as the British Commonwealth may best be reconciled with Irish national aspirations'.

For the first time the green, white and orange flag of Sinn Fein flew legally in the capital of the Empire against which the Sinn Feiners had fought. But this outward and visible sign of a spirit of reconciliation gave too sanguine an impression of the bitter arguments which raged between the British and Irish delegates and within the Irish delegation itself. Just how close to shipwreck the talks were was disclosed by one of the Irish party, Robert Barton:

> 'The Downing-street negotiations had broken down on the Sunday and the outlook was black indeed. Then contact was re-established, and in the struggle that ensued Mr Griffith tried repeatedly to have the alternative, which was war, referred to Dail Eireann. Mr Lloyd George directly negatived this proposal. He claimed that we were plenipotentiaries, and that we must either accept or reject. The signature of every delegate was necessary, or war would follow immediately.
>
> 'Mr Lloyd George gave us until ten o'clock to make up our minds. It was then about 8.30 and we returned to our rooms to discuss the situation. Mr Gavan Duffy and I were for refusal, war or no war, but an answer which was not unanimous committed us to immediate war, and the responsibility for that war would rest directly on the two delegates who refused to sign.
>
> 'For myself I preferred war but for the nation without consultation I dare not accept that responsibility. I signed.'

The treaty that was signed on 6 December, 1921, fell a long, long way short of the dearest hopes of the irreconcilables. An Irish Free State was created with its own Parliament and executive wholly on par with the dominions of Canada, Australia, New Zealand and South Africa. British troops were to be withdrawn immediately. But responsibility for Irish naval defence would rest, for some years anyway, with Britain; essential Irish ports would remain open to the Royal Navy; Irish MPs would take the oath of allegiance to King George V and, above all, Ulster could choose to remain wholly separate from the Free State and part of the UK – which she duly did.

When the treaty came up for ratification in the Dublin Dail, the two men who would seal its fate stood face to face: Eamon De Valera, the lined, ascetic academic who had spent most of the time of Ireland's anguish in America, urging outright rejection, and Michael Collins, the tall, broad-shouldered, cheerful, self-educated soldier who had spent all the time fighting the English in Ireland, advocating acceptance. The irreconcilable versus the reconcilable; the political purist against the practical soldier.

'I cannot do anything that would make the Irish people hang their heads. . . . I would rather see the same thing [war] all over again,' cried De Valera.

'We did not go to London to dictate terms to a vanquished foe. We knew we had not vanquished the foe. He did not come to us to sue for peace,' retorted Collins and counselled: 'The treaty has not secured ultimate freedom, but it has secured freedom to achieve it.'*

Collins won the day. But it was a short-lived triumph. The irreconcilables, defeated in the debating chamber and at the polls, took to armed insurrection and formed a new kind of Irish Republican Army, one dedicated to killing fellow Irishmen. A violent and bloody civil war ensued.

Eamon De Valera, Rory O'Connor, Liam Mellowes and Erskine Childers led the battle for the irreconcilables. Collins crushed them in Dublin and was clearly winning in the rest of the country when, on 23 August, 1922:

> Michael Collins fought his last fight a few miles from his native village of Clonakilty, Co. Cork, and died, rifle in hand, facing foes who were once his schoolmates.

---

* Collins had a premonition of what lay in store. 'I have signed my own death warrant,' he remarked as he appended his signature to the treaty.

He and his escort were trapped on a lonely road which winds its way through a desolate mountain country. Rebels who had received word of his approach lay in wait for hours.

A single shot rang out. Collins, although mortally wounded, continued to fire his rifle while lying on the road.

He suddenly asked for Major-General Dalton, who, with General Sean O'Connell, ran to his side. They whispered a few prayers and recited the Act of Contrition as General Collins died. His last words were: 'No reprisals, boys! Forgive them!'

Ireland was stunned by Collins' death. Their beloved 'Mick', the Big Fella, had been about to marry Kitty Kiernan of Co. Longford, who, in his Robin Hood Days, had once walked six miles in pouring rain to warn him of the approach of British troops.

Tim Healy, a fellow Irish nationalist, revealed on the morrow of Collins' death that De Valera had urged that he, Collins, and not De Valera, the President of the Provisional Irish Government, should go as a plenipotentiary to London to negotiate peace – and so bring on himself the odium of compromise; a compromise which had finally brought Collins to ambush and death at the hands of De Valera's insurgents. By a strange quirk of fortune it was Michael Collins who had organised the escape of Eamon De Valera from Lincoln gaol!

A fearful vengeance now supervened. One after another the Free State executed the leaders and followers of the revolt. On a single day eleven. One of the most dramatic executions was that of Erskine Childers, a renegade Englishman, son of a British Cabinet Minister, secret agent for Whitehall, author of *The Riddle of the Sands* – and, according to Collins, Ireland's evil genius. Two weeks later, in reprisal for the killing of a Free State MP four IRA chiefs, including Rory O'Connor and Liam Mellowes, were shot by firing squad.

Lives had also been claimed in the UK. Field-Marshal Sir Henry Wilson, former head of British military intelligence and a leading figure in the Ulster Unionist movement, was shot dead in front of his home at 36 Eaton Place. His assassins were caught and hanged.

Journalists were just as likely to die in this civil war as partisans of the warring factions. Robert Henrey, a veteran reporter of Ireland's troubles, recorded:

> Five ruthless looking men in ragged coats and leather leggings approached me. A shining little revolver was held a few inches from

my forehead, and I was ordered to put up my hands. I did so, and was thoroughly searched.

They escorted me at the point of their revolvers to the court house, past the sentries and through a large dimly-lit hall into a room where a fire was trying to burn brightly.

'You will see that we always treat our prisoners well,' said one of my captors.

I was told that my message to my newspaper would soon be brought, and I should be judged thereon. If it took up the case of the IRA, well and good.

'And if not?' I asked.

'Then you will be shot,' was the reply. Conversation lagged after that.

Henrey's message was considered reasonable. He was freed.

After another year of bloodshed, the policy of the Free State Government 'to meet terror with terror until it is crushed' finally prevailed.

An *Express* report ushered in 1924 with the words: 'Straight, stern Government has worked a wonderful change in the Irish Free State. The gunmen have put their guns away and gone back to work.'

Not quite. Three years later Kevin O'Higgins, the man who donned the mantle of Michael Collins to conduct the struggle against the insurgents, was shot dead on his way to mass. The shadow of the gunman still lay over the Emerald Isle.

As for Mr De Valera, he disappeared for a while, to emerge as the leader of the Opposition Fianna Fail party which denounced the Treaty but disclaimed violence. He won the election of 1932 and a few years later took Southern Ireland out of the Commonwealth and proclaimed a Republic under the green, white and orange tricolour.

CHAPTER SIXTEEN

India and Israel: Seeds of Conflict

Six thousand miles away another banner with the green, white and orange (the colours of the Congress Party) was being raised against the British: India was in ferment; or rather parts of India were displaying a reluctance to accept the British as the God-given rulers for aye. In the Indian tradition this rejection took the form of protests and riots. At almost exactly the same moment that Ireland erupted – the spring of 1919 – India experienced her most horrific civilian slaughter since the Mutiny of 1857. Before dealing with the episode that marks the beginning of the decline of British dominion it is necessary to look at how Britain bore sway over India.

Britain's vast Indian Empire, comprising upwards of 300 million souls was controlled by a comparative handful of European public servants, a British-officered Indian Army and a purely British force composed of the overseas battalions of British regiments who served on a rota basis. Like Rome, Britain governed indirectly: using local rulers in the princely states, which formed about one-third of the sub-continent and even where the Viceroy's writ ran directly, carefully refraining from interfering with religious dogma – so much at the heart of Hindu and Moslem life.

Since the Mutiny, the British had had little trouble. The Indian masses acquiesced in the Raj and probably greatly preferred it to the corruption and petty tyranny of domestic overlords.

Yet the nationalist fervour which had catapulted Europe into war could not be confined within that continent. It spilled over into India: carried first by Sikh emigrés returning from America to India in 1914 so as not to be cut off from their relatives by war and given immense, unfathomable, influence by the arrival of Mohandas Gandhi, lawyer and civil rights campaigner, from South Africa in 1915. This tiny wisp of a man – prophet, great soul, 'naked fakir' (to use Churchill's description) held an exceptional aura. In a land devoted to holy men, Gandhi was a holy one with a difference. He had political nous as well. He could always plead innocence when he was discovered in what less saintly beings would call double dealing.

Nonetheless Gandhi represented the quintessence of Hindu India. He was of this world and yet not of it. He wanted to return to a simple, homelier past based on the village and rural industry, which was why he carried a spinning wheel wherever he went, both as a symbol and a way of life for himself. He was as much opposed to the industrialization of India as to the British Raj: a fact which was later to put him at odds with his principal allies Nehru and Patel who were devout partisans of industrialisation.

Indeed in 1915 Gandhi was not politically opposed to the British. He had championed his fellow countrymen in race-conscious South Africa, but he blamed the Boers not the British for race bigotry and he stoutly favoured the British war effort.

The British Empire was neither brutal nor oppressive. It gave peace, order, dignity and justice to one-quarter of the globe.* The Englishman may have lacked imagination, his memsahib may have revelled in her husband's lordly estate and sometimes been a bit beastly to the servants (though a great deal less beastly than equally favoured Indians to those placed under them) but, by and large, the British believed their mission to be beneficial and totally necessary. Most Indians agreed with them. The upper caste Hindus and the better-off Moslems longed to be more English than the English. They copied the customs of their conquerors: afternoon tea, cricket, polo (the idea was Indian, the practical rules governing the game were wholly British), polite debates, 'fair play' and eventually the socialism of the London School of Economics. The Anglo-Indian Congress, from which emerged the nationalist All-India Congress, was established to bring Indians and Britons together so that the former could learn about government from the latter. Even if one disliked individual Britons, the British Empire was such a massive, majestic fact that one might as well rail against the weather as against the Empire.

Its scope may be gauged from the *Express* description of the Wembley Empire Exhibition:

* In the thirty years following the end of Empire there were ten wars between territories, races and creeds who had worked peacefully under the benign folds of the Union Jack.

India and Israel: Seeds of Conflict 223

Imagine the paradox of a vast miniature.

Even then you will only begin to have an inkling of the wonder and impressiveness of what is phlegmatically called the 'Overseas Section' of the British Empire Exhibition.

One passes from the astounding virility of Canada and Australia to the mud walls of West Africa, along to the rioting colour and romance of India, across to the Mandalay Road, and to the tinkling bells and dim-lit mysticism of Burma, back a few yards and up Union approach to see the wonders of South Africa, so on through the wonders of New Zealand, Newfoundland, Ceylon, Hong Kong and Malaya.

It seems like a fairyland journey, along which is displayed unassessable mineral wealth, jewels, and precious possessions of rare kinds, the fruits of the earth in an almost unimaginable abundance.

That the British presence in India was necessary to the welfare of the peoples may be measured by this item, chosen at random and published on 6 February 1925:

The prevalence of human sacrifices among the Naga hill tribes on the frontier of Assam has now caused the British Government to intervene.

The Naga chiefs, however, during a conference with the Governor, Sir J. H. Kerr, refused to promise that the sacrifices would cease.

The Governor replied that such sacrifices could no longer be tolerated and that slaves must be freed. A British officer will report annually.

The Empire's long reach to seize those who attacked its servants is attested by this news report from December 1927:

A punitive force is moving out from Khartoum to avenge the double murder by tribesmen of Sudan District Officer Captain V. H. Ferguson, OBE, and Mr Andres Paniatopoulous, a Greek trader.

Captain Ferguson was killed while attempting to restore cattle stolen from the Dinkas by the Nuong tribe of Nuers, near Lake Jor, in the Bahr-el-Ghazel province of Southern Sudan.

Gandhi, the realist, was acutely aware that in the matter of humanising Hinduism, the British were light years ahead of his fellow countrymen whose lives were ruled by the most rigid caste system, fossilised traditions and bewildering religiosity. As a visionary, Gandhi wanted India purified and that naturally meant eventually getting rid of the intruding British. But his prayer as he returned to his native soil in 1915 might well have been: 'Not yet, oh Lord, not yet.'

What then caused him to change so radically and so rapidly? That event which changed so much else: The Great War.

To mobilise India for war, the British chopped away civil rights which Indian writers, thinkers, politicians had long enjoyed. This authoritarianism appeared at odds with the Allies' proclaimed aim to be fighting for liberty, democracy and individual freedom. If Belgian independence was worth plunging the Empire into war to defend, what about Indian independence? Gandhi, by 1918 a highly-esteemed barrister, had raised an ambulance unit, had made recruiting speeches for the Indian Army and been awarded medals for his endeavours. Was loyal India to be denied the fruits of freedom's struggle?

Of course it was not nearly as simple as that. Without a strong hand India could break out in bitter communal strife.* Gandhi was a pacifist; some of the members of his Gujerati race were Jains who carefully swept insects out of their way to avoid treading on them; but millions of other Indians were anything but pacific and protest demonstrations could easily degenerate into 'goonda raj' -mob rule. Fearing just this, the British passed in 1919 a law to embalm wartime restrictions in peacetime India. At this Gandhi and the Congress Party which was now the instrument of Indian nationalism rebelled. Days of mourning and silence were proclaimed. At a place called the Julianwalla Bagh in the Punjab city of Amritsar the mourning became real.

The Punjab, directly ruled by a British governor responsible to the Viceroy who, in turn was accountable to the India Office and Parliament in London, was the most volatile of the provinces of British India. Split roughly half and half between Muslims and Hindus it was also the home of the warlike Sikh people. In 1919 all kinds of crazy rumours were sweeping India: 'The Sahibs are going to abolish the caste system' (anathema to the Hindu); 'The British are going to give the police the right to search private homes' (invasion of women's quarters and therefore anathema to the Moslems.) Add a touch of Communist subversion and the memory of the Indian mutiny that still haunted British Imperial administrators and the powder trail was laid.

It was set alight on 10 April 1919, when, following the murder

* After the British quit India in 1947 Hindus and Moslems massacred each other on a colossal scale: 450,000 died: one million were wounded; five million rendered homeless.

of five Europeans and the rape of an English missionary, the local military commander at Amritsar, General Dyer, forbade a protest demonstration on a large piece of waste ground with few narrow exits – the Jullianwalla Bagh. The meeting went ahead in defiance of Dyer. Fifty troopers were ordered to disperse the crowd – and fired. They fired in all 650 rounds and killed or wounded 1,516 people. From then on the London establishment increasingly distanced itself from its military and civil agents in India. General Dyer was court-martialled and retired on half-pay. His supporters among the British community in India however raised £26,000 for his retirement and the guardians of the Golden Temple (Sikhdom's holiest of holies) made Dyer an honorary Sikh. Why? Because they held – as did most Anglo-Indians – that Dyer had, by one ruthless blast, saved the Punjab from a blood bath, from the terrible, unrestrained, mayhem of religious disorder and mob rule. This view was not shared by India's political masters in Westminster and was violently repudiated by many Indians who had previously accepted the Raj.

Sir Rabinranath Tagore (he gave Gandhi the title *Mahatma*, Great Soul), India's leading poet and a knight of the Indian Empire, asked to be relieved of his knighthood. He wrote to the Viceroy on 3 June:

> Knowing that our appeals have been in vain, and that the passion of vengeance is blinding the noble vision to statesmanship in our Government, which could so easily afford to be magnanimous – as befitting its physical strength and moral tradition – the very least I can do for my country is to take all the consequences upon myself in giving voice to the protest of millions of my countrymen who have been surprised into dumb anguish and terror.
>
> The time has come when badges of honour make our shame glaring in their incongruous context of humiliation, and I, for my part, wish to stand shorn of all special distinctions by the side of those of my countrymen who, for their so-called insignificance, are liable to suffer degradation not fit for human beings.

The 'degradation' he referred to included Dyer's order that all natives passing the spot where the English woman missionary had been raped should crawl on their bellies. Another method of cowering the mob was to seize the ringleaders and whip them in front of their comrades. Short, sharp, public punishment was reckoned to be the best deterrent – according to the security forces in Delhi. In the eyes of London it was no longer acceptable to treat the Indians in this fashion and a committee of inquiry under Lord Hunter reported accordingly.

Mahatma Gandhi reacted to Amritsar with uncharacteristic venom.

He pronounced, firstly, a boycott of everything British: food, textile manufactures, courts, schools, police and secondly a civil disobedience campaign, unavoidably involving violence 'as the only assurance we have of beating them'. Uproar, riot and bloodshed ensued.

From the *Express* of 7 February 1922:

A grave statement was issued by the India Office yesterday. Outbreaks in which Mr Gandhi's illegal volunteers played the principal part occurred at two points in the United Provinces during the week-end.

At Chauri Chaura a mob attacked the police office, and killed seventeen sub-inspectors and constables, whose bodies were stripped and burned.

Gandhist agents are causing trouble at Cawnpore and Agra, where a railway strike is in force.

Appalled at the consequences of his thoughtless campaign, Gandhi called off his crusade and surrendered himself to the courts:

Bombay, March 1922

'I consider the sentence as light as any judge could have inflicted.' – Gandhi, the Indian agitator.

The news of the sentence of six years' imprisonment passed on Gandhi has been received quietly throughout the country, and in some districts with apathy by the extremists. His admissions in court have made a great impression, and appreciation of the fairness of the trial has gone far to remove any feeling of resentment.

Gandhi, until his removal to gaol, maintained an attitude of restraint and characteristic modesty. Sobbing men and women gathered round him after the sentence had been passed, but he smilingly reassured his followers.

It is understood that instructions have been issued for Gandhi to be treated with every possible consideration.

He was released three years later and retired, chastened, to meditate in his house at Ahmedabad on the non-violent future of his crusade to bring India back to first principles and away from westernism. There he was joined by a new disciple, Miss Madeleine Slade, daughter of British Admiral Sir Edmond Slade. On 29 November 1925 the press picked up this vignette which summed up Gandhi's quirky personality:

The new convert is living in Mr Gandhi's household studying Indian conditions, and when one of Mr Gandhi's followers took advantage of her presence to ask for lessons in French he was taken severely to task by Mr Gandhi, who said:

'Miss Slade's sacrifice for the cause is greater than ours. She is here to learn and give all her time to the service of our people. Nothing which happens in her home will swerve her from her task here. French is a luxury. Miss Slade must not waste time in teaching and you must not waste time in learning it.'

Mr Gandhi has ordered that his follower, instead of receiving French lessons, should give Miss Slade lessons in Hindustani and Sanskrit. His parting words were: 'You may read as much French as you like after India obtains *Swaraj* (Home Rule) but till then none.'

While Gandhi pondered, Imperial Britain saluted the completion of magnificent New Delhi:

The New Delhi was born today, when Lord Irwin, the Viceroy, opened with a golden key India's magnificent new Parliament Buildings, which are to house the Chamber of Princes, the Council of State and the Legislative Assembly.

Guns thundered a salute, and a maelstrom of humanity gaped open-mouthed as the Viceroy rode towards the Parliament building in a carriage drawn by six magnificent horses.

Banners and pennons fluttered above, and facing the gathering was the great circular building, six hundred feet in diameter, which forms the heart of still another new Delhi, destined to be the greatest of all, and perhaps the heart of a new India.

It is surrounded by cool grass lawns and shady trees.

Lord and Lady Irwin were seated during the ceremony on thrones of solid gold.

Every phase of life which finds expression in India's Legislature was represented here.

The Maharajah of Patiala was six foot three of glistening gems surmounted by an enormous turban in which shone a cluster of some of the finest diamonds in the world.

A Swarajist (Gandhi-ist) leader a few yards away was dressed simply in white at a cost of probably a few shillings.

Some of the hereditary princes, through whom Britain controlled one third of India, were described in a later despatch:

> Most striking of the figures is the Maharajah of Kashmir, ruler of over 84,000 square miles and reputed to be one of the richest men in the world.
>
> One of his official titles is 'Shield of the British Empire,' granted to his House because he defends three of India's frontiers – the Chinese, Russian and Tibetan. He is one of the five princes of India entitled to a permanent sovereign's salute of twenty-one guns.
>
> The Maharajah of Kapurthala is India's greatest traveller, and is famed for his elegance and luxury. His palace at Karpurthala is an exact model of the Palace of Versailles.
>
> The Gaekwar of Baroda possesses a jewelled carpet worth more than a million pounds; he has a carriage built of solid silver, while his diamond necklace alone is said to be worth £200,000.
>
> The most popular and best known to the British public is the famous cricketer, the Jam Sahib of Nawanager, 'Ranji', as he was popularly known in his great days on the cricket field, while another great sportsman is the young Nawab of Bhopal who has the reputation of being the finest polo player in India.

It was however the man in the simple white cloth 'costing a few shillings' who was the most significant figure at the New Delhi gathering. For he and politicians like him were to inherit the splendid glittering buildings. As the crowds gaped in awe at Sir Edwin Lutyens' hymn to Imperial glory, as 80,000 people gathered in Hyde Park that year of 1927 to commemorate Empire Day, 24 May, by singing 'Land of Hope and Glory', as Sir Mitchell-Thomson, the Conservatives' Postmaster General warned socialist leaders who campaigned against British military ventures: 'They will end up with their backs to the wall and a firing party in front of them' India was moving irreversibly towards fully representative government, Dominion status and, eventually, independence.

Mr Gandhi, emerging from his isolation, found he had to keep up with successive governments in London now bent on shedding responsibilities and making the Indians responsible for their own affairs. He promoted the use of homegrown *khadi* and people wearing clothes imported from England were liable to have their hats knocked off. He led a passel of followers to a seaside village where they ceremoniously filled pots with sea water, left them to dry in the sun and then passed around the salt – as a display of defiance against the revenue-raising salt laws. He protested against the despatch of 1,000 Marines to protect British lives and property in Shanghai, pointing out that the British might as well proclaim sovereignty over China, so great was their economic control!

Yet, for all this posturing, Gandhi was falling behind events. In January 1931 the British Prime Minister, Ramsay MacDonald, told the Round Table Conference of British and Indian statesmen: 'Britain accepts the scheme for an all-India federation which will be self-governing with control of defence, foreign affairs and minorities remaining with the Viceroy.'

To outbid this declartion Gandhi launched another civil disobedience campaign. Violent scenes of the early period were repeated. The authorities struck back. On 4 January 1932 Gandhi was arrested. The wily mystic was paradoxical to the last:

> One of Gandhi's last acts in preparing for his departure was to purchase two watches for presentation of the two Scotland Yard detectives, Sergeant William Evans and Sergeant William Rogers, who were his bodyguard in England at the recent Round Table Conference, and, in an address to his training camp followers he said:
> 'The fight is imminent. Endure its hardships. Welcome bullets. In your hands rests the honour of India.'

In reply British India showed the flag:

> The Union Jack is fluttering in the breeze from the flagstaffs of public buildings, and is being borne through the streets by marching troops, honoured by martial music.
> Sailors and marines, with a naval gun, were landed at Chittagong to-day from the flagship Effingham.
> They were joined by Gurkha and Mahratta troops and armed police, and marched through the town with a band playing, bearing the Union Jack.
> The imposing display was quietly watched by thousands of Indians.
> The King's Own Scottish Borderers are to carry the Union Jack through the Sholapur district. A battalion set out for there from Poona today.
> At Patna police raided the Congress headquarters, arrested all

revolutionaries, struck the Congress flag, and hoisted the Union Jack over the building.

The same procedure is going on elsewhere in India.

'Civil disobedience,' declared Mr Edward Villiars, President of the European Association of India, 'must entail civil disability.' That was exactly what happened. The subversive campaign gradually came to a close and India moved steadily towards Home Rule.

Showing the flag was a brave echo from the past. The terrible shadow of the future was contained in a small two paragraph item, dated April 29, 1929:

> Two serious riots, in which two persons were killed and sixteen injured, were provoked in Bombay last night, the first by a Hindu procession before a Mohammedan mosque, which the Mohammedans pelted with stones.
>
> Hindus retaliated in the second riot by attacking a Mohammedan funeral procession, and sporadic fighting took place throughout the night.

Soon the Empire which had united Moslems and Hindus in the same Army, under the same law, with the same privileges and duties, would make way for the new banners of communal hatred that would tear India into four feuding territories and cruelly mock Gandhi's dream of pastoral tranquillity and racial harmony.

Meanwhile the seeds of another conflict had been planted in another part of the Empire, the newly-acquired land of Palestine.

*

More perhaps than the evil men do is the unforeseen consequences of their actions that live after them. On 9 November, 1917 the newspapers carried a report which commanded nothing like the prominence given to the grim news from the Western Front and the cataclysmic collapse of Russia. Yet the item was one of momentous significance.

Headed simply:

STATE FOR THE
JEWS
EXILE ENDED

it stated:

The Government have for some time considered a scheme which had as its object the establishment of a Jewish Protectorate in Palestine. They have now accepted it in principle.

Following on the victory of Gaza comes the announcement of a new Jewish State. The Colonisation scheme – when the war is over – will include Jews from all over the world.

British Jews are not unanimous on the subject. The majority of Jewish MPs are against it on the ground that Judaism is a religion not a nationality. On the other hand, the Government had been moved by the fact that the opinion of the majority of Jews all over the world is in favour of the colonisation scheme.

The following letter from the Secretary of State for Foreign Affairs has been addressed to Lord Rothschild :

Foreign Office, Nov 2

Dear Lord Rothschild – I have much pleasure in conveying to you on behalf of his Majesty's Government the following declaration of sympathy with Jewish Zionist aspirations which has been submitted to and approved by the Cabinet :

'His Majesty's Government view with favour the establishment in Palestine of a national home for the Jewish People and will use their best endeavours to facilitate the achievement of this object, it being clearly understood that nothing shall be done which may prejudice the civil and religious rights of existing non-Jewish communities in Palestine or the rights and political status enjoyed by Jews in any other country.'

I should be grateful if you would bring this declaration to the knowledge of the Zionist Federation.

ARTHUR JAMES BALFOUR

The *Jewish Chronicle* says : 'It is the perceptible lifting of the cloud of centuries, the palpable sign that the Jew, condemned for two thousand years to unparalleled wrong, is at last coming to his right.

'In place of being a wanderer in every clime, there is to be a home for the Jew in his ancient land. The day of his exile is to be ended. It is a triumph for civilisation and for humanity.'

Thus was the famous Balfour Declaration – the foundation stone of the State of Israel – presented to the world. The Zionist Federation to which Mr Arthur Balfour had addressed his letter was the political arm of a world movement designed to facilitate the return of Jews everywhere to their ancient homeland. Zionism was given a political impetus in the nineteenth century following the anti-Jewish pogroms in Russia, but the movement was by no means universally endorsed. Many Jews held that Judaism was a religion, not a nationality, and that to develop a Jewish state would jeopardise the position of Jews in the lands in which they had made their homes.

The Balfour Declaration changed all that. At a stroke a Jewish state became a real, immediate, possibility. The British Imperial Army operating under General Allenby was driving the Turks – Germany's allies – helter skelter from the Holy Land. Gaza and Jerusalem were British; the rest of Palestine soon would be, so the temptation to play God must have been a factor: the British Empire remedying the guilt of Rome, reuniting the Israelites who had been dispersed two thousand years previously.

Balfour certainly was a man to whom such an historic mission would have immense appeal. A philosopher by nature, a politician by circumstances (he was the nephew of Disraeli's successor, Lord Salisbury, and himself a former Conservative Premier) and a Judaist* by inclination Balfour was, from the Zionist point of view, the right person in the right place at the right time.

This alone would not explain the Declaration. There were other reasons. Not the least was the remarkable personality of Dr Chaim Weizmann, a brilliant Jewish chemist from Russia whose work had been extremely valuable to the British munitions industry. Dr Weizmann was the President of the Zionist Federation. With his natural charm and intellectual depth he made astonishing swift headway with members of the British Cabinet.

A third factor, more pressing than the other two, was Britain's paramount need to stir the sluggish American war effort. Russia was finished. France was staggering. The Americans, who had declared war in April 1917, were taking an unconscionable time to get into it. The Jews were important in American business and while not all of them were Zionists, a pro-Jewish proclamation from the conquerors of Palestine could do nothing but good for the Allied cause in the USA.

Natural justice to the Jews who had been persecuted for so long also coloured Balfour's thinking, as did gratitude for Jewish service to Britain. The ancestor of the man to whom the letter was addressed – Lord Rothschild – had for example provided Britain with the money to buy the Suez Canal.

Justice to the Jews – yes, but what about the existing population in Palestine? What about the Arabs?

In 1915 Sir Henry McMahon, British Commissioner in Egypt, acting

---

* Though personally he was at odds with many Jews in Britain.

on the instructions of the Foreign Office, promised King Hussein, ruler of Mecca that if the Arabs would come into the war against Turkey Arabia would be independent – from the Gulf to the Mediterranean, from the Persian frontier to the Red Sea. This area embraced Palestine. In return for this pledge the Arabs followed T. E. Lawrence, 'Lawrence of Arabia', into revolt against the Turks. Now here was the Foreign Secretary of 1917 apparently contradicting the Foreign Secretary of 1915 and deliberately deceiving the Arabs who had put their lives and property at risk.

Apparently. For the Balfour Declaration was careful to say: 'The establishment *in* Palestine of a national home for the Jewish people,' not *of* Palestine. In other words, the Foreign Office envisaged a Jewish enclave within Arab Palestine in an Empire governed from London. Whether the Cabinet realised what they were doing is another matter. Distracted by a world war Ministers almost certainly did not think out the full consequences of their decision. 'Get the Arabs on our side', 'Get the Americans into the fight' – these were the imperatives of national survival. Post-war problems could keep until the war was won.

The chickens were not slow coming home to roost after Armistice Day. On 6 September, 1922 the *Express* published this excerpt from the English language, Arab-orientated *Palestine News*:

'Palestine is on the brink of revolt.

'The return of the Arab delegation to the Holy Land, dissatisfied, flouted by British statesmen, and with its appeal unheeded by the League of Nations, has fanned the smouldering flame of resentment against the British policy in Palestine.

'The murder of prominent Zionists in various parts of the Holy Land, gives some indication of the real and imminent peril of an Arab revolt.

'There are more than 500,000 Moslems in Palestine, as compared with 60,000 Christians and the same number of Jews, and unless something is done, and done quickly, we shall have an Arab rising on our hands.

'The Arab genius for intrigue has not been repressed, but forced into other channels. The country is honeycombed with secret societies, plotting and planning, with dreams of a pan-Islamic empire from Mesopotamia to Arabia, and including Syria and Palestine.'

The British had to move in special units composed largely of forces freed from Ireland – members of the Royal Irish Constabulary, the

Auxiliaries, the Black and Tans – to contain the upsurge of Arab nationalism which they themselves had aroused. While the Turks, indolent and apathetic, had been able to hold Palestine with a few hundred soldiers and police, the British, by 1923, needed more security forces in Palestine than in the rest of the Colonial Empire put together.

Yet even as early as 1923 the yearning for a separate identity and the pain of lacking it was being articulated by leading Jews in the arts and sciences. From the *Express* of 14 November, 1923:

> Mr Israel Zangwill attacked Charlie Chaplin in a speech at the Brooklyn Academy of Music last night for refusing to acknowledge that he is a Jew.
>
> 'Of course, Chaplin is a Jew,' Mr Zangwill said, 'and he ought to be ashamed not to own it. There are a lot more like him. You tell other people you are not Jews and they know you are and scorn you for your lie.
>
> 'It is this eternal pursuit of Gentiles and the terrible crawling to them you perform that makes Anti-Semitism. One nation has been trying to prove it is the lost ten tribes, while we – we're trying to get lost.'

That heartcry was to become the lamentation of an entire race within ten years.

During the twenties the Jewish population of Palestine grew steadily but not dramatically. In 1933 however with the advent in January of Adolf Hitler the Jewish inflow soared – and the Arabs rose in anger.

On 25 October the press reported 'wild anti-Jewish rioting by Arabs yesterday in Jaffa led to 20 people being killed and more than a hundred wounded. Jewish families, fearing trouble, are moving out of outlying districts . . .'

The headline was:

JEWISH FAMILIES SEEK SAFETY
IN CONCENTRATION CAMPS

PART THREE

Prologue to Another War

CHAPTER SEVENTEEN

'No More Money in the Bank'

It has been a commonly held belief that the Great Slump was responsible for the rise of Adolf Hitler. Such an interpretation alone cannot explain the fearful phenomenon of the Fuehrer and his National Socialist Party: many other factors in addition to economic circumstances went to seed the soil for Nazism. But the slump was certainly an important element in destabilising Europe and America and opening the way for extreme solutions.

The term 'The Slump' has come to be applied peculiarly to that period between the Wall Street crash of 1929 and the start of rearmament, about 1935, in Western Europe. Slumps, however, were regarded as endemic to the capitalist system long before 1929 and occasioned little surprise, let alone anger. It was considered natural that international trade should progress unevenly, surging ahead one moment as technical advance – steam engines, railways, coal-fired ships, refrigeration – gave impetus to the exchange of goods; stagnating when demand was temporarily sated and stocks built up before price cuts (or another dramatic technological innovation) re-started the machine. As well complain about whooping cough as about slump.

Such was the general informed – and uninformed – view of the market. Beliefs began to change when Socialists started to preach the virtues and practicalities of a state-managed economy and the argument gained ground that booms and slumps could be evened out by demand control and that unemployment was an avoidable waste of human resources. Socialist analysis, however, had not penetrated very far in 1921 when the first post-war slump hit the United Kingdom. Conventional wisdom taught – and 150 years of free enterprise success had apparently proved – that wage cuts led to economic recovery. Anything which promoted this desirable development was to be applauded, anything that hindered it was to be deplored. According to this thinking, if the state extracted money from the wealth makers and paid it out to the unemployed the process of recovery would be hindered; thrift and enterprise would be impaired, profligacy and idleness encouraged.

Reflecting a view held by the majority of people – who regarded many of the poor as having brought poverty on themselves – the *Express* published this report on dole (unemployment) payments in August 1921. At this time local authorities settled the rates of poor relief and administered budgets while the State concerned itself with labour exchanges and dole to short-term unemployed:

Islington has found a substitute for the now unpopular dole.

The guardians have adopted a new scale of poor relief, by which many families will receive a larger weekly income than if the head of the household were fully employed.

A family composed of man and wife and six children, for example, will receive a total of £3 13s 6d weekly, made up by the addition to the following items:

Husband	12s 6d
Wife	12s 6d
6 children (5s for each child)	£1 10s 0d
Rent	15s 0d
1 cwt of coal	3s 6d
Total	£3 13s 6d

Poor Law administration cost the ratepayers of Islington £200,000 during the first six months of this year, as compared with £89,000 for a similar period in 1918.

Slumps had always followed major wars – the decline in trade after Waterloo was constantly referred to – and readiness to work, at anything, was the recipe for beating recession, as this news story on 12 October, 1921, bore out:

The great race is developing in the small advertisement pages of the *Daily Express*. 'Situations Vacant' are trying hard to overtake the 'Situations Wanted' columns.

For every man who, buoyed up with hope, inserts a notice in our columns saying he needs work, we want to find an employer who can send us a message that will bring work and happiness to a workless man.

We are trying to force up the numbers of the 'Situations Vacant' notices, and it is employers alone who can help us to win. It is not only large jobs which are going to count. The small 'odd jobs' are going to help us too. Householders, for instance, have numerous little pieces of work which need doing. The garden fence requires repairing, perhaps, or the fallen leaves should be swept up and burned. Does the drawing-room carpet need a half-yearly beating or do the windows want a weekly cleaning for which task the maid cannot find time.

These little jobs may seem insignificant to householders, but the few shillings which a workless man would earn by doing them would mean a great deal to him.

Let us know when you have found that 'odd job'. We will then tell the unemployed what you want. You find the job, we find the man. Is it not a fair exchange?

Thrift and self-denial were also essential ingredients. It was announced in the autumn of 1921 that:

The King, in a letter to the Prime Minister, announces that 'in the grave financial situation with which the country is confronted' he has decided that the Civil List should be reduced by £50,000.

It is mentioned in the letter that the Queen and the other members of the Royal Family who receive Parliamentary grants all desire that the grants should be reduced 'during this time of national crisis'. At the same time the Prince of Wales – who receives no Parliamentary grant – informs the Premier that he proposes to contribute £10,000 to the Exchequer.

Woe betide those who dodged their responsibilities or were suspected of defrauding the Poor Law by making out they had less money than they actually possessed:

Jarrow Guardians have suspended the payment of poor relief to about twenty people who went for a motor coach trip costing five shillings each. The trippers have been ordered to appear before the relief committee.

Aggrieved farmers in Worcestershire reported in 1925 their dismay at the fact that they could not get extra labour at harvest time even though there were 1,000,000 unemployed. The dole, it was assumed, was to blame for this reluctance to toil.

The 'irreducible million' of workless stubbornly refused to go down during the twenties (other nations had a similar percentage of their population out of work). After the first flush of post-war activity a sickness seemed to have descended on the economy. Lord Beaverbrook, the proprietor of Express Newspapers and a perennial optimist, spoke of his fears that 'by 1935 England will be completely de-industrialised'. Despite evidence of some scrimshanking, the bulk of the unemployed just could not get work – at whatever price they offered their labour. This item, from December 1923, was not untypical of a situation that dragged on and on:

> Mr Henry E. Daly, who has walked hundreds of miles in search of work, looked up from the 'Situations Vacant' column of a newspaper in Holborn Public Library yesterday morning and saw Mr George McDermott, aged sixty-five, of College-place, Camden Town, drop dead.
> Mr Daly had walked breakfastless from his home in Delhi-street, King's Cross. The room swam, and he crashed to the floor. He woke in an ambulance on the way to Charing Cross Hospital.
> Mr Daly told a tragic story of his search for work. He is an ex-service man, thirty-seven years old. He was wounded in the head at the front. He has good references, and has worked as a railwayman and hotel porter.

A million unemployed was heavy, in all conscience, but it was to treble before the mid-thirties.

The first rumbles came from across the Atlantic. America had emerged from the World War as the land of opportunity for all, the Golden West. Just how golden could be gauged from the happy experience of an Army lieutenant:

> Lieutenant Osborne Wood, aged twenty-six, the son of the Governor-General of The Philippines, General Leonard Wood, expects to resign from the army and enter the Diplomatic Service in consequence of his spectacular successes on the Stock Exchange. He has made nearly £200,000 since the autumn of 1922.
> He began with a small sum and invested it in Standard Oil of

Lancashire miners
The flat cap brigade: Lancashire miners on parade. Had picture been taken of city gents in London the bowler hat would have been in as much evidence as caps here.

Jarrow marches
Contrast between rural tranquillity and industrial deprivation. Protestors against unemployment on the road to London.

New Jersey when the stock was booming. It advanced 169 dols. a share to 250 dols. and then a 400 per cent dividend was declared. Lieutenant Wood caught the rising market and made sixty points, then reinvested in other stocks with unvarying success.

His speculations were conducted in New York through the medium of his father-in-law, Mr H. B. Thompson, on whose advice he has now ceased speculating.

Lucky Mr Wood. Millions of other, less well-advised investors, continued to pour their money into the stock exchange. It was like a fruit machine that paid out every time. Shares were no sooner issued than they were snapped up in the sure and certain knowledge that they would appreciate (they didn't all do that but enough did to give the impression of universality). Using the higher base of issued capital as evidence of financial strength, firms then borrowed more from the banks, expanded output and went back to the investing public for more. And so it went on, spiralling ever upwards, ever forgetful of the cautionary aphorism that what goes up must come down. Small and not so small investors – gamblers would be a more accurate description – borrowed money to buy on the margin, a sort of hire-purchase arrangement, hoping to make enough profit on the stock to meet the debt, or even to sell within the accounting period without ever being called on to purchase the stock outright and so merely pocket the difference 'on the turn'.

America seemed the land where everything was possible; Disneyworld before its time. Lord Castlerosse, bon-vivant and *Sunday Express* columnist, gleefully recorded the grotesqueries of the fabled home of the free. Such as: 'More Americans have died from prohibition – murdered or from bad alcohol – than were killed in the Great War.' And of Jacob Ellerman, murderer of twenty-three women whose reputed reply to the question did he have a last request, while seated in the electric chair, was: 'I would like to offer my seat to a lady.'

It was a glib generalisation that America quipped and jazzed her way to economic perdition in the twenties. There were scores of millions of Americans who simply worked hard, and gambled not a cent. Unfortunately they too were caught up in the storm that broke in October 1929.

It had to come. Yet the first faint rumblings of the Crash rated no more than a couple of paragraphs in the European press:

Large offerings of principal trading stocks were thrown into the market shortly before noon, and violent recessions were forced in all parts of the list by traders' growing apprehension regarding the security of the market.

These developments induced many traders to throw their holdings on the market with little regard to price, causing violent declines in leading issues.

Thus began the panic which now produced the vortex of fear:

Monday, 21 October, 1929:
A sensational crash is taking place in the New York stock markets.

Shrewd speculators have been selling for some time past, and now the newly formed investment trusts and the main army of America's 20,000,000 speculators are coming in to try to save their rapidly vanishing margins of profit.

Dear money is killing itself. Money has been too dear for genuine borrowers who require it to carry on constructional work. The result is that building construction has dwindled and with it has been a general downward trend in industry, which in turn makes for reduced dividends.

The paper millionaires are waking up and finding that their fortunes are vanishing.

The people who were so optimistic that they could never see the top of the market may soon be so pessimistic that they cannot see the bottom.

Wednesday, 23 October, 1929:
The market opened listlessly, but soon gathered downward momentum under the increased pounding which began on Bethlehem Steel and quickly spread to a large number of other stocks.

Many small speculators were wiped out, and clerks in many brokers' offices were kept for hours at their offices to-night going over the accounts so as to close out those who had lost their entire holdings.

29 October, 1929 – 'Black Tuesday':
Wild crashes occurred on the Stock Exchange at the opening to-day amid scenes of confusion and disorder, as huge blocks of stocks were hurled into the market in an opening rush to sell which was without precedent in the Stock Exchange's history.

All regard for values was discounted. Quotations went down

several points at a time, with the brokers unable to handle selling orders at the prices which had been given them. They were compelled to accept whatever offered or to wait from fifteen to twenty minutes while quotations were privately arranged.

Never before have there been such tremendous drops in prices during the opening period of trading: 3,259,000 shares were sold within half-an-hour after the exchange began business, breaking all previous records.

Long after the market closed, saddened groups of men and women continued to gather outside the brokers' offices.

Their first news of the crash that had ruined them came from the afternoon papers, which displayed to-day's events with flaming headlines. They hurried to their brokers to learn the worst. A number of times men and women broke down and wept when they were informed that their accounts had been wiped out without the brokers having had time to notify them to put up more margins.

At the end of the most disastrous week in the history of the American Stock Exchange the twenties' balloon was well and truly pricked. The svelte sophisticates not less than the merely credulous found they had not discovered the secret of perpetual prosperity. A despatch from the US on the last day of October 1929 sadly observed:

New York's Great White Way is the gloomiest part of the city today. Actors and actresses have comprised the largest single group of speculators in the market during the past several years, and almost everybody connected with the theatre has been plunging, urged to do so by the depression in the theatrical business, and the hopes of making up the deficits by lucky speculations.

Advertisements are appearing in the newspapers offering luxury articles for quick sale, including a number of expensive motor-cars, especially attractive if there is anybody left with ready cash to afford them. Five Rolls-Royces are among the motor-cars advertised for sale, including one which the advertiser 'must sell'. Among the jewellery advertised for sale is a platinum diamond bracelet with eighty-seven diamonds, the owner stating: 'Recently purchased; must sacrifice immediately.'

American show business was not the only one to suffer. The ripples of the Wall Street crash lapped the boulevards of Paris. Les Night Clubs patronised by wealthy Americans closed their doors. By April 1930 Le Parroquet, the Florida, the Rat Mort, the Moulin Rouge had folded. Victor Perosino reported that the sale of champagne in his cabaret-bar had fallen from 200 bottles a night to two. The froth had gone flat. Very flat.

This was a financial crisis of extraordinary dimensions. What people didn't realise in 1930 was that it was more, much more than that. In 1907 Wall Street had shuddered to a horrifying low; many fortunes vanished; houses and jewellery were sold up and the luxury trades groaned dreadfully. But then some rich and powerful men got together, started buying stock again and confidence had been restored. This time the efforts of the rich and powerful were of no avail. The depression deepened and widened. Unemployment in America rose inexorably: from 6 million to 13 million. Desperate for ready cash to pay their creditors, Americans jammed the banks. The banks themselves foreclosed on loans and mortgages, adding to the numbers in distress – and to the customers clamouring to withdraw their deposits. The US banking system, more localised than in the UK, less buttressed by law, buckled under the strain. Many small banks went bankrupt, adding to the sense of confusion and despair.

Two despatches highlight the banking scare. They are from March 1933 just as Franklin Delano Roosevelt, proclaiming 'We have nothing to fear but fear itself', took office as President:

6 March:

> Hastily-engraved 'token' notes were being rushed through the printing presses in America last night for issue to millions of people who cannot draw cash from their banks. Every State in the Union has now imposed bank restrictions.
>
> Police in squads of a dozen each were on duty in New York streets to prevent looting of the shops.
>
> Cheerful New Yorkers gathered outside the banks and sang the theme-song: 'No more money in the bank, No cute baby we can spank. . . .'
>
> Congress is to meet on Thursday. Meanwhile an extension of the New York 'bank-holiday' – suddenly sprung on the city on Saturday – is being considered.
>
> Communist demonstrations have occurred at Detroit, Chicago, and Pittsburg. In Pittsburg several people were injured in a battle with police.

11 March:

Hollywood and its 60,000 inhabitants are living on paper.

Diana Wynyard explained that even the breakfast she was eating was not paid for. Her coffee and rolls had been bought on credit. A slip of paper had procured the flowers that stood in the middle of the table.

'It's fantastic,' she exclaimed. 'The most imaginative director in Hollywood could never have conceived so mad a plot. We are each of us living daily a life that no one would have dared to put on the screen. The banking crisis has turned Hollywood topsy-turvy.

'We work, eat and play on IOUs. I have seen Wallace Beery give a waiter a slip of paper to denote that he owed him a dollar for a tip. Clark Gable has paid for his taxicab with his signature scribbled on a slip of paper. Anyone who has a dollar bill left can find a hundred friends in a moment.

'Paid? Yes, but still on paper. Of course, all the studio staffs from director to extra have accepted a fifty per cent. cut in pay for the next eight weeks. That is the only thing that has saved Hollywood from disaster.'

Why did the slump of 1929-41 (for the US did not emerge fully from the depression until the war industries fuelled recovery) prove so appalling as to be different in kind from any recession that had gone before? The answer is: the Great War, the watershed of post-Renaissance civilisation.

Before 1914 the fabric of international trade, though apparently delicately balanced and subject to occasional panics, was robust. While Britain, Germany and France were relatively advanced manufacturing economies, their surplus investment could find rich returns in Russia, now emerging, quite rapidly, from feudalism. Free trade was the accepted norm and the empires of Britain, France, Germany, Austria decreed large areas of stability for capital. After 1918 nothing was the same. Russia, from being a welcome home for Western capital, was now a closed society sworn to the destruction of capitalism. The Austrian and German Empires had been swept away to be succeeded by factious little states at odds with one another, and jealously protecting infant industries against competition. A de-stabilising element had replaced a stabilising one in Europe. The British Empire, financially drained by the war, had already imposed tariffs (in 1915) and was contemplating counter-protective measures. The dollar was in process of emerging as the world currency in place of the £ sterling but America did not have the same need to oil the wheels of global commerce as did Britain, for America, a self-sufficient continent, was not dependent on international trade. Moreover America had conquered the last frontier of the West, and so there was no internal challenge to evoke a fresh industrial/agricultural impulse.

Post-war replacement and America's overwhelming economic predominance gave rise to excessive optimism in the stock market boom. For a while the boom fed upon itself in a spiral of rising expectations. Almost anything – low cost competition from outside, financial fears about Germany, a sudden unwillingness among consumers to purchase the latest car models – could bring things crashing down. And when they fell, as they did in 1929, no simple confidence booster could get them going again.

A whole painful process would be required; including Government job-creation schemes that would have been beyond the contemplation of an earlier generation and were still abhorrent to many in America who clung fiercely to the self-help ethic of their Puritan forebears. How successful these myriad agencies established by President Roosevelt were in dragging America away from the abyss cannot really be measured. Unemployment remained stubbornly around the ten million mark for his first two terms and only fell dramatically with rearmament. What action in Washington *did* do was reassure the country that democracy did have an answer and that the Administration was aware of the scope of events. In striving to pull America out of depression Roosevelt's New Deal may not have created that many new jobs, but it helped save an old institution : the Constitution. Despite the hardships, the soup kitchen queues, the broken farmers, America remained true to her democratic traditions.

*

In England a Labour Government met the full brunt of the slump as first the American and then market after market closed. An early sign of the size of the problem was the unemployment figure for April 1930 which disclosed a rise of 17,000 out of work in a single week and an increase of half-a-million on the previous year.

As the year wore on despair spread :

28 April :
Thirty women arrived here at Luton by motor-coach last night exhausted, weary, and sick at heart.

They were a Lancashire contingent of the national hunger march to London, who left home a week ago on their self-imposed trek for the demonstration in Hyde Park on 1 May.

They had tramped the streets of Sheffield the previous night in drenching rain rather than accept shelter at the workhouse.

They were found at daybreak. A collection was made for them and they were sent on by motor-coach.

A Scottish contingent passed merrily out of Glasgow singing the 'Red Flag', but to-night when they had almost completed their hundred hours' marching, they were tired and wondering what would be the result of it.

They sank to the floor of the Aylesbury town hall to rest. Some dropped off to sleep, using their knapsacks as pillows. The majority of them were mere boys.

19 September:
Despite the Government's guarantee to assist in meeting the heavy insurance risks of the giant new Cunard liner, none of the underwriters at Lloyd's has accepted any of the insurance on the vessel, and construction is at a standstill.

That was the ship destined to be the *Queen Mary*. In the autumn of 1930 one ship was building on the Clyde: a motor yacht for a Greek millionaire.

Farming prices collapsed as cheap produce flooded in from low-cost countries and unemployed workers were unable to purchase any but the barest necessities. At Dengie, Essex, 400 acres of good corn land with a fine farmhouse and outbuildings were sold for £1,700. At nearby Bradwell 600 acres of rich wheatland and farmbuildings were knocked down for £2,000. Farmers sacked their labourers and put themselves on labourers' pay. And that was starvation cheap. On 26 October, 1930, wages in Lincolnshire were cut by 1s 6d a week to 33s 6d.

Textiles, like shipbuilding and farming, were grievously affected as this picture of Lancashire unemployment in the loom town of Burnley shows:

On either side of the street groups of men in the eternal clogs and cloth caps stand at the kerbstone. Many of the doors are open and in some of the houses the cracked breakfast dishes are still lying on the tables. The mere act of clearing them away has become a futile burden. Yet the front steps are meticulously washed and 'stoned'.

That is part of the queer houseproud integrity of the Lancashire woman. She may be too poor to buy margarine but she is never too poor to buy rubblestone for her steps.

Bewildered by the economic blizzard the minority Labour administration of Mr Ramsay MacDonald – relying on Liberal support for its survival – waited for something to turn up as unemployment doubled from 1,000,000 to 2,000,000 between 1929 and 1931.

Philip Snowden, Labour's Chancellor of the Exchequer, looked a fanatic; drawn, ascetic, the shrivelled body more than offset by the blazing eyes of the zealot. He ought to have been the flaming sword of the Socialist revolution, a dedicated disciple of Lenin and Marx. In fact he was an old-fashioned Cobdenite free trader.

For many nineteenth- and early twentieth-century politicians, free trade was a kind of economic Methodism, closer to the revealed religion than to commerce; something that transcended ordinary party politics. To Snowden Socialism came a long way second to free trade and according to free trade doctrine it could never be wise or good to raise tariff barriers against other people's products. If everyone in the world played to free trade rules everyone would benefit. The trouble arose when other nations broke the rules. Even so, balanced budgets and tariffless trade routes should be maintained by the righteous to lead the miscreants back to the true road. And if foreign lands dumped their goods – at less than cost price – on the British market, was not that clear gain to the consumer?

In essence that was the Snowden case. His orthodoxy had won over his chief Ramsay MacDonald and was enthusiastically endorsed by a small number of fellow Labourites and a large section of the Liberal Party. It was not, however, Socialism.

The Labour Party was pledged to nationalise the means of production, distribution and exchange; to transform capitalism and create the New Jerusalem of equality, fraternity and social justice. What had such a crusade to do with balanced budgets, gold standards, free trade and other capitalist nostrums?

This was just one – though the biggest – of the splits in the Labour movement. Sir Oswald Mosley, Chancellor of the Duchy of Lancaster, caused another. He advocated a planned revival of internal activity by launching State-sponsored schemes: road building, land improvement, paid for, if necessary, by printing money. Better, he argued, a slightly depreciated currency than 2,000,000 unemployed. When his plan was turned down Mosley quit office and the Labour movement to found the

New Party taking several Socialists with him, including John Strachey, the rising hope of Labour's young intellectuals. Later, spurred by the example of Mussolini 'getting things done in Italy', Mosley established the British Union of Fascists.

Labour's allies, the Liberals, were also divided on what to do about the crisis. Lloyd George's blueprint for dealing with unemployment bore a strong resemblance to Mosley's, but was anathema to the Liberal apostles of Gladstonian retrenchment. Lloyd George was supported by John Maynard Keynes, a highly articulate economist who was to influence generations of civil servants on both sides of the Atlantic. Keynes did not believe in the all-seeing State but he did hold that in a crisis of such dimensions and complexity the State was obliged to prime the pump by selective spending and so induce a multiplier effect whereby workers employed on, say, road building spent their increased incomes on, say, furniture, thereby bringing furniture workers back into employment and so on and so on.

Possible inflationary effects of these policies could be discounted as taxes and prices in 1930-31 were at rock bottom, practically back to 1914 levels, as these figures testify (translated into decimal currency):

Annual Income Tax

	Married, 1 child	Married, 2 children
£150	nil	nil
£200	nil	nil
£250	nil	nil
£300	nil	nil
£400	£3.60p	nil
£500	£13.20p	£3.10p
£600	£21.15p	£23.45p
£700	£36	£22
£800	£54.70p	£23.45p
£1,000	£87	£83

(multiply by 12 approximately for late 20th century values)

Food Prices

Bread, 2p the 2 lb loaf
Butter, from 5p to 9p a lb
Tea, from 5p to 13p a lb

Sugar, granulated 1p; lump 2p a lb
Bacon, 2½p to 10p a lb
Margarine, 3½p to 5p a lb
Potatoes, 8lbs for 3½p
Eggs, 5p to 12½p per dozen
Cheese, 4p to 7½p a lb

The four main-line railway companies offered these return fares from London:

Aberdeen	£4.03p
Edinburgh	£3.75p
Leeds	£1.55p
Yarmouth	£1.03p
Nottingham	£1.03p
St Ives	£2.78p
Torquay	£1.65p
Liverpool	£1.65p

This brought rail charges to the 1914 level.

Despite the depression and the fear of unemployment it evoked among millions – fear of disgrace as much as loss of earnings – living standards were rising for those in jobs. It was the miasma of uncertainty, the humiliation of the Means Test (examining a claimant's capital and possessions, including furnishings, before awarding him extended relief after short-term unemployment benefit had run out) which provoked the desperate search for remedies.

Lord Beaverbrook possessed one of the most appealing and one, moreover, that chimed with traditional Toryism: tariff reform or, as his Lordship called it with public relations prescience, Empire Free Trade. He enunciated it in the pages of his newspaper at the precise moment Wall Street was collapsing. Beaverbrook wrote:

The policy is first to break down so far as possible the tariff walls which now divide the different members of the British Commonwealth, so that trade can flow between them without hindrance; and second, to give adequate protection to all the producers of the Empire, whether industrial or agricultural, by imposing a duty on imports from foreign countries.

The British Empire is potentially the greatest producer of wealth that the world has ever known. It covers a quarter of the earth's surface and contains a quarter of its population. Every variety of climate and of soil is to be found within its frontiers. Yet at the present time it is largely dependent on foreign sources of supply for its necessary requirements.

The food stuffs that we need in this country could all be raised either on our own soil or in the British Dominions, Colonies and Protectorates.

The coal, machinery and textiles that the increasing populations of our new territories overseas demand could be supplied by the mines and factories of Great Britain and its Dominions.

We ask, therefore, that the producers of the Empire should co-operate to supply each other's needs. We believe that they can do so. We believe that if only they are given the opportunity they will seize it and achieve a measure of prosperity which under our present fiscal system is unimaginable.

With the regular markets and increased demand which Empire Free Trade would create, unemployment would drop.

To this credo almost the whole of the Tory Party could rally, for Beaverbrook was simply repeating the doctrine of Joe Chamberlain now being re-echoed by his younger son Neville, a rising power in the Tory Party. Moreover the doctrine of protection against artificially cheap foreign foods had been expounded by Tories from Wellington to Disraeli. With practically every country turning in upon itself there really was no alternative to protection for British industry.

No free trader could answer the charge of British shirt-makers that they could not stay in business with the Japanese dumping men's shirts in English warehouses at seven pence a garment.

The Conservatives could thus offer a traditional policy that was popular and garnished with patriotic Imperialism into the bargain. They were united. The Liberals were divided. Labour was positively distracted.

The classical economic response to depression was to stimulate demand by cutting the price of supply, i.e. wages, salaries, public overheads. This was precisely what Chancellor Snowden proposed to do in the summer of 1931. His economies embraced wage reductions in all public service jobs including the police and the Armed Forces and cuts in welfare spending including the dole. At this the Labour Cabinet jibbed. Unemployment benefit was the Ark of the Covenant; it must not be touched. The Government split wide open: Premier MacDonald,

Chancellor Snowden, Colonial Secretary J. H. 'Jimmy' Thomas, and a handful of junior ministers offered to go into coalition with the Conservatives and Liberal parties (excluding a quartet of Lloyd George irreconcilables) and ask the country for a 'doctor's mandate' even though the medicine was extremely distasteful. The pay of the armed services, for instance, was originally to be cut by 14 per cent and this provoked a near mutiny in the Atlantic Fleet. The Admiralty issued a statement on 16 September, 1931:

> The Board of Admiralty have given their earnest consideration to representations received from officers commanding the Atlantic Fleet as to the hardships involved to certain classes of ratings by the reductions ordered by the Government in naval rates of pay.
>
> Their Lordships have directed the ships of the Atlantic Fleet to proceed to their home ports forthwith.
>
> Personal investigation will then be made by the Commanders-in-Chief and representatives of the Admiralty into those cases of cuts in which it is alleged the reductions press exceptionally on those concerned.
>
> The Government have authorised the Board of Admiralty to make proposals for alleviating hardship on these classes as soon as the facts have been ascertained by the contemplated investigation.

The cuts were partially restored but they still exceeded 10 per cent and this applied to all in the public service employ including police and teachers. To sweeten the pill the coalition cabinet, now including Tory leaders and eminent Liberals, cut their own salaries by 20 per cent.

Going to the country on a programme of swingeing economies the National Government (in fact overwhelmingly Conservative although nominally led by Ramsay MacDonald) triumphed by the greatest landslide in British history. The Labour Party, fighting a bitter campaign against the 'traitors' were, in the words of the exultant Tory *Morning Post*, 'sunk without trace'. They returned a mere 52 MPs – 560 fewer than the Conservatives and allies.

Later there were defections from the National Administration. Extreme free trade Liberals could not stomach the Ottawa Agreement which set up an Empire trading area at the expense of Europe, America and other competitors. Then Beaverbrook hived off in a huff because the Government had not gone far enough in establishing tariff barriers against foreign food. But these were minor distractions; by and large the National Government remained firmly in the saddle and slowly,

slowly the worst of the depression, reaching 3,000,000 unemployed in January 1933, passed.

When house prices reached bargain basement prices (see page 172), homes were snapped up; demand rose, and confidence surged back into the building trade. Constant exhortations in the newspapers to buy, buy, buy had a considerable effect. The Government too gave an upward twist to the multiplier by guaranteeing John Brown, shipbuilders, payment for Cunarder 534 (the number of the berth) to allow work to resume. The glorious news for the Clyde was given in the Commons in March 1933, appropriately to the Labour MP David Kirkwood, who has worked unstintingly to get 534 and its successor, later to be the *Queen Elizabeth*, moving again.

So protection, pump priming and the iron laws of supply and demand joined forces to bring Britain up from the slough of despond. In seven years the country had endured a general strike and a horrifying slump – and survived with the social fabric intact.

Mr Neville Chamberlain waxed enthusiastic about the extent of the country's recovery:

> 'Our credit has been fully restored. We are almost embarrassed by the amount of money that is coming into London from other countries brought to England by people who feel that this is a safer place than that from which it came.
>
> 'From having slipped back to the position of the third exporting country of the world we have once again regained our position as the first exporting country.'

Mr Neville Chamberlain, a true son of Birmingham (Lloyd George once cuttingly described him as 'one who would have made a good mayor of Birmingham in a bad year'), was totally at home with commerce. He came of sound business stock and was proud of it. The day was coming, however, when he would have to deal with men and systems so removed from his experience that he could never begin to comprehend them.

A new world was fashioning: not suitable for businessmen and frighteningly unsafe for democracy.

CHAPTER EIGHTEEN

Believe. Obey. Fight

The statesman who coined the phrase 'making the world safe for democracy' addressed his fellow Americans on 'the wireless' in November 1923. Woodrow Wilson, who as President had led the USA into the Great War, was tired, sick and disillusioned. His vision of a world-wide League of Nations devoted to the maintenance of peace and the redress of grievances had been rejected by his own people. The League existed. America was not part of it. As early as 1923 Wilson saw the mortal peril of another struggle. Yet his analysis revealed the very flaws that would make the struggle inevitable. For Wilson mistook moral righteousness for effective defence against aggression. If he had urged his countrymen to back peace with military preparedness his advice would have been invaluable. Instead he implied that membership of the League *by itself* without the arms to buttress resolutions would suffice. In doing so he rendered his country and democracy a grave disservice.

He called America to exalted standards of conscience and right 'to moral obligations', to 'devotion to the highest ideals of disinterested service'. Noble sentiments however did not stop bad men from committing wicked deeds; they merely lulled the good into abdicating their responsibilities.

The League of Nations *sounded* a fine ideal; every country pledging itself to come to the aid of any member who was attacked. In truth it was not an instrument for action but an excuse for inaction. The corridors and conference rooms of its Geneva headquarters echoed to sonorous oratory while outside the sounds of the real world were rifle shots and the tramp of armed men.

Of all countries in Western Europe Italy was the most violent in the early twenties. Rewarded somewhat extravagantly at the expense of the Austrian Empire for a less-than-glorious war effort the Italians were nevertheless angry that their war sacrifices hadn't earned them a better, more vital, more satisfying life. Democracy degenerated into anarchy, albeit a winsome Italian anarchy. Agnes Egerton Castle, a socialite traveller and writer, despatched an account of Italian journeyings in March 1921:

> On the flank of a little church, lost in the mountain mists between Recco and Santa Magherita 'Morte ni Pretil'. Death to the priests.
> There is something rather charming in the disdain which allows such a sentiment to remain conspicious upon such a place; unless indeed it is but a manifestation of Italian indolence. This Italy is a strange, sloppy country as we find it to-day.
> Is it a war result? Is it the relaxation due to the new conceptions of existence general throughout the world, and more marked here, perhaps, because of the character of the people? Certain it is that, with apparently this fierce spirit of revolt seething among the working class, the officials have almost a Gilbertian conception of their duties.
> You cannot even find the exact hour of a train. Everything fluctuates, nothing is fixed. Your tram may start to meet a train which, with luck, may leave the station two hours after the time marked in the guide-book.
> Your luggage, labelled and registered for Genoa, goes to Rome, because it is too much trouble to unload it at the intermediate station. But no one is surprised at your luggage having gone to Rome. It happens every day, you are told. It will be returned, perhaps the day after tomorrow, anyhow near that date. And eighteen other trunks have gone on with yours. How can you be so unreasonable as to complain?

Not for nothing, apparently, was it to be a Fascist boast that Mussolini made the trains run to time!

Fascism was raising its banners all over Italy. The bound rods signifying the unity and strength of ancient Rome symbolised the Fascist creed. Nationalist, patriotic, authoritarian, the creed was succinctly expressed by its leader, Benito Mussolini: 'Believe, Obey, Fight.'

Fight they certainly did:

> 8 March 1921:
> Little authentic news is coming out of Italy on account of the

stringent censorship but it is known that throughout Central Italy there is fighting between the Socialists and Fascists. Hundreds of people were killed last week, and the list of wounded runs into thousands.

The Government is powerless to act, because each warring faction watches it closely in order to see that the other side does not profit by undue protection. The Government is unable to count on the assistance of the army to put down the riots, although the Carabinieri have so far proved loyal.

9 March 1921:
After a banquet held at Casale Monferrato yesterday, the Turin Fascisti leaving the city passed the workmen's council hall, and were greeted with a volley of shots, three men being killed.

18 April 1921:
A general strike was declared at Leghorn and Pisa yesterday after a fierce street fight between Socialists and Fascisti at Leghorn. The combat was started by a Socialist who struck a Fascisti. The latter's comrades hurried up to avenge the insult and soon firing was general.

A feature of this affray was that numbers of ordinary citizens joined in, hurling crockery and tiles, and even firing shots at upstairs windows on both parties impartially. Two persons were killed and nine wounded.

16 July 1921:
The Fascists throughout Italy have reached a point at which they openly arrange punitive expeditions against any Communists who have defied their edicts. At Treviso the Fascists warned two local newspapers. The threat was ignored and last night 3,000 Fascists collected in various quarters of the town.

The Fascists then advanced to the offices of the two newspapers and completely destroyed everything even penetrating to private apartments in the same building. They then patrolled the streets terrorising the population. They still hold the town.

One man represented Fascism, Benito Mussolini, who embodied the physical and moral force of the movement and proclaimed it so forcefully and energetically that by the summer of 1922 Fascism was the paramount political force in Italy. While the traditional parties played musical chairs, with Ministry following Ministry as the country slid

Benito Mussolini
"Beethoven for me is indefinable. I have an indescribable love and passion for him." Mussolini also loved women. Unfortunately for himself and his country he lusted still more for power and glory.

Hitler, Roehm, Himmler
Within a few months of this picture being taken Adolf Hitler had his 'old fighter' Roehm (with scar) executed. The man in black is Captain Heinrich Himmler.

Lenin with Stalin
The man who succeeded him as the Communist autocrat of Russia. In his political testament Lenin warned his contemporaries against Stalin's dangerous temperament, but within four years of Lenin's death Stalin had eliminated all opponents to his absolute rule.

into chaos, Mussolini promised Italy order and strong government. Democracy had no place in his scheme of things, but then democracy was manisfestly failing in Italy. In its place Mussolini proposed a corporate state in which government would be de-politicalised. Instead of parties, trades and professions would choose representatives – rather like the craft guilds of old. Real, effective power would reside; not with Parliament but with the Fascist Grand Council and, in truth, with Benito Mussolini himself.

In October 1922 events rushed to a climax. The Fascists demanded a share in the Government commensurate with their power in the country. Signor Facta, the last of a long line of futile, despairing Premiers, asked King Victor Emmanuel to sign a declaration of martial law to crush the Fascists. The King refused. He knew full well that the Army could not be relied on to implement it. In addition, Mussolini was a professed 'King's Man', a Royalist. So Victor Emmanuel called on him to form a government and the Fascists, who had been threatening to seize office by *coup d'état*, marched into Rome unopposed.

Sensing that this was more than the usual strongman act and that the assumption of power represented a fundamental ideological divide, the *Express* of 30 October 1922, painted this picture of Il Duce, the first Fascist:

Benito Mussolini, a black-haired, hard-featured man with dark flashing eyes and a chin that looks as if it were chiselled in granite, has become Prime Minister of Italy. This is an event likely to have an enormously important effect far beyond the bounds of the country in which he has so rapidly sprung to the position almost of a dictator.

Less than two years ago Mussolini called to the youth of Italy to band themselves together in an organisation called the Fascisti. The avowed object of the movement was to fight the Bolshevism and Communism which was eating into Italy.

An eye for an eye was its guiding principle. Force was the weapon. A few weeks of organisation and recruiting brought the membership up to a few hundreds. To-day it has swollen to a million. Many thousands of them are armed 'Black Shirts'.

Your Fascist never goes into a picture gallery or stares at a fresco: for him all that kind of thing is a relic of the musty past. What he wants is an Italy full of factories, flowing with money and as free from labour troubles as pre-war Germany.

Nine months later foreign correspondent H. J. Greenwell was taking soundings of the new Italy:

> There is something changed in the state of Italy. One feels it in the very air: travellers remark it, chat about it, forget it until they say to each other: 'Why, have you noticed? The train is on time.'
> Not only is the train punctual now, but letters are delivered promptly, and the telegrams come to hand with despatch. Up and down the length and breadth of Italy there is not a murmur of a strike. What has brought about this remarkable condition of things?
> The answer is: Benito Mussolini and his Fascists. From the Sicilian village children who hurl stones at your motor-car to the ragpickers of Naples who sweep down the Via Roma at nightfall all shout the Fascist greeting, 'Alala' to you.
> Everywhere, too, friend greets friend with the right arm outstretched as in the days of ancient Rome. Sometimes, I think, the gesture and greetings are made with derision, but there is no doubt even those who mock recognise the renaissance of Italy under the dictatorship of Mussolini.
> Mussolini had been a Socialist, almost a Communist, before he revived Fascism and taught the world the real meaning of the word which is, in effect, to govern.

But early on the dark side of Fascism made its appearance:

> Maestro Arturo Toscanini has resigned as conductor of the Scala in Milan because of a Fascisti demonstration at the Opera House last night during a performance of *Falstaff*, which was being given in honour of the Italian Navy.
> The orchestra had finished playing the National Anthem at the request of the Fascisti in the audience when they shouted for the orchestra to play their hymn. Signor Toscanini declared that the orchestra was not prepared to play Fascisti songs and this caused a riot.
> After vainly shouting a protest to the vast audience, he threw down his baton in disgust and left the hall.

Shortly afterwards Toscanini quit Italy for America. From a despatch published in July 1928 comes this description of the oppressive aspect of Fascist Italy:

'The Signor will be able to accompany me?'

You may be having your breakfast, writing letters, attending to your affairs, or talking to your wife, it matters not a jot: if you hear these words and see a policeman with a scrap of paper in his hand, all you have to do is to pack your bag and follow him. This is one of Mussolini's ways when he has decided to send you to the *confino*.

The total suppression of all personal liberty in Italy has led, inevitably, to a reign of terror. The *confino* is the place where the Duce sends his political enemies. At the moment of writing there are on the Lipari Islands, situated north of Sicily, nearly one thousand men who had been fetched away by a policeman and personally conducted to the islands.

But it is rare for a man to be detained for more than one year on the Lipari Islands. The prisoners are allowed to live as they like. They either board themselves on the villagers, or stay at some small inn. They can live fairly easily on the money allowed them. They may receive newspapers and letters, of course, only after they have been censored.

Far harsher sentences, ranging up to 25 years in gaol, were imposed on former deputies of the banned Communist party. All political associations and movements, of course, having been abolished to leave the Fascists in full control.

Within two years of coming to power Mussolini had quadrupled the strength of the Italian Air Force and in a fly-past to mark the second anniversary of the March on Rome 300 warplanes took part. That was three times as many aircraft as the RAF's total strength.

Meanwhile artistic Italy expressed its admiration for the new Order. Thus in February 1927:

Dear, Great Mussolini, you must defend the new beauties of concrete and electricity, defend luminous sky signs which are most important elements in the great art now in formation. You know that every night airmen joyfully observe the lighting of the luminous advertisements which form the proud, palpitating nocturnal crown of Imperial Fascist Italy.

The above outburst is contained in a letter written by Marinetti, the Futurist poet, to Signor Mussolini.

Luminous advertisements are the enticing flowers, the succulent fruit and dancing cherubs of our future aesthetics, of swift steel and audacious concrete. Sky signs are the hygenic devaluation and denial of sickly twilights, of the homesick moon and the stars, that provokes melancholy and depression.

To counter alarm at Fascist Italy's quirky militaristic oppressive nature, Mussolini wrote this brief guide of himself for the foreign press in 1927:

'My evenings are quiet and simple. Work must be prepared for the next day sometimes, but generally I indulge those cultural activities.

'My real passion for the evening is for the violin. I consider it a perfect instrument on which the artist creates. Gypsies love it because it is supported on the breast of the player, above his heart. The tone is the creation of the gentle touch of the violinist.

'It is when I take my bow and draw it over the string that I feel completely united with the instrument. The touch on the string and the movement of the bow to produce the mellowness and velvety qualities of the tone, captivate me. I vibrate with emotion, as I sink into the rapture of the strains.

'I delight in the works of the eighteenth century Italian composers in the suites of Monteverdi, of Corelli, and the operas of Veracini. I have a passion for liturgical music and am devoted to Palestrina.

'I devote not less than an hour each evening to music such as this. I find that this time is sufficient, as the passion I put into it exhausts me rapidly, and more than an hour would leave me a nervous wreck. My whole psychic being vibrates.

'Beethoven for me in indefinable. I have an indescribable love and passion for him.

Whether the world noted that the word 'passion' occurred four times in five paragraphs is not recorded, but it gave a vital value to the volcanic nature of Mussolini's temperament. He loved women as much as music. Unhappily for Italy he did not confine himself to women and song: the world stage claimed him and he translated theatricality into bloody reality. For Mussolini, Beethoven was not enough.

*

Italian Fascism had its admirers and imitators. The admirers were many and diverse. Winston Churchill declared that Mussolini had shown there was an iron fist answer to Bolshevism. Mayor Cernick, the noted crime-buster of America, boasted that he was known as 'the Mussolini of Chicago'.*

Among the imitators were the British Fascists (this was before they were re-organised by Sir Oswald Mosley. He was still in the Labour Party). They had a rather dotty appearance to one critical young woman who wrote to the *Express* in March 1924:

> I have attended a meeting of the British Fascisti but I shall not join them.
>
> The movement is organised on military lines, but the leaders are apparently so ignorant of the Army meaning of the letters BF that they propose labelling themselves as such by wearing BF on their armlets.
>
> A Fascist friend took me to a meeting of the newly formed women's unit in the Hon Gabrielle Borthwick's restaurant over her Piccadilly garage.
>
> The women were bidden to learn how to change the tyres of their cars. Older women whose enthusiasm did not run to tyre-changing were expected to do propaganda work.
>
> A Mr Sebright made a speech, stating that the Army was treacherous, and would not fire on revolutionaries, but the Fascists would, whether legal or not.
>
> The secretary said she hoped women would learn to shoot and another woman speaker added that 150,000 Communists, most of them armed, are at large in London.

A rather more disturbing paragraph appeared a year later:

> Trouble is brewing at the nightly meetings of the National Fascisti. I cannot but admire the stalwart sincerity of the young black-shirts: but, on the other hand, I deplore much of the narrowness of their views. Racial feeling of the bitterest type is being engendered: now and then, whenever a bystander protests, a woman supporter of the Fascisti shouts: 'Are you employed by some Jews?'
>
> There were sneers from the platform about races with heavily pigmented skins. Two Hindus stood by listening. There were attacks, too, on firms that employ foreigners. It sounded very patriotic; but there will be trouble.

Nevertheless when the 3,000 Fascisti at Liverpool offered their services as special constables in October 1925 the Chief Constable eagerly

---

* Mayor Cernick founded the gang-fighting untouchables. He was shot by gunmen attempting to take the life of President Roosevelt.

accepted them. They drilled under their own officers but took the oath to act constitutionally under police direction.

There was, however, one fanatical admirer and imitator of Fascism who had no intention of acting constitutionally or taking anyone's orders but that of his own divine inspiration – Adolf Hitler.

*

Germany at the close of World War I was in a shambles. Just before the Armistice of 11 November 1918, the Navy had mutinied on being ordered to sail on a death-or-glory mission against the British. Swiftly the revolt encompassed other elements of the German forces and as the Kaiser slipped across into Holland and permanent exile his country slid towards anarchy. For a short period it seemed that the Communists might fall heir to the Hohenzollerns: Bolsheviks seized power in Bavaria and a 30-year-old ex-corporal helped report on their activities to the regular Army which ousted the Communists. Adolf Hitler had tasted violent politics and turned it to make it a profession when he joined the infant (six-member) National Socialist German Workers Party, one of a score or so of zealot movements struggling for one thing or another, but, above all, for recognition. Germany's traditional political parties however curbed the extremists of the Left and Right and established a middle-of-the-road Social Democrat regime in Berlin.

Indeed a spurious prosperity gripped post-war Germany after the initial shock of defeat and collapse of authority. Worried French and British businessmen reported in 1921 that despite being ordered to pay astronomic reparations for the injuries they had inflicted on the French and Belgians, the Germans were rising, phoenix-like, to challenge the commercial leadership they had so nearly grasped before the war. Baron Beaverbrook decided to reconnoitre Germany for himself and to do his own reporting. He proved to be extraordinarily accurate in his forecasting of the future from appraisal of the present. On 12 September 1921 his despatch appeared:

> Buildings are rising everywhere. I have seen the five great banks of Berlin, and they are all extending their premises. Where does all the money come from for this profusion and luxury in which both the rich and working classes share alike?
>
> There is one single cause: inflation. Germany is going through a postponed but prolonged boom which makes our post-war boom of 1919 a tiny thing.
>
> The boom on the Berlin Stock Exchange has ushered in gambling

on a tremendous scale. Shares and articles change hands at values differing widely from day to day, and as the mark continues to lose in value the shares of companies continue to rush up.

In this way it is all demand and no supply. Fortunes are reaped in a few hours and spent as rapidly as possible, while the price of stocks soars to figures which are perfectly ridiculous. German finance is thus heading towards a vast crisis.

These booms inevitably breed discontent as dirty huts breed vermin. The profiteers, real or supposed, were an object of dislike and a cause of class unrest in Great Britain after the war. In Germany they call them even more unpleasant names.

I watched the usual flow of cars drive down a Berlin main street, and the small boys shouted out to the passing line 'Schneber!' which means a profiteer who traffics illegally in forbidden goods, and then 'Pig of a Jew'!

After the boom the deluge, and if I had any commercial interest in Germany I should get out before the storm broke, but I would not take marks as the price of getting out.

The mark had been worth one shilling in 1914. In that 1921 September of Beaverbrook's visit it fell to 404 to the £. In the following months its descent gained momentum until it became an avalanche. Lack of confidence in the Republic had something to do with the collapse but the main reason was that the German Government deliberately depreciated the currency – reducing it to confetti money – to make nonsense of the Allies' reparations demands.

To most Germans the bill presented by the victorious powers was fraudulent. Germany hadn't provoked the war and the fact that, in the West, it was fought on French and Belgium soil merely proved the superior merit of the German soldier. Germany had honourably concluded peace on the basis of President Wilson's 'non-victimisation' offer and it was montrously unjust of the revenge-seeking French to impose intolerable burdens on the German people: ranging from the ceding of large slices of German territory to Czechoslovakia and Poland, the loss of 5,500,000 German folk and the payment in cash and kind of thousands of millions of pounds. To get their own back and reduce Allied accounting to a farce the German authorities let inflation rip – and so compounded the hatred which the great majority of Germans felt for the Versailles Diktat.

The French took an entirely different view. The Germans were reneging on their obligations. They had savaged France for four years.

They were going to pay. If they devalued their currency to worthlessness the French troops would take physical possession of German assets. The French invaded the Ruhr. German defiance grew. And German inflation grew apace. In April 1923 a small detachment of French troops sent to Krupps' factory to requisition motor cars were greeted by a threatening crowd of German workers. The French, fearing an attack, opened fire and killed ten Germans. The Germans countered by sabotaging deliveries of coal and steel to France. Bitterness and loathing infected relations between the two countries. And all the time the mark kept falling and falling. In June it reached 805,000 to the £. It had farther to go yet. A visitor discovered that in the time it took him to drink a cup of coffee the mark had slumped from 5 to 8 million to the £.

Desperately the Germans looked around for a scapegoat: they found the Jews. Beaverbrook had already remarked on the anti-Jewish tone of German children in 1921. Now, two years later, the cry was widespread.

From H. J. Greenwell's special despatch of 6 November 1923:

> 'Death to the Jews!' was the cry I heard in Berlin's Ghetto this morning when a small pogrom started.
>
> Unorganised bands of unemployed, headed by obvious scallywags, raided every shop in the Grenadiertstrasse.
>
> I saw dozens serve themselves in a butcher's shop. Men and women came out waving legs of mutton. A girl of the typist class seized a small steak and put it in her vanity bag. When she saw me look at her, she exclaimed: "This is the first meat I have seen for a week.'
>
> As the crowd worked their way through the Grenadierstrasse Jewish shopkeepers in adjacent streets took fright and hastily closed their shops, and this did not save them. People went into private houses and dragged Jews from their beds.
>
> The crowds – particularly women – dashed at them and began trying to tear them to pieces.
>
> Police arrived in large numbers. They did nothing to prevent the looting, merely looking on laughing: they had to arrest the Jews in order to protect them from the rage of the crowd.

Germany's thrifty middle class and her sober industrious tradesmen were the principal victims of inflation. Speculators were the beneficiaries and the Jews bore the brunt of popular rage. Juxtaposition of two reports of this period explains the sharpening conflict:

6 January 1924:
Herr Streseman, the Foreign Minister, who has just completed a ten days' visit to Lugano, has returned here worried and perturbed by what he witnessed among German visitors to Switzerland, where they far outnumbered other foreigners and poured out francs with a recklessness that both surprised and perplexed other visitors, who had heard so much concerning German poverty and distress.

A special Cabinet was called yesterday to discuss measures to deal with 'the German orgy of spending abroad' while nearly a million people in Berlin are officially receiving Government relief.

Professional men figured prominently among the depressed classes:

24 January 1924
Public kitchens where doctors can have free meals are called for by a number of eminent German physicians in an appeal published in Berlin.

Poverty among the doctors has reached such a degree that unless the State comes to their aid at least two thousand of the four thousand will be faced with starvation.

Owing to the general impoverishment of Germany the number of people who consult doctors is so greatly diminished that many who were once leading specialists have sometimes only two patients a week.

Owing to the depreciation of the mark, which severely hit the insurance companies, they reduced the rate to about $\frac{1}{2}$d a consultation.

Statistics show that during the last month one professor and several doctors have committed suicide but these figures do not tell of the many who have died of illness.

The great mass, however, are reduced to the dole for the unemployed. They receive two marks a day, but they have to clean the streets or shovel snow for eight hours before they receive the tiny fraction of a farthing.

From Dusseldorf this description of sullen resentment:

Hour after hour I have watched the unemployed and Communists, their faces drawn and sullen, tramping through the main thoroughfares of the city.

As an insurance against pillage, the hotels distribute food after each meal to two or three hundred unemployed, who scramble for the leavings of the guests.

A number of restaurants take a similar precaution. I was dining at one last night. I left a portion of food behind me, and I asked the waiter what would happen to it. 'Why, hundreds of men will fight for that tonight,' he replied. 'Between five and six hundred come to the back door every night after dinner.'

Something had to give. And it was the Right, the former soldiers who had seen the German glory they had fought for tarnished by 'the traitors of November 1918' who gave their answer. Revolt against the Republican Government.

Now surely was the moment for a German 'March on Rome' on the Mussolini model: but who was to be German's Mussolini? Adolf Hitler idolised the Italian dictator but at this point, November 1923, he led a fairly minor party confined to Bavaria. The big man, the one most likely to succeed, was General Ludendorff hero along with Hindenburg, of Germany's struggle against Russia, the master of the Second Reich's last mighty offensive in the West. Haughty, arrogant, egotistical and cold as ice, Erich Ludendorff embodied the virtues and defects of the great German General Staff. Politically however he was a babe in arms. The National Socialist Party with whom he allied himself – he didn't actually deign to join the organisation – was a local movement with no grass roots support in Prussia where the bulk of Germany's population and wealth lay. Hitler did not yet possess the lieutenant who would conquer the streets of Northern Germany for him: Joseph Goebbels was not yet a member of the party. Even in Bavaria the National Socialists were not the largest of the Right wing private armies. They were simply one among several. However on 9 November 1923 – ever afterwards commemorated as the Holy Day of National Socialism – the *Putsch* began. It was derisively dismissed in this despatch from H. J. Greenwell in Berlin:

The Ludendorff-Hitler adventure is finished. This evening both are prisoners in the hands of loyal Bavarian troops.

The story of the beginning of the coup reads like a cinema scenario written by an amateur.

There was a meeting last night in a Munich beer cellar which was to be addressed by Dr von Kahr. As he rose to speak one of Hitler's officers entered and announced 'Gentlemen, the revolution has begun.'

Then Hitler and some of his followers came into the brewery and, like screen cowboys, 'shooting up' a small town in the Western States of America, they fired their revolvers into the ceiling.

Then Hitler climbed on the platform, drew his revolver and pointing it in Dr von Kahr's direction forced him to make a speech favourable to the coup. Dr von Kahr eventually escaped.

After firing their revolvers the insurrection leaders seemed at a loss how to proceed. Finally they withdrew and barricaded themselves in the War Ministry and a brewery.

Actually Hitler, Goering and Ludendorff had been subjected to a whiff of grapeshot from the Bavarian police as they marched on the Feldherrnhalle, the royal palace in Munich. Ten of the insurgents were killed and duly became Nazi martyrs. Goering was wounded, Hitler was slightly wounded and Ludendorff just kept on marching, furious that ordinary police should fire on a German general. He was still at liberty three days later when his soldier servant, who had been killed during the *Putsch*, was ceremoniously buried in the black, white and red colours of old Kaiser Germany. Hitler too used the black, white and red flag but the black was in the form of a Swastika (an ancient Aryan emblem for virility and well-being), encased in a white circle on a scarlet background: a combination sinister and awesome. Hitler had not been an artist for nothing. The swastika banner carried at the Munich *Putsch*, the blood flag, became another of the Nazi's sacred symbols, worthy of the Fuehrer's mystical communion with Wagnerian legends.

Yet while not all the facts were contained in the Greenwell article, the tone of the report was accurate. The *Putsch* was a fiasco. So enormous was Ludendorff's prestige, so deferential were all civilians to a soldier that he was acquitted – even though Munich was the second *Putsch* against the Republican regime in which he had participated. Hitler was sentenced to five years and served nine months, using his time in Landsberg prison to write *Mein Kampf*.

What the Munich *Putsch* and the Communist counter-measures did was to alert the West to the real possibility of a civil war in Germany. Fearing such an outcome the Allies backtracked on reparations. The French quit the Ruhr and, eagerly urged on by peace-loving Americans, loans were arranged on reasonable terms. Germany's inflation abated and confidence surged back into the middle classes, with the election in 1925 of Field Marshal Paul von Hindenburg, the very model of the German father-figure, as President of the Republic.

On his release from jail Hitler found there wasn't much of a party left for him to pick up. Now, at last, it seemed tranquillity was returning to Germany.

It proved to be simply a remission. Mass unemployment and the rise of Nazism was just five years away.

CHAPTER NINETEEN

Failure of the Will

'No more war' was a feeling so axiomatic in the twenties that it did not need to be translated into a slogan. The League of Nations was there to ensure peace and it was buttressed by all kinds of high-sounding declarations from American statesmen – Mr Kellogg was one – and by the practical arrangement known as the Locarno Pact whereby Britain guaranteed France against German aggression and Germany against French aggression. Nobody was to change anything without everyone's approval (including the Rhineland which still belonged to Germany but was to remain eternally de-militarised). If proclamations and oratory could have secured peace, Europe would have been tranquil for 1,000 years.

What was lacking was the will to resist aggression. By itself the League of Nations was a paper tiger: at best a mechanism for adjusting international relations, a forum for discussing grievances; at worst it provided the Western democracies with an excuse for doing nothing towards national preparedness and fanatical pacifists with a 'cause' that nothing should be done.

The first major test to confront the League was Japan's seizure of Manchuria from China. The League did nothing. That was in 1931. The following year the Japanese shelled and occupied Shanghai. The League deplored Japan's action to which Tokyo replied that Japan would guard peace and order in the Far East and that the League could – in diplomatic terms of course – get lost. As China had no government worth the name many in the West agreed with the London *Times* comment: 'We cannot now complain if the Japanese are adopting the policy of the strong hand which was once our own.'

However for the League of Nations – pledged to uphold justice and punish transgression – Japan's successful defiance was an unmitigated disaster, although millions of the well-meaning shut their eyes tightly and continued to believe the League had outlawed war.

A popular argument of the period was that if only America had not deserted her offspring (the League being an American inspiration) all would have been well. But America in the twenties and the thirties had no intention of becoming embroiled in wars anywhere and would not have been of much use had she been prepared to intervene. In 1933 – the year Hitler came to power – the US Army was considerably smaller than the Yugoslav and possessed twelve tanks less than fifteen years old; machine guns that were expected to do duty against tanks and aircraft, and rifles of 1903 vintage. Total expenditure on the US forces amounted to £270 million: and that was subject to Congressional reductions.

Moral outrage against the profession of arms was expressed by 20,000 US Protestant pastors who said they would never again 'bless a struggle in which our country is involved'.

But perhaps the most significant affirmation of pacifist sentiment was made at Oxford University on 12 February 1933:

> *This House will in no circumstances*
> *fight for its King and country.*

This motion, passed by a majority of 122 votes in the Oxford Union debate on Thursday night, has stirred this lovely 'city of spires' into bitter war.

That the university where the Prince of Wales, the highest nobility of England, the greatest poets and patriots in British history have studied should so strongly proclaim a view which is regarded as highly Communistic, unpatriotic and un-British, has shocked the citizens of Oxford.

The most representative sentiment was given by the Mayor of Oxford, Alderman C. H. Brown.

'I sincerely believe that if all the great men, the lovers of England, the great soldiers and fighters who have studied in past years in the university were alive to know what these young men are doing to the noble traditions which they have passed down, then they would call these young men of to-day traitors.

'Even last November while I was marching to the war memorial a crowd of these young men walked alongside waving red flags and shouting and displaying nothing but sheer hooliganism and irreverence.'

Does the Union express the sentiments of the undergraduates of Oxford?

'Yes. It is the main body of thought in the University. What the Union thinks is the same as all those who are politically minded. It represents the political thought of the majority of the University.'

From the ranks of these young men – or their Cambridge equivalents – came the traitors Burgess, Maclean and Philby. No doubt some who voted for the trendy resolution later regretted their actions but the damage had been done and it was symptomatic of a widespread and implacable opposition to the most elementary forms of military preparedness.

David Lloyd George, 'the man who won the war' in Hitler's words, blamed the French for not disarming, as promised, in line with Germany's enforced disarmament in 1918. Did he imagine that Hitler, or Mussolini or Stalin, would have been persuaded towards pacifism, by a French self-denying ordinance or that Germany would not have broken the Versailles Treaty if France had not broken it first? Perhaps he did believe these things. His political instinct had gone. His rejection, once and for all, by the electorate in 1931 had grieviously wounded him. Within three years of taking Germany's side in the armaments dispute he would hail Adolf Hitler as Europe's saviour and give the Nazi salute in public.

Meanwhile the Conservative Government was behaving in almost as deluded a fashion as the Liberals and the Oxford students.

They had embarked on mutually irreconcilable foreign policy objectives:

* Persuade France to disarm so as to 'show willing.'
* Assure France of immediate British succour in accordance with the Locarno Pact should she be attacked by Germany.
* Reduce UK arms expenditure so as to make it impossible to offer any worthwhile assistance to France.

One man beyond others stood out in opposition to this 'policy': Winston Churchill stated in the debate of 15 March 1933 on cutting £342,000 from the Air Force estimates:

'If we advise France to disarm we shall be morally bound to help her in time of war.

'If we desire to remain independent in any European conflict we must be strong enough to preserve our neutrality.

'An adequate air force is almost a complete defence against foreign air attack on our civilian population.

'We should do nothing which exposes us to the French retort: "Very well, you are involved with us." I would far rather have larger estimates and be absolutely free and independent to choose our course than be involved on the Continent by well-intentioned methods.

'If we wish to lead our life free of European entanglements we have to be strong enough to preserve our neutrality. I am convinced that we require strength and armaments in the air and on the sea in order to make sure that we are the sole judges of our fortunes and our own destiny.'

Churchill's warnings went unheeded. He was charged with being a mad warmonger who wanted to relive his days of derring-do on the Khyber Pass or inflict another Dardanelles on another generation. Far more to the liking of the intellectuals was the policy propounded by Mr George Lansbury, a white-haired, lovable bundle of inanity and Labour leader. In October 1933 his Socialist party conference came up with a truly dazzling way of stopping Hitler: by calling a general strike in Britain in the event of hostilities:

> The resolution was passed unanimously in spite of the warning given by one delegate, Mr Elvin, of Cambridge, who heartily supported it, while pointing out that under the Trades Disputes Act a general strike is illegal.
>
> Not one hand was raised against the resolution, not even the hand of Mr Bevin of the Transport Workers' Union.
>
> Now, by his silent consent, Mr Bevin finds himself pledged, at least by implication, to the use of the illegal instrument of the general strike in the event of war.

Total pacifism was now de rigueur. Beaverbrook – always against European entanglements – declared in typical staccato style:

> Mr Baldwin says we will go to war if the east bank of the Rhine is fortified, if soldiers are trained in that area, if military encampments are established there. All these are provisions of the Treaty of Locarno.

Who is prepared to join with the French armies in driving the Germans back beyond Cologne?
Nobody, nobody, nobody.
You cannot persuade the British people to march.
There is not going to be any war, so far as Britain is concerned.
What is going to make us fight?
Not the Polish Corridor* nor the demilitarised zone on the east bank of the Rhine.

To ram home the message 'No More War' the *Express* published a book of heartbreaking pictures of the First World War. The response was staggering. Within 36 hours of the announcement 65,450 applications for the book, costing 7s 6d (37½p) about one tenth of the average weekly wage had been received.

Publication day also marked the climax of the East Fulham by-election. The Conservative candidate, defending a 14,000 majority, was in favour of arms and punishing aggression. His Labour opponent was a dedicated pacifist who campaigned on the slogan: 'No arms, no war.' The election erupted into violence not seen in any London constituency in the twentieth century:

Mounted and foot police were called out at East Fulham last night to deal with wild eve-of-poll demonstrations.

Two Conservative street platforms were overturned and a speaker, in falling, struck a woman. He had to take refuge from the crowd in the Conservative committee room. Fulham Town Hall, where a Conservative meeting was being held, was stormed.

Labour won the East Fulham by-election with a majority of more than 7,000. Politically, re-armament was the kiss of death and anyone advocating it was inviting angry, contemptuous repudiation.

Just once, in July 1934, Stanley Baldwin, effectively leader of the Government even though Ramsay MacDonald was the titular chief, spoke of the encroaching danger. 'The greatest crime to our own people,' he said, 'is to be afraid to tell the truth.' He went on:

'I am nervous of accepting obligations when I have not the means in my hand to carry them out.

'Without them our contribution to collective security is meaning-

---

* That was precisely the cause of Britain going to war in September 1939.

less. I have heard in the whispering gallery of Europe that our defences are so small as not to contribute to that collective security.'

Dealing with Germany his Foreign Secretary Sir John Simon observed:

'The sums of money to be spent in Germany under the heading "Civil Aviation" are very striking. Many commercial air machines are capable of a double use. If they can carry passengers and luggage in large quantities at high speeds, they can also carry bombs.'

However, adamant Labour and Liberal resistance to rearmament found an echo in the country at large. Apart from the development of exceptional fighter aircraft like the Spitfire and Hurricane Britain's defences remained pitiable. During the war that was to come the UK, inventor of the tank, did not put one outstanding armoured fighting vehicle into the field. Compulsory miltary service was delayed until April 1939, a mere five months before Hitler's attack on Poland – and even then the Labour opposition voted against conscription.

Collective failure of the will in Britain sapped the resolve of an already weakened France and made Adolf Hitler's advance appear preordained and irresistible. Honourable hatred of war dissolved into passionate refusal to face the facts and to declarations that Hitler should be stopped by moral counter-attack, as though you could cure cancer by resolutions.

In the Thirties, perhaps as never before in history, was the terrible truth driven home that the road to hell is paved with good intentions.

CHAPTER TWENTY

Triumph of the Will

When Adolf Hitler came out of Landsberg-am-Lech prison in 1925 he vowed never again to attempt a *coup d'état*. Mussolini, with less than a ten per cent representation in the Italian Chamber of Deputies, had seized Rome because the Italians loved the dramatic, exulted in the strong man's rape of democracy, had a Roman tradition of the seizure of power and no inherent respect for law and order.

How different were the Germans! As has been quoted before, if their revolutionaries decided to storm a railway station they would first of all buy platform tickets. So Hitler, the tempestuous Austrian, decided he would come to power legally, with a majority in the Reichstag.

The prospects were hardly auspicious. The Republic was settling down, business was picking up and there was little headway to be made in denouncing the Versailles Treaty, or blaming 'the November criminals' for Germany's woes. Hitler and his henchmen, now aided by the genius of propaganda, Dr Goebbels, worked unsparingly: speaking, writing, cajoling, arguing. The largely Bavarian NSDAP (Nazionale Socialist Deutsche Arbeiter Partei) spread its tentacles throughout the entire area of Germany. Yet despite these Herculean efforts the party won a mere 12 seats in Reichstag elections at the close of the twenties and was numbered among the 22 'also rans' in a Parliament which contained 27 parties. The Communists with 54 seats were the fourth largest. But this very multiplicity of parties, based on strict proportional representation, was to prove the Republic's undoing. All parties desired to govern, so no party truly governed. Along came the economic blizzard of 1930 and the German people who wanted work, order and pride were offered tumult, selfishness and the humiliation of mass unemployment. Within twelve months the German political scene was transformed. Now the people listened to Hitler as never before and his slogan 'Germany Awake' swept the land.

The Nazis – a slang term used often by their foes – deliberately sought confrontation with the Communists. 'We,' claimed the Nazis, 'are the true representatives of the German people; the Communists are the dupes of Russia; the 'democratic' parties are the pawns of the Jews. We promise you work, bread and national dignity. The others offer you chaos and Bolshevism.'

In September 1930 a general election was held long before it was due because Germany was becoming ungovernable and President Hindenburg hoped that the German public would coalesce round the parties of the Centre, Catholics and Nationalists. He could not have been more wrong. The election campaign polarised attitudes and provoked near civil war.

Berlin, Sunday, 14 September
At least six people have been killed and 247 injured – many of them seriously – in the rioting which yesterday and to-day has accompanied the German general election. Practically the whole of the bloodshed was caused by the strife between Communists and Fascists.

Lorry loads of Fascists, Communists, and Socialists, as well as police, drove through the streets all night, the demonstrators with ugly shouts of hoarse hatred, making sleep impossible for Berlin, on the eve of this most important poll in the history of the German Republic.

The results were a triumph for the Nazis. They increased their strength eight-fold. The *Express* explained to its readers what this meant:

Herr Hitler is a tall, English-looking man with fanatical blue eyes and clipped English moustache under an energetic nose.

He served as a private in the German Army and rose to the rank of sergeant, rejecting all offers of a commission.

His strength, and that of his 100,000 armed followers of the Fascist 'storm division' has been their obvious sincerity and the easy comprehensibility of the Fascists' political demands for the abolition of reparation payments, restitution to Germany of her former frontier, the abolition of parliamentary Government with its nefarious party interest in favour of a national Dictatorship.

Perhaps it was the unusual description of Hitler as 'an English-looking man' that sparked William Barkley the *Express* political correspondent to speculate on who could be Britain's Hitler:

> We like our dictator a little bit disguised. He will exert his absolute power in a way that we can accept – the iron hand will be hidden by the velvet glove, the sceptre will be a wand.
>
> Is there a dictator among us? Mr Churchill deserves pride of place.

Meanwhile the real Hitler showed the world what kind of man they would have to deal with. A week after his election victory he turned up in court at Leipzig as a witness for three Army officers accused of treasonably acting on behalf of the Nazis against the orders of their political superiors. Hitler used the occasion to shout:

> 'After two or three more elections, our party will be in the majority. If we are victorious then we certainly shall establish a new State tribunal whose duty it will be to deal with the criminals of November 1918. Then heads will certainly roll in the sand.'

As Hitler, smashing his fist on the desk of the witness-box, roared out this threat to the makers of the German Republic, witnesses, prisoners, and the crowd in the gallery rose as one man to cheer him.

Described as 'Germany's New Iron Man' Hitler granted the *Sunday Express* the first-ever interview with a foreign journal on 28 September 1930. It was headed:

'MY TERMS TO THE WORLD

'Our people have lost faith in promises and those who make them. Their confidence in the old political leaders and parties has gone.

'The National Socialist Party has been born out of the sufferings of the German nation. Our aim, our purpose, is to free Germany from political and economic conditions that mean enslavement; from burdens as unjust as they are impossible, burdens that no nation, no people, can carry for generation after generation.

'No people, I do not care who they are, can endure such conditions, carry such burdens, be conscious that they, their children and their children's children are foreign tribute slaves, and yet retain their self-respect. It is impossible.

'Even a camel will lie down and refuse to move, even a horse will baulk when cruelly overloaded. Why should not a people revolt against burdens they know they cannot carry, after having given the world the sincerest proof of their loyal efforts to do so? The policy and aim ruling all German Governments – Socialist and Democratic and Centre Parties – since Versailles have been the famous *Erfuellungspolitik* – the fulfilment of each and every demand of our former enemies.

'Then years of that policy has proved the futility of attempting it. It cannot be done.

'Instead of proving to the world that Germany cannot carry the enormous burden and live decently, the German political parties have been endeavouring to keep up the impression abroad that she can and will pay what is demanded.

'*We, the National Socialists, demand the revision of the Versailles Treaty.*

'*We demand the return to us of the Polish corridor, which is like a strip of flesh cut from our body.** It cuts Germany into two. It is a national wound that bleeds continuously, and will continue to bleed till the land is returned to us.

'All this is founded on the hypocritical basis that Germany was guilty of causing the world war. The National Socialists reject that accusation. It is untrue.

'I scheduled 34,000 meetings throughout Germany. We held 47,000. Within the next few months we expect to hold 70,000. That is why we get closer to the people than do those who sit in Berlin.

'We read in the Berlin Press that political parties who claim for themselves the monopoly in Republican sentiment in Germany are "conferring".

'Let them deceive themselves – if they are blind.

'The shock and the surprise of the election is nothing to the shock and the surprise that is coming to them.

'Those same elements trumpet that the coming of the National Socialist Government in Germany means a new war.

'As if an utterly disarmed, impoverished Germany, with no navy, no army, no air force, no tanks, no artillery worth speaking of could go to war with the ring of Powers armed to the teeth that surround her.'

Now Hitler was on his way. His Storm troopers, the *Sturm Abteilung*,

---

* The corridor gave Poland access to the sea and split East Prussia from the rest of Germany.

SA, under an ex-officer and soldier of fortune Ernst Roehm, won the streets from the Communists. In one of the many savage gutter fights a young SA man, Horst Wessel, was killed. Goebbels made a martyr out of him and turned lines written by the dead Wessel for his local SA group into the official hymn of the Nazi Party. The 'Horst Wessel Lied' encapsulated the brutal power that so fascinated Germans and gave them the conviction that such a movement with its brown shirted legions, massed banners of red, white and black and martial soul-stirring music was invincible.

> Raise the banners in firm formation.
> The SA march in close formation
> Clear the streets for the brown battalions
> Clear the streets for the Storm troopers.
> Millions look with hope to the Swastika
> Soon Hitler's flag will fly over all streets.

'Germany Awake', 'Heads will roll', 'Down with the November traitors' ... the slogans rasped the nerve ends. Hitler thought with the blood, going unerringly for the instincts of his audience. Germany was suffering the torments of poverty and 6,000,000 unemployed because 'Jews and democrats' had stabbed the German Army in the back in 1918 and signed a shameful surrender at Versailles. Old, self-seeking politicians were trying to keep the system going for their own selfish ends at the expense of decent Germans – and the principal gainers were (as always!) the Jews. If the voter did not support the National Socialists the Communists would exploit Germany's miseries and take over. As the Jews ran the Communists as well as the corrupt Republican capitalists they would win either way. Adolf Hitler was the only solution, the only salvation.

The message worked. Just as Hitler predicted at Leipzig, the movement did win more and more seats until it became the largest single party in the Reichstag.

President Hindenburg and his advisers were at their wits end. Between them the Nazis and Communists commanded 317 of the Reichstag's 594 seats. Whoever ruled could only do so effectively by allying himself to the Swastika or the Hammer and Sickle. Unemployment and violence were still mounting. In the July 1932 elections which produced the above result, 160 people were killed in street fighting in the six weeks before polling day in incidents such as this one:

The Fascist officer-in-command of 200 storm troopers, after they had been marching for about twenty minutes, gave his men the order to march down a dark lane which led to a noted Communist settlement.

The Communists had been expecting a raid, and had been lying in ambush for the Fascists.

Suddenly the sound of a gun rang out. It was the signal for a wild fusilade of revolver shots and stones to be opened from all sides on the advancing Fascists.

The Fascists at once returned fire.

Dr Goebbels had no doubt as to where the responsibility lay:

'Never forget this, comrades and repeat it a hundred times a day so that you will say it in your dreams: "The Jews are to blame. They will never escape the judgment they deserve."'

Still President Hindenburg's collaborators, Chancellor von Papen and Defence Minister General von Schleicher, cobbled together a moderate coalition to exclude Hitler for a little while longer. But already the spirit of militarism was abroad in the land, merely waiting the grip of the master craftsman to turn it into a terrifying instrument of German vengeance.

This account is taken from a despatch of 5 September, 1932, five months before Hitler came to power:

It is 1914, not 1932, in Berlin today.

The city, as in the bygone days of Imperial Germany, is full of uniforms. The climax to this historic 'throwback' came this morning with the review, in the presence of the ex-Crown Prince and other members of the Hohenzollern House, all of them in uniform, of an army of 197,000 men on the Tempelhof field.

Just think of it – 197,000 men, 11,000 more than the established strength of the British Army, almost double the size of the army of the German Republic.

They were soldiers of the Steel Helmet Association.

There was nothing but an armlet on the sleeves of their field-grey tunics, and the absence of rifles and machine guns to distinguish this magnificent looking body of men from the soldiers of the Republican Army.

It was an impressive moment when Colonel Franz Seldte, the Steel Helmet commander-in-chief, at the conclusion of his inaugural address, took from those 197,000 German men, stretched over the field like some great medieval army, an oath of loyalty.

'Swear,' he cried, 'to preserve obedience and loyalty of arms unto death in your leaders in the fight for Germany's freedom and greatness.'

'We swear,' the full-throated chorus echoed over the field.

'Swear,' Colonel Seldte resumed, 'to stand together like iron and steel in trusty comradeship against the enemies of the Fatherland.'

Again the great field-grey mass raised up their arms and swore.

'Swear that you will fight relentlessly, in word and deed, wherever you find it, the spirit of Marxism, pacifism, and internationalism – the spirit of softness and the fear of sacrifice.'

The answer swept over the field like a storm.

'We swear.'

A thousand flags were then paraded in the great square before Colonel Duesterberg, the second-in-command of this mighty army, which are trained most efficiently in exercise of modern warfare, even to the use of gas masks.

'On all the battlefields of the world,' said Colonel Duesterberg, before consecrating the banners, 'the German soldiers were victorious. Unvanquished they returned home.'

The march past then began. It went on for hours and hours. Battalion after battalion of Steel Helmets from Bavaria, from Pomerania, from the Rhineland, and from Silesia and from every corner of Germany filed past their leaders, past the generals of the Republican Army, and past Herr von Papen, the Chancellor, and other members of the cabinet.

Ten days later Hindenburg signed a decree creating a joint command for all the private political armies – Nazis storm troopers, Steel Helmets, Bavarian Home Defence Socialist Reichsbanner enabling them to train under the instruction of the regular Republican Army. German disarmament was dead.

On 30 January 1933 the German Republic died too. Hindenburg, assured by his fellow Prussian aristocrat von Papen that he could control Hitler and fearful of the military-coup ambitions of General von Schleicher appointed Hitler Chancellor. The Fuehrer still did not have an absolute majority in the Reichstag but he was resolved to hold another election to give him just that. What he wanted was an excuse.

He got it on Monday, 27 February 1933. Germany's House of Commons, the Reichstag, went up in flames. From Sefton Delmer, Berlin:

'This is a God-given signal! If this fire, as I believe, turns out to be the handiwork of Communists, then there is nothing that shall stop us now crushing out this murder pest with an iron fist.'

Adolf Hitler, Fascist Chancellor of Germany, made this dramatic declaration in my presence tonight in the hall of the burning Reichstag building.

A cordon had been flung round the building and no one was allowed to pass it.

After about twenty minutes of fascinated watching I suddenly saw the famous black motor car of Adolf Hitler slide past, followed by another car containing his personal bodyguard.

I rushed after them and was just in time to attach myself to the fringe of Hitler's party as they entered the Reichstag.

Never have I seen Hitler with such a grim and determined expression. His eyes, always a little protuberant, were almost bulging out of his head.

Captain Goering, his right-hand man, who is the Prussian Minister of the Interior, and responsible for all police affairs, joined us in the Lobby. He had a very flushed and excited face.

'This is undoubtedly the work of Communists, Herr Chancellor,' he said. 'We have succeeded in arresting one of the incendiaries.'

'Who is he?' Dr Goebbels, the propaganda chief of the Nazi Party, threw in.

'We do not know yet,' Captain Goering answered, with an ominously determined look around his thin, sensitive mouth. 'But we shall squeeze it out of him, have no doubt, doctor.'

It was then that Hitler turned to me. 'God grant,' he said, 'that this is the work of the Communists. You are witnessing the beginning of a great new epoch in German history. This fire is the beginning.'*

Van der Lubbe, a demented Dutch Communist, confessed and was executed. Whether he was a cat's-paw of the Nazis or a deluded loner has never been satisfactorily resolved. What was beyond doubt was the marvellous opportunity the burning of the Reichstag presented Hitler. He was able to point to it and say, 'but for us, all Germany would be

* The story is that after this dramatic exclusive Delmer was telephoned by a very junior sub-editor and asked 'How many fire engines were there?' Delmer's rejoinder is not recorded.

engulfed in Red destruction'. He had his election and victory. He actually won the greatest success ever achieved in German Parliamentary history and with his Nationalist allies gained an overall majority of 52 per cent of the votes. As the results of the 88 per cent poll were being broadcast the radio played the German marching song 'We shall conquer France'.

In full flood the Nazi revolution swept everything before it – including the last constitutional defences of German freedom. The Reichstag passed an enabling bill endowing Hitler with dictatorial powers for four years and then suspended itself sine die.

A squaring of accounts now began. 'For every National Socialist shot dead,' cried Count Heldorf, chief of the Berlin storm troopers, 'we shall shoot three Communists.'

Captain Himmler, of the new Secret State Police or Gestapo, for short, announced:

'If so much as a single shot is fired at Hitler there will be such bitterness among the majority of the population that we in Germany will see a blood bath and a pogrom such as the world has never yet experienced.'

Captain Himmler also announced that a concentration camp has been established for political prisoners at Dachau, in Bavaria, where 5,000 Communists and Socialists are to be confined.

A large force of Berlin police and storm troopers raided today the country cottage of Professor Einstein, who is at present in America.

Information had been received that a secret arsenal of arms and ammunition was stored at the cottage.

The police and the storm troopers searched and searched and searched. And what did they find? The official report says, 'Nothing.'

On the same day, 9 March, thousands of school children between seven and sixteen, members of the Hitler youth movement, marched through Berlin chanting 'Perish Judah.' While in Bremen the Peruvian consul, of swarthy appearance, was knocked down by a German who exclaimed: 'Take that, you Jew.'

Anti-Semitism, so much a part of the Hitlerian racial dogma, was rampant throughout Germany with the public burning of books by Jewish authors, boycott of Jewish shops, and disbandment of Jewish organisations. What has been forgotten, due to the subsequent holocaust, is that the Jews counter-attacked:

24 March 1933.

A strange and unforeseen sequel has emerged from the stories of German Jew-baiting.

Fourteen million Jews, dispersed throughout the world, have banded together as one man to declare war on the German persecutors of their co-religionists. Sectional differences and antagonisms have been submerged in one common aim – to stand by the 600,000 Jews of Germany.

Plans for concerted Jewish action are being matured in Europe and America to strike back in reprisal at Hitlerite Germany. In London, New York, Paris and Warsaw Jewish merchants are united for a commercial crusade.

Next day evidence of the effectiveness of the counter-action was reported in the press:

'German Agents cannot be seen.' That notice printed in huge red letters was posted on the door of almost every Jewish firm in London yesterday. Posters inscribed 'Boycott German Goods' were carried by motor cars and lorries. Orders valued at hundreds of thousands of pounds were cancelled. Letters were sent out by Jewish firms to thousands of customers asking for their support in the Jewish war against Hitler.

The letter said:

> The Jewish people have no concrete form of retaliation or protest and it is for this reason that we write you, whether you are members of the Jewish faith or otherwise, in the name of humanity and civilisation, to show the German Nazis and those who, with Hitler, are outside the pale of civilisation, that the deeds perpetrated by them will have a repercussion at least in their immediate commercial relations with other countries.
>
> We request you . . . that a specific boycott be made of German goods used in your business.

Many thousands of pounds worth of furs are sold at this time of the year in the East-end of London. Many of these came from Germany.

But now there will be no more German furs auctioned. The dealers, Jews and Gentiles, have agreed that the boycott shall be complete.

The owner of an important group of German trade papers was

notified that all advertisements contracted for by British Jews were cancelled.

An order for machinery valued at £50,000 was cancelled yesterday by telegram.

Goods from Hungary, formerly sent here through Germany, are now being sent through Switzerland and France at a higher cost. Every effort is being made to bring German export trade to a standstill.

British Jews say they will be satisfied with nothing less than a formal specific declaration by Hitler that the Jews are to have full civic rights restored to them.

German Jews, organised in the so-called Union of National German Jews, fearing reprisals, denied what they termed atrocity stories about Jews. They called them 'unfounded inventions of the foreign press'.

In the British Parliament the Marquis of Reading, a Jew, suggested respectfully that the Government should let Germany know its views on the persecution of the Jews. The Archbishop of Canterbury associated himself with the Marquis. The Government replied that it had no right to make representations nor to report Germany to the Council of the League of Nations as this was an internal matter outside the League's competence.

Nevertheless a few months later Mr Ormsby-Gore, British representative at the League, denounced Germany's Jewish policy:

'In my own country I belong to the Tory Party. Every April 19th, Primrose Day, my party goes on a pilgrimage to the statue of one who led it for a whole generation.

'I refer to Benjamin Disraeli, Earl of Beaconsfield, three times Prime Minister of England, a man descended from Spanish Jews driven out of Spain at the time of Ferdinand and Isabella.

'He was a devout and patriotic Englishman. He was baptised in the Church of England and buried according to the rites of that Church.

'Nevertheless, he proclaimed himself the proudest of Jews, a Hebrew of Hebrews. I say Jews form a racial minority which deserves the same treatment everywhere as all other minorities in all countries.

'We regret absolutely the German point of view,' he added.

Pembroke Stephens, another *Daily Express* correspondent in Germany, also spoke, much more unequivocally:

In a Berlin restaurant recently two Jews picked up the menu to order a meal. The waiter snatched the menu from their hands, flung it to the floor and turned his back on them.

The Jews were obliged to leave the restaurant without being served.

In a Berlin underground train some uniformed storm troopers began shouting in chorus: 'Jews must not sit in the train. Out with the Jews.'

Jews in the train were forced to vacate their seats and stand in the entrance to the carriage, which they left at the next station.

Dr Goebbels, Nazi Minister of Propaganda, is the man who releases the new attacks on the Jews. I am not the only man who believes that Goebbels is Germany's evil genius, and that, in his war on Jewry, not Zion but Nazi Germany may be destroyed.

Mr Stephens did not last long as foreign correspondent. He was arrested and deported for 'constant misrepresentation ... frivolous and disturbed reports not conducive to peace and good relations between England and Germany.' He described his experience in prison awaiting deportation:

> The surroundings prompted me to ask my companions if it was true that German criminals and political offenders were beheaded – as I have heard – lying on their backs gazing up at the headman's axe. The detectives denied this and said that felons were dragged by chains to a headsman's block and that the blow fell from behind.

The other side of the German picture, the one exhibited to the world by official propaganda, was contained in this piece of whimsy:

> Imagine the most beautiful prospect you have ever seen – snow-capped mountains, russet-coloured forests, green plains and hills, and you will understand why Hitler chose the little Bavarian village of Berchtesgaden for his home.
>
> Hitler's sister – her name is Frau Raubal – is a tall, stately woman, with a strong kindly face, greying hair and frank blue eyes.
>
> 'Hitler asked me if I would keep house with him. I was very happy. I accepted gladly, and here for the past five years my brother and I have made our home.
>
> 'This house represents all Adolf Hitler, the man, has in the world. He has no wife, no children, no hobbies.
>
> 'Two years ago he gave up eating meat.

' "I must not poison my nerves with nicotine and alcohol," he said. Before he gave up meat he used to suffer pain, but he has never been so fit as he is now.

'He arrives here pale and worn-out. He lies down for an hour, and comes downstairs red in the face and happy, whistling and singing as merrily as a bird.

'I do not think he will ever marry, but sometimes when he sees pretty blond-headed children – he loves blond hair – he sighs and says: "It is a pity I am not married. I should like to have children like that."

'At other times he will say: "I am wedded to politics. No wife would stand for that." '

Hitler had cause to whistle. Aware that the bully boys of the SA were giving Germany a bad image abroad he reined them in, slowed down the anti-Jewish campaign (though not before Einstein had renounced German nationality) and launched domestic projects which sent his popularity soaring.

Submitting to authority the Germans exchanged formless individualism for community spirit. Every aspect of the Third Reich (the first had been the ancient Holy Roman Empire, the second the Kaiser's) emphasised the *Volk* and their mystical communion with blood and soil. The Republic had been identified with night clubs, sardonic literature, 'decadent' art: the Nazis relentlessly extolled the glories of the open-air life and the virtues of physical exercise and endurance.

The Nazi concept of the dignity of labour was demonstrated by the creation of the *Arbeitsdienst*, labour service, whereby every German male, regardless of position was obliged to join at eighteen for six months. He worked hard digging ditches or building motorways and lived in spartan fashion to make him 'as tough as leather and as hard as Krupp steel'. The *Arbeitsdienst* had the additional advantage, from the Nazi point of view, of conditioning young men for the compulsory military service they were already planning.

Cakes and ale were not forgotten. To reward loyal German workers the Strength Through Joy movement took them on holiday cruises by ship, bus or train. The Party offered group activities of every conceivable nature ranging from motor cycling (not without military application) to mountaineering and gymnastics. And a people's car, Volkswagen, at cut-rate prices was planned so that dedicated workers who saved their pfennigs could use the new autobahns.

All this gave the impression of intense Nazi dynamism compared with slovenly, static democracy. The discipline, classlessness and sense of purpose of the new Germany was conveyed by reports like this in October 1933:

> Seven thousand German girls between the ages of sixteen and twenty-five have left their homes to join Hitler's new women's camps.
>
> Every day between four and five lecturers speak to the women on the political topics of the day.
>
> 'Have you any questions to ask?' said the lecturer at the conclusion of his speech.
>
> 'Please, teacher,' said a pretty blonde-haired girl, 'is it true that the prisoners in the big concentration camp at Dachau are badly treated?'
>
> 'What motive makes you ask that question?'
>
> 'Pity.'
>
> 'Well, that's a fine motive. As a matter of fact, I was at Dachau yesterday, and I can tell you that you are ill-informed. The prisoners look exceedingly happy.'
>
> The camp spirit is one of real sacrifice. As in the old days of the Teuton tribes, these women are working and thinking of German men, doing work for the adjacent men's labour camps, without proper pay, without thought of reward.
>
> On Sundays, Hitler's young men and women walk out together in their grey uniform, discussing what their teachers have told them during the week.
>
> Hitler hopes that at the end of the forty weeks some of these people will marry under his dowry scheme and build a happy future together.
>
> Under the new decrees an income-tax rebate of 15 per cent will be allowed on each of the first four children and 30 per cent for each additional child.
>
> Thus people with six children will pay no income tax at all.
>
> It is now revealed that 100,000 couples who could not otherwise have married have received the special Hitler marriage loan of £60 in the past five months.
>
> Thus £6,000,000 has already been spent in State dowries.

On foreign policy the Fuehrer was winning golden opinions from his people. He brilliantly presented and articulated German resentment at their inferiority in arms compared with their French and Polish neighbours (Germany was still barred by the Versailles Treaty from conscription and possessing offensive weapons – officially that is). When the League of Nations refused to tackle this grievance Hitler took Germany out of the League and a wildly enthusiastic public gave him 95 per cent endorsement at a referendum. At last, was the commonly held view, someone is speaking up for the Fatherland!

In Venice he struck an accord with Mussolini as, for the first time, the two dictators raised their arms in the outstretched Fascist salute to their adoring thousands roaring approval in St Mark's Square.

Yet there was a cloud on the Hitler horizon: a brown cloud, the 3,000,000-strong Storm Troop army headed by Ernst Roehm.

These young men fed on a diet of violence, yearning to exercise their newly acquired authority as district leaders or block wardens and to pay off old scores were the stuff of permanent revolution and as such were anathema to the officers of the German Army.

The Army still had a mystic aura of authority. It was small, limited by Treaty to 100,000 men but each of them was potentially an officer or senior NCO. Hitler stood in awe of the Army and he needed it, in 1934, far more than the Army needed him. The Reichswehr was Nazism's holy grail and to grasp it Hitler was ready to sacrifice the radicals of his own party.

These radicals were, at any rate, acting in a thoroughly alarming and belligerent manner. Early in June 1934 storm troopers marched through the streets of Munich chanting 'Down with Hitler' and making plain that their allegiance lay with their own rotund, hail-fellow-well-met, leader Ernst Roehm.

Whether Roehm really did plot a coup against Hitler will never be known with certainty; it is in the same class as the question of who fired the Reichstag. What Roehm did was to hand over a number of hostages to fortune.

He pranced around with boy friends, openly exhibiting homosexual tendencies. He lived riotously: drinking, carousing, lavishly extending hospitality at the public expense while the Fuehrer lived the life of an ascetic and most Germans had to watch every pfennig. He made speeches emphasising the *Socialist* element of National Socialism – just when Hitler wanted to play down all talk of socialism and indeed was re-defining the word to mean 'feeling of national communion, of caring for one another'. Roehm's final, fatal blunder was to underestimate the power of the new black guard – the *Schutz-Staffel*, protective force. Initially Adolf Hitler's own lifeguards, the SS, had by 1934 become a major unit in its own right armed with carbines, machine guns and grenades. The SS was honour-bound to serve Hitler alone, an élite whose loyalty could be counted upon to the end.

Roehm was also known to be seeing a great deal of General Schleicher, a former Chancellor, a perennial plotter with a record of intrigue among the officer class.

Hitler resolved to strike. Having sent Roehm on holiday to the Bavarian highlands and stood down the Brownshirt Army for two months, the Fuehrer conferred with his loyal lieutenants, chief among whom were Captains Goering and Himmler, and Dr Goebbels. It seemed clear that he – Hitler – was to be used as a front to bring in non-disaffected SA leaders who were to be persuaded that a 'night of the long knife' was required to launch a second revolution against the rich reactionaries who were allegedly polluting the clear ideals of the party. The phrase 'Night of the Long Knives' has been used to describe Hitler's removal of Roehm and his fellow plotters. In fact (according to Hitler's speech of 14 July) it was the plotters' own watchword.

On 1 July the world learned of what had happened the previous day at the lakeside resort of Wiessee in Upper Bavaria. The report came in a radio broadcast by Dr Goebbels himself. He charged his performance with the hectic melodrama that was to characterise the whole Nazi regime and the twelve years of the Third Reich:

> At one o'clock in the morning startling news reached Hitler as he was sitting on the terrace of the Rhine Hotel at Godesberg, listening to the music and looking out on the winding river below.
>
> He learned the storm troopers, acting under orders of two of Roehm's closest friends, Schneidhuber and Schmid, had gone out into the streets of Munich and were marching through them with the cry: 'Hitler is against us.'
>
> 'A short council of war,' said Dr Goebbels, 'and then Hitler's mind is made up. He decides not to wait till the morning but to fly at once to Munich to hunt down the conspirators in their nests.
>
> 'Half-an-hour later the airplane leaps into the fog-enshrouded night. It is two o'clock.
>
> 'Hitler is sitting silently in the foremost seat of the long cabin staring immovably out into the dark. At four in the morning we land in Munich. Dawn has broken.
>
> 'On the aerodrome Hitler receives a report on the situation. We immediately go to the Ministry of the Interior.
>
> 'There Hitler found Schmid and Schneidhuber the two rebel leaders under arrest.

'Adolf Hitler immediately goes to their rooms and faces them alone.

'In two sentences of immeasurable indignation and scorn he hurls their whole shame into the pale, scared faces of the two traitors.

'Then he personally tears the epaulettes off their shoulders. Their harsh but just fate will meet them in the afternoon.

'At racing speed we tear off to Wiessee. At seven o'clock we are there.

'Without the slightest show of resistance we are able to enter the house and surprise a band of conspirators asleep and take them prisoners at once.

'With unparalleled courage Hitler personally makes the arrests. I do not wish to dwell on the revolting scenes of debauchery which were witnessed by us, but let me quote the words of a simple Hitler guard who declared:

'I only wish the walls could collapse so that the whole nation could witness these happenings and understand how good it is that our leader acts in this way.'

'Hitler, armed only with a hunting crop, entered the bedroom of Roehm and declared him to be under arrest. Roehm surrendered without a word.'

Roehm was executed by firing squad, after refusing to commit suicide and spurning a blindfold. Also executed were a number of leading SA officers. General Schleicher and his beautiful young wife died under a hail of SS bullets 'resisting arrest'.

Two weeks later Hitler appeared before the Reichstag to justify the elimination of 77 people – that was the admitted total.

He said: 'I knew that if disaster was to be prevented I must act like lightning. Only ruthless and bloody intervention was possible . . . if anyone raised the charge against me that we did not use the ordinary courts for sentencing I can only say that I myself was the supreme court of the German people for 24 hours. . . . If traitors carry out a meeting, which meeting they kept secret from me against my direct order, then I have them shot.'

In these four sentences, screamed out at his baying, idolatrous followers, were encapsulated the entire *Fuehrer-prinzip*, the leadership principle which was the heart and core of National Socialism: unquestioning faith in the Fuehrer, unquestioning acceptance of his orders. From July 1934 onwards Adolf Hitler's wishes were to be Germany's law. *Ein Reich. Ein Volk. Ein Fuehrer.*

That year the annual rally of the party at Nuremberg was christened 'The Triumph of the Will'. It centred round Hitler, picked out by a single searchlight beam from the surrounding blackness, illuminating the world by his presence, bringing Germany into the light.

Even before the drum-fire of Fuehrer glorification had reached the crescendo of Nuremberg the world had been warned of what lay in store for it from Nazi fanaticism. Austrian Nazis had murdered the tiny Chancellor of Austria, Dr Dolfuss, to provoke an *anschluss* (union) with Germany. On 31 July the two ringleaders Otto Planetta and Franz Holzweber were sentenced to death. The report from Vienna recorded how the men went to their deaths three hours after the verdict:

> At exactly 4.35 the guards came to take Holzweber to the scaffold. He met them with head erect, and marched with them, utterly indifferent, with the same careless arrogance as had characterised his whole bearing before the court.
>
> As he left the door of the prison and entered the courtyard he paused. He saw the scaffold, and, lifting his hand in the Nazi salute, shouted time after time, *'Heil Hitler!* I die for Germany!' and marched to the gallows.
>
> As the Austrian gallows are only five feet high and have no drop it took ten minutes for Holzweber to die.
>
> Thirteen minutes afterwards Planetta followed his comrade, with the same stoic bearing. He, likewise, flung his arm in salute and marched to the scaffold shouting *'Heil Hitler!'*

On the day following these executions another death took place: that of Germany's aged President, Paul von Hindenburg. Now the last barrier between Adolf Hitler and total control over the life and destiny of Germany was removed. The office of President was abolished and Hitler became Fuehrer and Reichs-Chancellor. General von Blomberg, the War Minister, then made the crucial announcement that the Armed Services would take the oath of allegiance to Hitler. It was on the twentieth anniversary of Germany's declaration of war on France:

> 'I swear by God this holy oath that with unconditional obedience I will serve Adolf Hitler, Leader of the German Reich and of the German people, Supreme Commander of all fighting forces, and that I am ready to lay down my life for him at any time.'

Sefton Delmer, the *Express* correspondent, observed:

By this evening all soldiers, sailors, all officers, generals, and admirals of the German Army and of the German Navy had taken this oath.

And therewith the last hope of the anti-Hitler opposition has been buried.

The army has today sworn the decisive oath, and Hitler's power is more firmly laid than ever it was. Nothing but death can remove him.

The *Express* commented editorially:

History has not seen such an age since the Frenchmen of 1789 broke the feudal chains of centuries, letting loose a new torrent on the world.

Who would choose to live through any other than these eventful years?*

A week later, as Britain prepared to celebrate the August Bank Holiday, it was reported that 22 members of the Hitler Youth Movement had arrived at Gosforth Park, Newcastle-on-Tyne. They were on an exchange trip – with 25 Boy Scouts.

---

* There is a Chinese curse that says: 'May you live in interesting times.'

Index

Abbott, Mr, 197
Aberystwyth, 199
Agra, 226
Ahmedabad, 221, 226
Aisne, River, 88
Aitken, Max, *see* Beaverbrook, Lord
Albert, 50
Alcock and Brown, 190
Alexandra, Czarina, 117
Allenby, Gen., 232
Alsace, 17, 21, 86
Altkirch, 21
Ampthill, 176
Amritsar, 183, 224
Anderson, Jane, 43-5
Annabella, 167
Antwerp, 24
Arabia, 233
Arbuckle, Fatty, 161-3
Archer-Shee, 24
Arras, 109
Ashley, Edwina, 181
Asquith, H. H., 17, 18, 34, 40, 55, 60, 85, 95, 96, 97, 100, 102
Astbury, Mr Justice, 140
Australia, 19, 223
Austria, 15, 20, 53, 74, 115, 292

Bacon, H. L., 82
Bailey, Herbert, 119
Bailey, Councillor W. M., 33
Bairnsfather, Bruce, 64
Baldwin, Stanley, 134, 136, 138, 139, 140, 141, 143-4, 272, 273
Balfour, A. J., 85, 231, 232, 233
Baltic, 90
Banbury, Sir F., 193
Bangladesh, 19
Barkley, W., 277
Barnard, E. B., 84
Barnard, Jeffrey, 160
Barrie, J. M., 32
Barry, Kevin, 214
Bartlett, Private, 28
Battenberg, Prince Louis, 32

Beaverbrook, Lord, 97, 122, 239, 250, 262, 263, 264, 272
Beery, Wallace, 245
Belfast, 206, 216
Belfort, 21
Belgium, 18, 24, 79, 80
Belgrade, 16
Belin, Edouard, 176
Bell, Herr, 116
Bennett, Arnold, 151
Bennett, Belle, 165
Bennett, Sir Henry Curtis, 201
Benson, A. C., 27
Berchtold, Count, 17
Berlin, 19, 26, 32, 90, 92, 93, 111, 262, 264, 266, 280, 283
Berthelot, Gen., 20
Bethmann-Hollweg, Chancellor, 18
Bevin, Ernest, 133
Birmingham, 253
Bishop, Nellie and Thomas, 68
Black Sea, 54
Blomberg, F. M. von, 292
Bochkeroya, Mme, 126
Bonar Law, Andrew, 96, 97
Bond of Fear, The, 165
Bo'ness, 72
Booth, Bramwell, 107
Borneo, 19
Bradford, 153
Bremen, 283
Bridgeman, Viscount, 202
Bridgeton, 83
Brooke, Rupert, 75
Brown, Alderman C. H., 270
Brussels, 18, 79
Buchan, Lt Alastair, 61, 62
Buchan, John, 61
Buchanan, Mr, 193
Buchholtz, 91
Burgess, Guy, 271
Burleigh, Bertram, 165
Burlison, Mr, 187
Burma, 19, 223
Burns, John, 18

295

Bussy, Gordon, 175
Bywaters, Frederick, 199-204

Caillaux, Joseph and Mme, 87-8
Cairo, 166
Calmette, Gaston, 87
Cambrai, 102
Campbell, Rev. R. J., 78
Campbell Stephen, Rev., 193
Canada, 19, 45, 62, 84, 223
Canterbury, Archbishop of, 153, 194, 285
Caporetto, 85
Cardiff, 45, 132
Carlisle, Countess of, 154
Carr, Mrs, 176
Carson, Edward, 217
Caruso, 164
Casement, Sir Roger, 205, 206, 207, 208, 209
Castle, Agnes, 255, 256
Castle of Dreams, The, 166
Castlerosse, Lord, 241
Cawnpore, 226
Cavell, Nurse Edith, 35, 36
Ceannt, Eamonn, 209
Cecil, Lt E. R., 62
Cecil, Lady Gwendolen, 71
Cecil, Capt. V. A., 62
Cecil, Lord William, 62
Chamberlain, Joe, 251
Chamberlain, Neville, 253
Chaplin, Charlie, 158, 159
Chapman, Rev. Hugh, 148
Chappell, Henry, 28
Charlot, Andre, 166
Chicago, 244
Childers, Erskine, 218, 219
Chittagong, 229
Chu Chin Chow, 102
Churchill, Winston, 17, 18, 54-5, 89, 119, 124, 126, 129, 138, 194, 222, 271, 272
Citrine, Sir Walter, 141
Clancy, Alderman, 214
Clarke, Thomas, 209
Clemenceau, Georges, 88, 102, 111
Clive, Colin, 111
Cochran, C. B., 177
Collins, Michael, 205, 215, 216, 217, 218, 219, 220
Cologne, 91, 92, 213
Conan Doyle, Sir Arthur, 107
Congo, 207
Connolly, James, 209
Constantinople, 54, 55
Cook, Arthur, 133, 141

Corelli, Marie, 99
Cork, 212
Cornwell, Boy John Travers, VC, 59
Courlander, Alphonse, 21
Coward, Noël, 156, 191
Cowper, Jack, 178
Craig, Sir James, 217
Cunningham, John, 62
Cunningham, Catherine, 198
Cyprus, 19
Czechoslovakia, 115, 263

Daily Express, passim
Daily Herald, 111
Daily Mail, 55, 126, 136
Daily Telegraph, 85
Daly, Henry E., 240
Daniels, Bebe, 161
Dardanelles campaign, 53-55
Darling, Mr Justice, 154
Dartmouth, 24
Das Kapital, 115
Davenport, Lord, 98
Davies, J. R., 203
Davies, Lloyd, 191
Davis, Mr, 81
Davis, Roderick, 197
Davison, Sir W., 131
Davy, Dr, 57
Dean, Julia, 165
de Grey, Magistrate, 31
de Lyon, John, 196
Delhi, 225
Delmer, Sefton, 282, 292
Delmont, Mrs, 162, 163
Demi-Virgin, The, 156
Derby, Lord, 41, 76
De Valera, Eamon, 205, 210, 211, 212, 214, 216, 217, 218, 219, 220
Dietrich, Marlene, 168
Dolfuss, Dr, 292
Douglas, James, 145, 202
Drogheda, Earl of, 151
Dublin, 205, 206, 209, 210, 211, 213, 216, 218
Dunn, G. A. & Sons, 83
Durham, 197
Dusseldorf, 92, 265
Dyer, Gen., 225

East Africa, 19
Eastbourne, 68
Eckhardt, Herr von, 93
Edinburgh, 187
Edington, May, 151, 152
Edward, Prince of Wales, 183-6, 189, 239, 270

Index

Einstein, Prof., 283
Eliot, Walter, 191
Elizabeth, Princess, 141
Ellerman, Jacob, 241
Engelhardt, Col., 117
Englefield Green, 99
Entwistle, Major, 153
Estonia, 115
Evans, Sgt W., 229
Evening Post, USA, 32
Evening Standard, 111

Fairbanks, Douglas, 157-9
Falmouth, 92
Farrar, T. C. L., 179
Ferguson, Capt. V. H., 223
Figaro, Le, 87
Flushing, 25
Foch, Marshal, 88
Folkestone, 25
Fordham, Mr, 76-7
Frampton, Mr, 83
France, 17-101 *passim*, 116, 130, 153, 263, 269
Franz Ferdinand, Archduke, 15, 16, 110
French, General, Sir John, 24, 38, 53, 54, 212, 214
Frohman, Charles, 32
Fuller, Lance-Corp. Wilfred, VC, 40

Gable, Clark, 245
Gallipoli, 54-5
Gamage, Eric, 137
Gamages, 46
Gandhi, Mohandas, 221-230
Gape, Mr, 83
Garbo, Greta, 168
Gates of Duty, The, 165
Gaza, 231, 232
Genoa, 255
George V, King, 19, 56, 96, 97, 178, 179, 183, 184, 207, 216, 218, 239
Germany, 11-101 *passim*, 116, 118, 119, 130, 234 ff
Gibraltar, 19
Gingold, Baroness Helene, 34
Glasgow, 80, 97, 136, 147, 169, 174, 192, 206, 247
Goch, 25
Goddard, Mr Justice, 199
Goebbels, Dr, 275, 282, 286
Goering, Hermann, 267, 282, 290
Goldman, Emma, 128
Gore-Langton, Lady Mabel, 99
Gothein, Georg, 92
Gough, Gen. Sir Hubert, 101

Govan, 80
Graham, Henry and Gladys, 73
Gray, Private George, 31, 32
Greenford, 174
Greenwell, H. J., 49, 51, 213, 264, 266, 267
Grenoble, 153
Grey, Sir Edward, 18
Griffen, Sybil Catherine, 73
Griffith, Arthur, 214, 217
Griffiths, D. W., 164
Grisewood, Freddie, 178
Gueydan, Mme, 87
Guynemer, Lt. Georges, 88

Haifa, 234
Haig, Gen. Sir Douglas, 54, 101, 132
Haldane, Lord, 18, 27
Hall, Admiral, 93
Hamburg, 20, 25, 26, 90
Hamilton, Cosmo, 167
Hamilton, Ontario, 62
Hamilton, Lord George, 48
Hamilton, Sir Ian, 55
Handley-Seymour, Mme, 181
Hapsburg dynasty, 115
Harrods, 46, 97, 171
Hayward, Mme, 181
Hedges, Dorothy, 154
Heldorf, Count, 283
Henderson, Arthur, 47, 78
Henrey, Robert, 219, 220
Herts Advertiser and St Albans Times, 83
Hibberd, Stuart, 178
Himmler, H., 283, 290
Hindenburg, F. M. von, 26, 267, 276, 280, 281, 293
Hitchens, Robert, 201
Hitler, Adolf, 11, 75, 102, 111, 234, 237, 262, 267, 268, 269, 271, 274, 275, 278 ff
Holland, 18, 31, 78, 91
Holman, W. S., 107
Hopwood, Avery, 156
Hore-Ruthven, Hon. Alison and Margaret, 154
Hötzendorf, Conrad von, 15
Huff, Louise, 165
Hungary, 20, 115, 285
Hunter, Lord, 225
Hussein, King, 232
Hyndman, H. M., 180
Hypatia, 152

India, 11, 19, 84, 124, 183, 221-230
Inskip, Thomas, 200

Irvine, John, 49
Irwin, Lord, 227
Ireland, 11, 124, 205-220
Israel, 230-4
Italy, 11, 85, 255, 285
Ivan the Terrible, 127

Jacot, Bernard, 166
Japan, 16, 93, 94
Jazz Singer, The, 166
Jellicoe, Adm., 89
Joffre, Gen., 21, 48, 49
Johnson, Amy, 190
Johnson, Mr, 196
Johnston, Beulah, 154
Jolson, Al, 166
Jones, Private, David, 45
Journey's End, 111
Joynson-Hicks, Sir William, 107, 127
Jutland, Battle of, 59, 110, 182

Kahr, Dr von, 267
Kamenev, 127
Kapurthala, Maharajah of, 228
Kashmir, Maharajah of, 278
Kealey, Lt. F. W., 176
Kerensky, Alexander, 119, 121
Kerr, Sir J. H., 223
Ketchum, C. J., 128, 129, 142
Keynes, J. M., 249
Keyworth, Lance-Cpl. Leonard, VC, 64
Kiernan, Kitty, 219
Kipling, Rudyard, 61
Kirkwood, David, 180, 253
Kitchener, Lord, 20, 21, 22, 41, 42, 49, 54, 55, 56, 67, 75
Kuusinen, Comrade, 126

Labori, M., 88
Lane, Franklin D., 164
Lansbury, George, 180, 272
Lansdowne, Marquess of, 84, 85
Lascelles, Lord, 181
Latvia, 115
Lauder, Harry, 61
Lauder, Capt. John, 61
Lawrence, T. E., 233
Lawrence, Lily, 177
Laventie, 38
Leeds, 47, 132, 147, 174
Lehrmann, Harry, 162
Leipzig, 277
Lenin, Vladimir, 80, 115, 116, 118, 119, 121, 122, 123, 124, 139, 192
Leningrad, 89

Lewis, S. T., 199
Lichnowsky, Prince, 17
Lier de Ste Marie, 28
Lincoln, 212
Lindbergh, Charles, 190
Lithuania, 115
Little Nelly Kelly, 177
Liverpool, 41, 131, 132, 196, 261
Llewelyn-Davies, George, 32
Lloyd, Marie, 67
Lloyd George, David, 18, 56, 57, 58, 85, 96, 99, 100, 101, 102, 103, 104, 111, 117, 212, 213, 216, 217, 248, 249, 252, 253, 271
Lockwood, Colonel, 97
London, 31, 35, 46-7, 65, 71, 73, 76-7, 82, 104-5, 107, 127, 139, 140, 149, 160, 170, 171, 174, 175, 184, 185, 186, 197, 199
London, Bishop of, 35
Londonderry, 206
Long, Sidney, 138
Lonsdale, Frederick, 156
Loos, Battle of, 47, 53
Lorraine, 17, 86
Louvain, 28
Lubbe, Van der, 282
Ludendorff, Gen., 102, 266, 267
Lullaby, 155
Lush, Mr Justice, 203
Lusitania, 32, 80, 92, 93, 131
Lutyens, Sir E., 228
Lyon, Ben, 161

McCardle, Mr Justice, 197
McCormack, John, 187
McCurtain, Thomas, 212
McDermott, G., 240
McGillcray, Private A., 29
McMahon, Sir H., 232
McSwiney, T., 214
MacDiarmads, Sean, 209
MacDonagh, Thomas, 209
MacDonald, Ramsay, 78, 127, 142, 229, 248, 251, 252, 273
Maclean, D., 271
Maclean, John, 80
Macquiston, F. A., MP, 148
Macready, Sir Nevil, 132
Malaya, 19
Malta, 19
Manchester, 31, 132, 174
Manchester Guardian, 77
Mansfield, 143
Marinetti, 259

Index

Marne, Battle of the, 24, 25, 53, 88, 89
Marshall, Sir Horace, 131
Marseilles, 172
Martin, Lt. Col., 40
Marx, Karl, 115
Mary, Princess, 180, 181, 182
Mary, Queen, 59, 60, 179, 182, 183
Mauberge, 24
Maud, Princess, 184
Maugham, Somerset, 156, 191
Maurice, 146
Maurice, Maj.-General Sir Frederick, 100, 101, 102, 105
Maxton, James, 83, 193
Maxwell, Gen. Sir John, 210
Maxwell, Mary Mortime, 68
Mead, Frederick, 196
Meath, Earl of, 141
Mecca, 232
Mediterranean, 54-5
Meers, Superintendent, 99
Mellowes, Liam, 218, 219
Mexico, 93, 94
Michael, Grand Duke, 117
Middlesborough, 198
Miller, Irene, 70
Mitchell, Rosslyn, 194
Mitchell-Thomson, Sir, 228
Mollison, Jim, 190
Moltke, Helmut von, 17
Mons, 22, 72, 105
Moore, Lady Patricia, 151
Morris, Sam, 168
Morris, William, 180
Morton, H. V., 137, 149
Moscow, 124
Mosley, Oswald, MP, 191, 192, 248, 249, 261
Mountbatten, Lord Louis, 181
Mulhausen, 21
Muller, Herr, 110
Munich, 75, 267, 290-1
Mussolini, Benito, 164, 248, 255, 256, 257, 258, 259, 260, 261, 266, 271, 275, 289

Nehru, 222
Nell, Peter, 31, 32
Nelson, Capt., 62
Neuve Chapelle, Battle of, 37, 38, 39, 40, 41, 49, 56
Newbold, Comrade, 126
Newcastle, 41, 132, 293
Newfoundland, 223
New York, 92, 149, 155, 163, 240, 241, 242, 243-253

New York Herald, 32
New York Times, 32
New Zealand, 19, 223
Nicholas II, Czar, 16, 53, 117, 119
Nielsen, Amelia, 168
Normand, Mabel, 166
Northampton, 81
Northcliffe, Lord, 55
North Sea, 37
Nottingham, 84
Nuremberg, 292

O'Callaghan, Mr and Mrs, 214
O'Connor, Rory, 218, 219
Odette, Mary, 166
O'Doherty, Dr, 146
O'Grady, J., 118
O'Higgins, Kevin, 220
Ormsby-Gore, 285
Ottoman Empire, 115
Our Betters, 156
Oxford, 149, 270-1
Oxford, Bishop of, 71

Pakistan, 19
Palestine, 11, 232, 233, 234
Paniatopoulous, Andres, 223
Pankhurst, Christabel, 68
Pankhurst, Emmeline, 68, 120
Pankhurst, Sylvia, 68
Papen, von, Chancellor, 280, 281
Paris, 18, 19, 23, 51, 86, 88, 284
Patel, 222
Patiala, Maharajah of, 227
Pearse, J. H., 209
Peck's Bad Girl, 166
Perosino, Victor, 244
Peter Pan, 32
Petrograd, 117, 121, 122
Philby, K., 271
Phillips, Percival, 103, 109
Pickford, Mary, 157-9
Pittsburg, 244
Plekhanoff, M., 118
Plunkett, Joseph, 209
Plymouth, 132
Poincaré, Pres., 17
Poland, 135, 274
Poona, 229
Primrose, Neil, 60
Prussia, 21, 36, 88, 89
Pugh, Arthur, 141

Queen Mary, 247

Radio Times, 179
Rainford, Violet, 177

Rappe, Virginia, 162, 163
Rattigan, Sir Terence, 24
Raubal, Frau, 286
Reading, Marquis of, 285
Reid, William, 165
Reith, John, 178
Renaix, 28
Rennenamf, Gen., 89
Reynolds, Mr, 83
Rhondda, 142
Ridder, Hermann, 35
Rio de Janeiro, 207
Roberts, Henry, 23
Robeson, Paul, 197
Rodzianko, M., 117
Roehm, Ernst, 279, 289, 290, 291
Rogers, Will, 163
Rogers, Sgt W., 229
Rolfe, Samuel, 106
Romanov dynasty, 115, 128
Rome, 221, 255
Roosevelt, Franklin D., 155, 244, 247
Rosebery, Lord, 60
Rothschild, Lord, 231, 232
Ruling Passions, 165
Rumania, 93, 120
Russell, Mrs Bertrand, 152
Russia, 11, 16, 17, 20, 21, 24, 28, 36, 53, 54, 74, 78, 79, 88, 89, 115, 116, 117, 118, 119, 120, 121, 122, 126-7, 128, 130, 133, 230, 245
Rykov, Alexis Ivanovitch, 127

St Davids, Lord, 47, 48
St Petersburg, 19
St John, 190
Sadler, Rev. G. T., 79
Saklatvala, Mr, 194
Salford, 31
Salisbury, Lord, 84
Samms, Alphonso, 79
Samsonov, Gen., 89
Samuel, Sir Herbert, 141
San Francisco, 162, 163
Sarajevo, 15
Scapa Flow, 109, 110
Schleicher, Gen. von, 280, 291
Schmitt, Marguerite, 35
Scotland, 57
Scott, Adm. Sir Percy, 110
Sea Waif, The, 165
Secrets, 151
Seldte, Col., 281
Selfridge's, 46
Serbia, 15, 16, 17, 24
Shaw, G. B., 78, 151
Shoulder Arms, 159

Shirley, R. T., 81
Sicily, 259
Simon, Sir John, 138
Singapore, 19
Slade, Sir E., 226
Slade, Madeleine, 226, 227
Smallwood, Mr, MP, 60
Smith, F. E., 133, 208
Smith-Dorrien, Gen. Sir Horace, 72
Snagge, John, 178
Snow, James, 196
Snowden, Mrs Philip, 180
Snowden, Philip, 248, 251, 252
Soissons, 23
Somme offensive, 48-53, 109
South Africa, 19, 53, 222
Speyer, Sir Edward, 33
Spring Cleaning, 156
Sri-Lanka, 19
Stalin, Joseph, 115, 122, 127, 271
Stephens, Pembroke, 285, 286
Stewart, Mary, 177
Stevenson, Frances, 101
Stopes, Marie, 152
Strachey, John, 176
Strathmore, Lady, 182
Streseman, Herr, 265
Sullivan, Serjeant, 208
Sunday Express, passim
Sunday Herald, 61
Swaffer, Hannen, 158
Swan, Annie S., 74
Switzerland, 37, 119, 265, 285

Tagore, Sir R., 225
Taylor, Annie, 73
Taylor, Ellen Mary, 73
Tcheidze, Mr, 118
Temple, Emma, 203
Thayer, H. B., 175
The Times, 101
Thomas, J. H., 139, 142, 252
Thompson, Edith, 199-204
Thompson, Percy, 199, 200, 204
Thompson, H. B., 241
Thompson, Herbert, 108
Tilden, 'Big Bill', 195
Toscanini, Arturo, 258
Travers, Inspector, 32
Triumph of Nationalisation, The, 124
Trotsky, Leon, 115, 118, 119, 121, 127
Turkey, 54, 115

USA, 32, 85, 89, 92, 93, 94, 116, 119, 124, 125, 130, 133, 145, 154, 155, 159-164, 174, 239, 240, 241, 242, 243-253, 254, 258

Index

Valentino, Rudolf, 163, 164
Verdun, 88
Vernon-Hunt, Mr, 188
Versailles, Treaty of, 110-112
Vicars, Sir Arthur, 215
Victor Emmanuel, King, 257
Victoria, Queen, 17
Vidal, Mrs, 154
Vienna, 15, 16, 19
Villiars, E., 230
Vimy Ridge, 109
Vincent, J. C., 196
Vladivostok, 119
Vortex, The, 156
Vorwarts, 93

Wagner, Richard, 34
Waizmann, Dr Chaim, 232
Wales, 18
Washington, 92, 245
Waterford, 211
Wellington, Duke of, 205
Wells, H. G., 78, 122, 124, 125, 126, 129, 151
Welwyn Garden City, 172
Wertheim, Councillor, 33
Wessel, Horst, 279
West Africa, 19
West Indies, 19
What Price Glory?, 165

Wheatley, Mr, 193
Whiteley's, 46
Wilhelm II, Kaiser, 16, 17, 24, 28, 68, 92, 101, 105, 106, 115, 118, 206, 287
Wilson, Dr Arthur William, 154
Wilson, Frank, 197
Wilson, F. M. Sir Henry, 26, 219
Wilson, Pres. Woodrow, 92, 94, 111, 254, 263
Windsor, 73
Winslow Boy, The, 24
Wood, Gen. L., 240
Wood, Lt. Osborn, 240
Woking, 82
Wolter, Martha, 96
Wraysbury-on-Thames, 172
Wynyard, Diana, 245

Yapp, Sir Arthur, 98
Yate, VC, Major Charles, 29
York, Archbishop of, 194
York, Duchess of, 141, 181, 182
York, Duke of, 141, 182, 185
Ypres, 38, 45, 61
Yugoslavia, 115

Zangwill, Israel, 234
Zimmerman, Herr, 35, 93
Zinoviev, 126-7